The Selected Works of

MAULANA ABUL KALAM AZAD

Volume X
(1956-57)

Chief Editor
DR. RAVINDRA KUMAR

ATLANTIC PUBLISHERS & DISTRIBUTORS

Published by
ATLANTIC PUBLISHERS AND DISTRIBUTORS
B-2, Vishal Enclave, New Delhi - 27
Phone: 5413460

Sales office
4215/1, Ansari Road, Darya Ganj
New Delhi - 110002
Phone : 3273880

Typeset at
APD Computer Graphics
B-2, Vishal Enclave, N. Delhi - 27

Printed in india at
Mehra Offset Press
New Delhi

To

MOTHER INDIA

Preface

Dr. Shri Ravindra Kumar is an admirer of Maulana Abul Kalam Azad. This is nothing unusual. Maulana Azad had numerous admirers in the course of India's struggle for freedom. The number increased appreciably after India attained freedom. Partition of India was the heavy price India paid for this freedom. Maulana Azad had throughout his whole political life opposed forces which encouraged separatist trends in our national life. It was in the partitioned India that people realised more vividly the soundness of the views Maulana had expressed on the communal problem.

Maulana Azad was among the major figures in our unique struggle for freedom waged under the leadership of Gandhiji. The Selected Works which Dr. Ravindra Kumar has edited bring out the greatness of Maulana Azad in several fields of life. He was most assuredly an outstanding scholar, a great journalist, a matchless orator but with equal ease he was also a great statesman who played a significant role in every crisis which India and, in particular, the Indian National Congress, faced from time to time in its struggle to make our country free and independent.

He had also his due share in shaping India's destiny in her first decade of Independence. He was an outstanding member of the union cabinet but what was more important was the mature advice he made available to his comrade and fellow warrior Pandit Jawaharlal Nehru as the latter sought to grapple with India's difficult and daunting problems in the first crucial phase of her independence.

Dr. Ravindra Kumar may not yet be a mature scholar but the enthusiasm he has shown in portraying the intellectual and political life of Maulana Azad deserves commendation. The country is still faced with problems which greatly exercised the Maulana's mind. What he thought and said on these problems would still be a source of inspiration and enlightenment to his countrymen in the difficult days through which we are all passing.

Sadiq Ali

Introduction

Maulana Abul Kalam Azad was a great Parliamentarian who proved himself to be pillar of strength to the veterans of the Congress Party and the Union Cabinet headed by Pandit Jawaharlal Nehru. Being an outstanding educationist and thinker, he became the stoutest champion of all progressive causes in the fields concerned.

He was a man who, through his ideas on the role of religion and politics, strengthened national unity and integrity. It was his fundamental belief that being a Hindu or a Muslim or a Sikh or a Parsi or a Christian or a Buddhist, a person can be a true nationalist by observing his or her religion. But in order to realise that it is necessary that India's old culture and civilization should be properly linked with modernism. He, in this regard, pointed out clearly:

> 'If in our midst there are Hindus who believe that there can be restoration of Hindu life of thousand years back then they should be clear in their mind that this is merely utopian and obviously such a dream can never be fulfilled. Similarly it applied to Muslims who if they labour under the illusion that they can revive their old culture and civilization of a thousand years back which they brought from Iran, Arab or Central Asia then this is also a well nigh impossibility. My only appeal to such people is that they should not entertain such a misconception because such a concept is far removed from reality.'

Thus, in Maulana Azad's thinking nationalism was a matter of faith and conviction and not merely based on antiquated concepts. To quote himself again:

> 'I am that fundamental element who has himself made India, therefore, I never abandon my claim to be Indian.'

I am grateful to the staff of National Archives of India specially to its Director General, Dr. R.K. Parti and Assistant Director Shri P.R. Malik, Mrs. Meena Kapoor, Mrs. Manju Sehgal, Shri Pramod Mehra and Shri N.P. Sharma, President Shri Sadiq Ali and other staff of Gandhi National Museum and Library, Rajghat, New Delhi, Dr. Ravindra Kumar, Director and Dr. Hari Dev Sharma, Deputy Director,

Shri A.K. Awasthi and others of Nehru Memorial Museum and Library, Teen Murti House, New Delhi, Librarian and other staff of Parliament Library, Sansad Bhavan, New Delhi, official and staff of Sardar Vallabhbhai Patel National Memorial and Navjivan Trust, Ahmedabad and staff and officials of Kakasaheb Gadgil Pratishthan, Pune, for providing me important literature in their possession.

I am greatly indebted to His Excellency, Hon'ble Dr. Shankar Dayal Sharma, Vice President of India, Hon'ble Shri Shivraj V. Patil, Speaker, Lok Sabha, His Holiness, Maulana Syed Abul Hasan Ali Nadvi, Rector, Nadwatul Ulama, Lucknow, Hon'ble Dr. (Mrs.) Najma Heptulla, Deputy Chairperson, Rajya Sabha, His Excellency, Hon'ble Shri B. Satya Narayan Reddy, Governor of U.P., Dr. Karan Singh, Dr. Akbar Ali Khan and other officials of Abul Kalam Azad Oriental Research Institute, Public Gardens, Hyderabad, Shri Babubhai Jashbhai Patel, Shri V.N. Gadgil, Shri Hitendra Desai, Shri Jitendra Thakorebhai Desai, Com. E.M.S. Namboodiripad, Shri Nathubhai Naranji Naik, Shri A.J. Jalali, Shri S.G. Mohiuddin, Mrs. Kamlesh Ravindra Kumar, Dr. Malti Malik, Prof. K.L. Malik and others for their kind encouragement, guidance and co-operation in many ways in preparation of this Volume (No. 10).

My special thanks are due to Dr. K.R. Gupta and Shri Manish Kumar Gupta of Atlantic Publishers and Distributors for undertaking the publication of Maulana Abul Kalam Azad's works courageously.

– RAVINDRA KUMAR

Abbreviations

A.E.O. - Appointment of Educational Officers.
A.P. - American Psychologist.
A.T. - American Teachers.
B.E. - Basic Education.
B.E.T.C. - Basic Education Training Centres
B.S.T.S. - Basic Salary of Teachers in Part 'C' states.
C.I. - Constitution of India.
C.S.L. - Council of Secondary Education.
C.U. - Central Universities.
D.O.P.V.E.A. - Damage to Oil Painting in the National Exhibition of Art.
D.P. - Delhi Polytechnic.
D.T.I.U.P. - Discovery of a Temple and Images in U.P.
E.E.O.U. - Educational Experts Committee on Osmania University.
E.I. - Educational Institutions.
E.M. - Excavation in Mathura.
E.M.I. - Education Minister of India.
E.O.B.C. - Educational Officer in Bombay and Calcutta.
G.B. - Governing Body.
G.B. - General Budget.
G.I. - Government of India.
G.J.B.M. - Grants to Jalianwala Bagh Memorial.
G.U.A.W.L.E.P. - Grants to Universities under the American Wheat Loan Educational Programme.
H.I.J.K. - Historical Imortance in Jammu and Kashmir.
H.S.S. - Hindi Shiksha Samiti.
H.T.T. - Hindi Technical Terms.
I.F.L.E.I. - Interest Free Loans to Educational Institutions.
I.I.T.K. - Indian Institute of Technology, Kharagpur.

L.S.G.A.E.	- Loans to Students Going Abroad for Education.
M.E.	- Ministry of Education
M.H.I.	- Monuments of Historical Importance.
M.V.I.	- Missions Visiting India.
N.L.C.	- National Library of Calcutta.
N.R.S.R.	- Natural Resources and Scientific Research
O.U.	- Osmania University.
P.C.B.S.T.	- Production of Children's Books on Selected Topics.
P.E.M.	- Personnel of the Education Ministry.
P.F.A.U.	- Property For Aligarh University.
P.R.M.E.H.	- Publication of the Reports of the Ministry of Education in Hindi.
P.S.M.E.	- Parliamentary Secretary to the Minister for Education.
P.T.L.H.O.I	- Promotion of The Learning of Hindi Outside India.
Q.G.S.	- Qualification for Government Services
R.H.E.C.	- Rural Higher Education Council.
R.H.E.R.A.	- Recommendations on Higher Education in Rural Areas.
R.L.I.	- Regional Languages in India.
R.P.C.	- Research and Publication Committee.
R.S.B.	- Reorganisation of States Bill.
S.A.C.C.	- Second Asian Cultural Conference.
S.H.I.L.	- Students' Hostel for Indians in London.
S.S.T.S.M.B.	- Scholarships for Scheduled Tribes of Madhya Bharat.
S.S.T.I.	- Study of Social Tensions in India.
T.S.I.I.T.K.	- Teaching Staff in the Indian Institute of Technology, Kharagpur.
T.T.P.	- Teachers Training Programme.
T.T.C.M.	- The Teachers' College, Mysore.
U.K.	- United Kingdom.
U.G.S.W.	- Universities for Geological Survey Work.

U.I.E.L.	-	University Institute of Education, London.
W.P.D.M.	-	Withdrawal of Protection from Delhi Monuments.
W.S.S.A.	-	Women Students Studying Abroad.
Y.A.D.	-	Yoga Asharam in Delhi.
Y.M.C.A.	-	Young Men's Christians Association.

List of Documents

Cotents

Document No. 1

Answers dated 28-8-1956, of Maulana Azad, to the Questions asked in the Rajya Sabha

NATIONAL COMMITTEE OF ARCHIVISTS

Dr. Raghubir Sinh: Will the Minister of **Education** be pleased to state:

(a) whether any meeting of the National Committee of Archivists of India was held recently; and

(b) if so, what was its agenda and what decisions, if any, were taken at the meeting?

The Minister of Education and Natural Resources and Scientific Research (Maulana Abul Kalam Azad): (a) Yes, Sir; on 6th and 7th July 1956.

(b) A statement is laid on the Table of the House. [See Appendix XIV, Annexure No. 58.] The minutes of the meeting have, however, not yet been finalized.

Document No. 2

Answers dated 28-8-1956, of Maulana Abul Kalam Azad, to the questions asked in the Rajya Sabha

PUBLICATION OF RARE MANUSCRIPTS AND OTHER WORKS OF MERIT

Dr. Raghubir Sinh: Will the Minister of **Education** be pleased to refer to page 61 of the Report of the Ministry of Education for 1955-56, and state:

(a) which are the rare manuscripts or works of merit whose publication has been helped or subsidised by Government so far;

(b) what sums have been sanctioned so far in respect of each of these items; and

(c) how is the selection of deserving manuscripts or works made from those applying for such help or subsidy?

The Minister of Education and Natural Resources and Scientific Research (Maulana Abul Kalam Azad): (a) and (b) So far no grant has been given for the purpose.

(c) On merits.

Document No. 3

Answers dated 28-8-1956, of Maulana Azad, to the questions asked in the Rajya Sabha

TEACHING OF HINDI TO INDIAN CHILDREN IN BURMA

Shri Nawab Singh Chauhan: Will the Minister of **Education** be pleased to state:

(a) whether Government incur any expenditure on the teaching of Hindi to the children of Indian origin in Burma;

(b) if so, how much; and

(c) how many institutions are receiving aid and since when?

The Minister of Education and Natural Resources and Scientific Research (Maulana Abul Kalam Azad): (a) No, Sir.

(b) Does not arise.

(c) Does not arise.

Document No. 4

Answers dated 28-8-1956, of Maulana Azad, to the questions asked in the Rajya Sabha

BUDDHA'S IMAGE FOUND IN STOCKHOLM

Shri Nawab Singh Chauhan: Will the Minister of **Education** be pleased to state:

(a) whether it is a fact that an old image of Lord Buddha has recently been found in an island near Stockholm in Sweden; and

(b) if so, whether Government have obtained any information in regard to the same and if so, what is that information?

The Minister of Education and Natural Resources and Scientific Research (Maulana Abul Kalam Azad): (a) and (b) The Government have no information in the matter.

Document No. 5

Answers dated 28-8-1956, of Maulana Azad, to the questions asked in the Rajya Sabha

HISTORICAL RUINS AT UNAKUTHI, TRIPURA

Shri S.N. Mazumdar: Will the Minister of **Education** be pleased to state:

(a) whether the attention of Government has been drawn to the historical ruins at Unakuthi in Tripura; and

(b) if so, whether any steps have been taken by Government to preserve these ruins as historical monuments?

The Minister of Education and Natural Resources and Scientific Research (Maulana Abul Kalam Azad): (a) and (b) Information is being collected and will be laid on the Table of the House in due course.

Document No. 6

Answers dated 28-8-1956, of Maulana Azad, to the questions asked in the Rajya Sabha

EXCAVATION OF RELIGIOUS TEMPLES

Shri M. Valiulla: Will the Minister of **Education** be pleased to state:

(a) how many Hindu, Jain, Buddhist and Christian temples were excavated by the Department of Archaeology during the last five years and where; and

(b) what is the period of history to which these discoveries are ascribed?

The Minister of Education and Natural Resources and Scientific Research (Maulana Abul Kalam Azad): (a) and (b) A statement is attached. [See Appendix XIV, Annexure No. 59.]

Document No. 7

Replies of Dr. Shrimali (on behalf of Maulana Azad), to the questions asked in the Rajya Sabha on August 28, 1956

GRANTS TO CENTRAL UNIVERSITIES

Shri B.B. Sharma: Will the Minister of **Education** be pleased to state:

(a) the amount of grants sanctioned in March 1956 for each of the Central Universities;

(b) the dates on which applications for the said grants were received and the dates when sanctions were accorded; and

(c) whether these grants were sanctioned in response to applications made for the same or Government sanctioned them on their own initiative?

Dr. K.L. Shrimali: (a), (b) and (c) A statement is laid on the Table of the Sabha [See Appendix XIV, Annexure No. 57.]

Document No. 8

Replies of Dr. Shrimali (on behalf of Maulana Azad), to the questions asked in the Lok Sabha on Sept. 21, 1957

UNIVERSITY GRANTS COMMISSION

Shri C.R. Iyyunni: Will the Minister of **Education** be pleased to state whether any discrimination exists between the colleges directly run by the Universities of Madras and Travancore and those affiliated to them in regard to the pay-scales of their teachers, as recommended by the University Grants Commission?

Dr. K.L. Shrimali: The University Grants Commission is not at present dealing with the affiliated Colleges. The question of discrimination, therefore, does not arise.

Shri C.R. Iyyunni: May I know whether the case of affiliated colleges will be taken into consideration?

Dr. K.L. Shrimali: Yes, the University Grants Commission is considering the question.

Shri A.M. Thomas: What sort of aid has the University Grants Commission promised to give in the matter of these colleges which are directly run by the University?

Dr. K.L. Shrimali: As I said, the University Grants Commission is dealing at present only with the Universities, in the absence of any modification of the regulations. Regulations have not been made with regard to affiliated colleges which may come under the purview of the University Grants Commission at a later stage. At present the University Grants Commission is only dealing with the Universities.

Shri A.M. Thomas: I want to know what sort of aid has been promised to the Universities.

Dr. K.L. Shrimali: The University Grants Commission has decided to improve the salary scale of University teachers who are in the direct employment of the Universities as follows:

Professors	Rs. 850–1,250
Readers	Rs. 500-25-800
Lecturers	Rs. 250–500

And the Commission has decided that the additional expenditure will be shared between the University Grants Commission and the State Governments in the ratio of 80:20.

Shri B.S. Murthy: Arising out of the answer given by the Deputy Minister, may I know whether the question of the pay scales of teachers in the affiliated colleges formed a part of the enquiry by the University Grants Commission?

Dr. K.L. Shrimali: I can only repeat what I have already said, namely, that the University Grants Commission, according to the Act, deals only with the Universities and the question of affiliated colleges does not come within its purview at the present moment.

Shri B.D. Pande: I want to know from which date these revised pay scales mentioned by the hon. Minister will come into operation.

Dr. K.L. Shrimali: I am afraid I cannot give the date. We have already written to the Universities. If the hon. Member tables a separate question, I will be able to give the date.

Shri C.R. Iyyunni: May I know whether the policy of dealing only with the institutions under the University will not create dissatisfaction in the minds of the teachers who are employed by the affiliated colleges?

Dr. K.L. Shrimali: I have full sympathy with the affiliated colleges, and as soon as more funds are available, that question will be taken up.

Dr. Rama Rao: Since the majority of our Universities are affiliating Universities, and since most of the College Lecturers and Professors are out of this aid, will Government reconsider the question of giving aid to the affiliated colleges also?

Dr. K.L. Shrimali: The University Grants Commission has already appointed a Committee to go into this question; and the Committee does consider that the revision of the salaries of the Professors and Teachers in the affiliated colleges is of basic importance. As I have said, Government are already considering that question. I can only say at this stage that this question will be kept in view, because the Government attaches the greatest importance to improving the quality of the teaching profession.

Shri M.K. Moitra: The University deals mainly with post-graduate classes and the affiliated colleges deal with under-graduates.....

Mr. Speaker: Are we arguing out this matter. The hon. Minister has already stated that as the rules stand at present these colleges do not come within the Commission's jurisdiction. They are trying to find ways and means to include them also. Why should there be an argument about this matter?

Shri M.K. Moitra: I am simply stating the fact.

Mr. Speaker: That is all right but we are not considering this now.

Document No. 9

Answer of Maulana Azad to the question asked in the Rajya Sabha on 22-11-1956

NATIONAL REGISTER OF SCIENTIFIC AND TECHNICAL PERSONNEL

Shri M. Valiulla: Will the Minister of **Natural Resources and Scientific Research** be pleased to state the number of scientists and technologists who are unemployed according to the latest information available from the National Register of Scientific and Technical Personnel?

The Minister of Natural Resources[1]: According to the information available with the Council of Scientific and Industrial Research 1348 Scientists and Technologists are unemployed.

1. Maulana Abul Kalam Azad.

Document No. 10

Answers dated 22-11-1956, of Dr. M.M. Das[1], to the questions asked in the Rajya Sabha

RECOGNITION OF PRIVATE INSTITUTIONS FOR NATIONAL DIPLOMA AND CERTIFICATE COURSES IN COMMERCE

Shri M. Govinda Reddy: Will the Minister of **Education** be pleased to state:

(a) whether private institutions have been recognised for training and conducting examinations in National Diploma and Certificate Courses in Commerce; and

(b) if, so, which are those institutions and what are the terms on which recognition has been accorded to them?

Dr. Mono Mohan Dad: (a) and (b) A statement giving the required information is laid on the Table of the House.

STATEMENT

Parts (a) and (b):

The following six private institutions have been granted affiliation by the All India Council for Technical Education for conducting the National Diploma and National Certificate Courses in Commerce. The examinations for the award of the Diploma or Certificate are held by the All India Council and *not* by the institutions.

Private Institutions affiliated to the All India Council for Commerce Courses:

1. Fatima Mata College of Commerce, Quilon (Travancore-Cochin State).
2. Y.M.C.A. College of Commerce, Madras.
3. College of Commerce, Patna.
4. Sanatam Dharam College, Alleppey.
5. The Travancore Co-operative College, Trivandrum.
6. Davar's College of Commerce, Bombay.

---

1. On behalf of Maulana Azad.

The affiliation has been granted subject to the following conditions:

(a) The Institutions should have properly constituted Managing Committee.

(b) The financial position of the institution should be satisfactory. For this purpose, the All India Council has prescribed in certain cases that the institutions concerned should build up a reserve fund of Rs. 25,000 or Rs. 50,000 in the course of two years.

(c) The instructional facilities by way of staff, equipment and accommodation required for the courses should be provided by the institution.

Shri M. Govinda Reddy: May I know the number of centres for conducting these examinations or is it only at the headquarters of these institutions that the examinations are conducted?

Dr. Mono Mohan Das: Does he mean the centres for conducting these examinations? I have not got information regarding that at my disposal.

Shri M. Govinda Reddy: Is it true that the Diploma in Commerce is recognised as equivalent to the B.Com. degree?

Dr. Mono Mohan Das: Yes, Sir, a National Diploma is equivalent to a B.Com. degree and a national Certificate equivalent to an I. Com.

Shri M. Govinda Reddy: Is it recognised also for purposes of recruitment to the services?

Dr. Mono Mohan Das: Yes, Sir, I think so.

Shri M. Govinda Reddy: Who, on behalf of Government, examines the schemes of examinations of these National Diploma and Certificate courses?

Dr. Mono Mohan Das: The All-India Council for Technical Education.

Shri M. Govinda Reddy: The Council for Technical Education originally sanctioned the scheme but who supervises the conducting of these examinations and the standards of teaching in these private institutions?

Dr. Mono Mohan Das: There is the Board of Technical Studies. There are seven such Boards, one for Commerce, and Business Administration. that Board goes into these details.

Shri M. Govinda Reddy: My question is, does this Board supervise the standards of teaching in these institutions?

Dr. Mono Mohan Das: That Board prepares the syllabus and other details but I do not know whether it supervises or not.

Document No. 11

Answers dated 22-11-1956, of Dr. Shrimali, on behalf of Maulana Azad to the questions asked in the Rajya Sabha

TECHNICAL TRAINING CENTRE FOR THE DEAF

Shrimati Savitry Devi Nigam: Will the Minister of **Education** be pleased to state:

(a) whether it is a fact that the Ministry of Education has not yet finalised the scheme for starting a model Centre for the technical trainining of the deaf and dumb; and

(b) whether it is also a fact hat some institutions which are doing useful work for the education and rehabilitation of the deaf and dumb have applied for grants starting such a model centre?

Dr. K.L. Shrimali: (a) Yes.

(b) No.

Shrimati Savitry Devi Nigam: May I know whether any work for the rehabilitation of the deaf and dumb has been done by the Education Ministry?

Dr. K.L. Shrimali: As far as I am aware, the whole scheme is in the initial stages and no actual programme has been undertaken but this is subject to correction.

Shrimati Savitry Devi Nigam: May I know the number of educated deaf and dumb persons who are unemployed? Has any survey been made in this connection?

Dr. K.L. Shrimali: Surveys have been made but I am not sure whether those surveys are correct. We are trying to make sample surveys.

Shrimati Savitry Devi Nigam: May I know whether Government is going to make a correct survey in the near future?

Dr. K.L. Shrimali: Government propose to make a sample survey.

Shrimati Savitry Devi Nigam: May I know the occupations wich are taught in the schools for the deaf and dumb run by Government?

Dr. K.L. Shrimali: I do not have the details but there are various kinds of crafts which they take up. There are various kinds of technical courses also taught in these institutions.

Shrimati Savity Devi Nigam: May I know whether there is any such institution in India which gives college and university education to the deaf and dumb persons?

Dr. K.L. Shrimali: As far as I am aware, there is no such institution which gives higher education to the deaf and dumb.

Shri V.K. Dhage: May I know whether any disadvantage is suffered by the deaf and dumb in the matter of employment in educational institutions if they are otherwise properly qualified?

Dr. K.L. Shrimali: The whole question is very difficult. There are certainly difficulties for the deaf and dumb and the handicapped people to find cmployment in ordinary educational institutions. Unfortunatley, there is a lot of prejudice in our country regarding the employment of these unfortunate people. It has been found by experience in various foreign countries that these people, if they find proper opportunities, can do jobs as well as normal persons. The whole question is now being considered by the Education Ministry and steps are being taken to rehabilitate these people.

Document No. 12

Answers dated 22-11-1956, of Dr. Shrimali[1], to the questions asked in the Rajya Sabha

INTER-UNIVERSITY YOUTH FESTIVAL

Shri V.K. Dhage: Will the Minister of **Education** be pleased to state:

(a) what expenditure was incurred on the Inter-University Youth Festival held in October 1956;

(b) how many universities participated in the festival;

(c) whether there is any proposal to hold a world Inter-University Festival in India; and

(d) if so, when and where?

Dr. K.L. Shrimali: (a) The accounts have not yet been finalised but it is hoped to meet the entire expenditure within the sanctioned amount of Rs. 2.5 lakhs.

(b) Thirty-one.

(c) No.

(d) Does not arise.

Shri V.K. Dhage: May I know whether there has been a demand for holding these Inter-University Youth Festivals in places other than Delhi?

Dr. K.L. Shrimali: Yes, Sir, there have been proposals from time to time.

Shri V.K. Dhage: Did the Government consider the feasibility of holding these festivals in other places also?

Dr. K.L. Shrimali: The experiment has just been started. I do not say that that consideration is ruled out but at present the Government have not yet decided to hold the festival in places other than Delhi.

Shri V.K. Dhage: May I know the reasons why Government is thinking like that in this matter?

---

1. On behalf of Maulana Azad.

Dr. K.L. Shrimali: As I said earlier, this scheme has been started just now and Government is taking steps to encourage these competitions in other places also. Last year, we encouraged the universities to organise festivals in their own areas and several universities did organise such festivals. As I said earlier, I do not say that the proposal is ruled out but at present we are organising the whole festival and it is proper that it is held at Delhi.

Shri V.K. Dhage: May I know whether Government will consider the feasibility of financing or assisting some of the other Universities if they decide to hold such festivals.

Dr. K.L. Shrimali: Yes, Sir, we have been giving financial assistance for inter-collegiate competitions and festivals.

Document No. 13

Replies by Dr. M.M. Das[1], to the questions asked in the Rajya Sabha on 22-11-1956

CULTURAL DELEGATION TO U.S.S.R.

Shri V.K. Dhage: Will the Minister of **Education** be pleased to state:

(a) whether a Cultural Delegation visited the Union of Soviet Socialist Republic recently;

(b) if so, who were the members of the Delegation;

(c) who bore their expenditure; and

(d) whether they have submitted any report to Government ?

Dr. Mono Mohan Das: (a) Yes, Sir.

(b) A list of the members of the Indian Cultural Delegation to U.S.S.R. is attached.

(c) The expenditure on the transportation of the delegation from India to Prague and back; travelling charges in India; equipment and daily allowances and monthly honorarium to Artists, etc., was borne by the Government of India while expenditure on local hospitality including travel within the Union of Soviet Socialist Republics was borne by the host Government.

(d) Not yet.

Composition of the Indian Cultural Delegation to U.S.S.R.

1. Shri Anil K. Chanda, Deputy Minister for External Affairs	Leader of the Delegation
2. Shrimati Rani Chandra	

Artist Members

Kathak:

1. Kumari Sitara Devi	Dancer Soloist
2. Śhri Krishna Panicker	Accompanist

3.	Shri Durga Prasad Misra	Accompanist
4.	Shri Govind Prasad	Accompanist

Kathakali:

1.	Shri Raman Kutty	Dancer
2.	Shri Krishnan Kutty	Dancer
3.	Shri Balakrishnan Nair	Dancer
4.	Shri K. Kumaran	
5.	Shri T. Chandran	Accompanist
6.	E.K. Achutan	Accompanist
7.	Shri Vasudevan Nedungadi	Accompanist

Santiniketan Group:

1.	Shri Narendra Kumar	Dance Director
2.	Shri Biren Palit	Vocalist
3.	Kumari Mitra Dutt	Dancer
4.	Kumari Kiran Mahajan	Dancer
5.	Kumari Ushana Aryanayakam	Music
6.	Kumari Manjula Dutta	

Bharata Natyam Group:

(From Kalakshetra Adyar)

1.	Kumari A. Sarada	Dancer (Soloist)
2.	Kumari Pushpa Makhijani	Dancer
3.	Shri D. Pasupathy	Accompanist
4.	Shri K. Lakshman	Accompanist

Ravindra Sangita:

Shri Dwijen Mukerjee

Sitar:

1.	Shri Vilayat Khan	(Soloist)
2.	Shri Imrut Husain	(Surbahar)

Tabla:

Shri Shanta Prasad

Folk Music:

1.	Shri Nirmalendu Chowdhury	
2.	Shri Nirendu Chowdhury	Accompanist

Sarod:

Shri Bahadur Khan

Hindustani Classical Music:

Shrimati Lalita Sivaram Ubhayakar

OFFICIAL MEMBERS

1.	Shri Romesh Bhandari	Secretary to the Delegation
2.	Miss Kapila Malik	Programme Director
3.	Shri S.L. Vasudeva	Private Secretary to the Leader
4.	Shri D.N. Sharma	Assistant

Shri V.K. Dhage: May I know as to what is known as the "Santiniketan group dance"?

Dr. Mono Mohan Das: Perhaps the hon. Member is aware that this Santiniketan was an organisation established by Poet Tagore many years back. Now, this has been taken over by the Central Government and a Central University has been established there and that is Santiniketan.

Mr. Chairman: He wanted to know as to what is the Santiniketan special dance.

Shri V.K. Dhage: Yes, Sir.

Dr. Mono Mohan Das: It is not a special dance, Sir. It is a dance performed by the students of that institution.

Shri B.P. Basappa Shetty: How many members of the delegation belong to the same family?

Dr. Mono Mohan Das: We have given the list of the artists in the statement submitted to the Members. Will the hon. Member kindly point out the particular artist he has in mind?

Shri H.C. Dasappa: What is the expenditure borne by the Indian Government?

Dr. Mono Mohan Das: The total expenditure borne by the Government of India will be about Rs. 3,68,800.

Shrimati T. Nallamuthu Ramamurti: May I know the names of the members of the delegation?

Mr. Chairman: The list is there.

Dr. R.P. Dube: May I know who selected these artists? Is there a panel?

Dr. Mono Mohan Das: The Government of India is responsible for the selection of the artists.

Dr. R.P. Dube: Who selected them on behalf of the Government of India? Who are the persons who selected the members of the delegation —experts in cultural matters, is it the Education Ministry that selected these persons or is it the Ministers themselves who made the selection?

Dr. Mono Mohan Das: I have said that the responsibility of selection lies on the Government of India as a whole. Now, in the Government of India we have got our Information and Broadcasting Ministry which deals with artists. We consult them. Then there is a special body, the Sangeet Natak Akadami which has been established by a Resolution of the Government of India and we also take their advice.

Dr. R.P. Dube: But what is the special body?

Mr. Chairman: The Government of India, Information and Broadcasting Ministry is number one; Education Ministry another; External Affairs Ministry is the third and Sangeet Natak Akadami is the fourth.

Shri V.K. Dhage: May I know whether the hon. Minister is aware of an interview given by one of the dancers criticising the selection of these delegates?

Dr. Mono Mohan Das: Criticising what? Is it that the number was too small or too big?

Shri S.N. Mazumdar: About the calibre of the artists.

Shri V.K. Dhage: I will read out the criticism. The artist is Miss Sitara Devi. This is what is stated here: "She pulled up the leaders of the delegation for their complete mismanagement of the whole show and alleged that they got the maximum benefits from the Moscow tour in comparison to the hard-worked artists who had to content themselves by merely making formal complaints and no more." Is the hon. Minister aware of this?

Dr. Mono Mohan Das: I am sorry that we cannot corroborate this view at all. We have got our own information received from more than one source and they all show that all the performances given by this delegation were successful.

Shri V.K. Dhage: My point is.....

Mr. Chairman: He says that they would not accept this criticism. They have got their own sources of information which made out that the performances were quite successful.

Shri V.K. Dhage: Is he aware of the criticism made by the newspapers before this delegation left for Europe and is he aware that they gave a performance in New Delhi?

Dr. Mono Mohan Das: I am aware of the criticisms that were made on the eve of the departure of the delegation from Delhi and I am also aware of the reports of foreign correspondents of Indian newspapers which were sent from the countries visited by this delegation.

Shri S.N. Mazumdar: For the statement which Mr. Dhage read out, it seems that there are two parts of the criticism. One is about the success or otherwise of the functions; another is about the treatment meted out by the leaders to the other members of the delegation. The hon. Minister is silent on the second point. Has he any information on that?

Dr. Mono Mohan Das: I did not catch him.

Mr. Chairman: He concedes that the performances may have been successful but he wants to know whether there has been any criticism of leadership and team work.

Dr. Mono Mohan Das: At least we have not received any complaint from any of the artists so far.

Dr. R.P. Dube: In the delegation how many were artists and how many were non-artists, that is, people who went there just for making the trip?

Mr. Chairman: Dr. Dube, from the statement you will find that non-artists were six and artists were about 20 or 25.

Document No. 14

Answers dated 22-11-1956, of Dr. M.M. Das, on behalf of Maulana Azad to the questions asked in the Rajya Sabha

RAMANUJAM INSTITUTE OF MATHEMATICS, MADRAS

Shri S.C. Karayalar: Will the Minister of Education be pleased to state:

(a) whether Government are aware that the Ramanujam Institute of Mathematics at Madras is engaged in fundamental research in mathematics; and

(b) if so, whether Government have granted any facilities to this Institute for encouraging such research?

Dr. Mono Mohan Das: (a) Yes, Sir.

(b) The Central Government have endowed a Chair of mathematics in the Institute at a cost of Rs. 18,000 per year. A research scholarship of the value of Rs. 200 per month has also been sanctioned.

Shri Kishen Chand: May I know from the hon. Minister whether, in view of the importance of the work carried on in this Institute, the Government is thinking of increasing the number of scholarships?

Dr. Mono Mohan Das: We have given a large number of scholarships for research work and one of these scholarships has been given to this Institute. There are other scholarships given to universities and other institutions.

Shri G. Ranga: How many students are there now?

Dr. Mono Mohan Das: I have got no information on this point.

Shri Kishen Chand: But is Government thinking of giving more scholarships to this Institute?

Dr. Mono Mohan Das: At present there is no proposal for increasing the overall number of scholarships. About the particular number of scholarships to be given to this Institute, that will be considered on the applications.

Document No. 15

Answers dated 22-11-1956, of Dr. Shrimali[1], to the questions asked in the Rajya Sabha

DEPUTATION OF PROF. SIGSGARD TO INDIA BY UNESCO

Shri J.S. Bisht (on behalf of Shri Nawab Singh Chauhan): Will the Minister of **Education** be pleased to state:

(a) whether the famous Danish educationist Professor T. Sigsgard deputed by UNESCO, has arrived in India;

(b) if so, how long he will stay here; and

(c) what are the various fields in which he is assisting the Education Ministry and what co-operation he has sought from the Ministry?

Dr. K.L. Shrimali: (a), (b) and (c) A statment is laid on the Table of the Sabha.

STATEMENT

Prof. T. Sigsgard, a UNESCO Expert in testing has since arrived in India and is working at the Central Bureau of Educational and Vocational Guideance, Delhi. His services have been obtained under the Expanded Technical Assistance Programme of UNESCO. Mr. Sigsgard will be in India for a period of 13 months *i.e.* till the end of September 1957. He is to assist the Central Bureau (i) in the preparation of Educational and Vocational Guidance posters; (ii) in the adaptation of a foreign non-verbal test of intelligence (Raver's Matrices 1956); and (iii) in the management of the UNESCO equipment comprising psychological tests and apparatus, with accessories.

Prof. Sigsgard is also expected to assist the Director, Central Bureau in the field of educational and vocational guidance in general.

He has started working on the construction of a battery of selection tests for use in the final year of the Middle Stage of Secondary Education with the help of the Bureau's technical staff. The Ministry will fully give him such co-operation as he may seek from time to time in the discharge of his duties.

---

1. On behalf of Maulana Azad.

Shri J.S. Bisht: Here in the statement it is said '.... to assist the Central Bureau (i) in the preparation of Educational and Vocational Guidance posters, (ii) in the adaptation of a foreign non-verbal test of intelligence (Raver's Matrices 1956) ....' and all that. What is all this?

Dr. K.L. Shrimali: This UNESCO expert has been invited to assist the Educational and Vocational Guidance Bureau in developing techniques for educational and vocational guidance and also to prepare suitable material so that educational and vocational guidance can be carried on in this country.

Shri G. Ranga: Including posters.

Dr. K.L. Shrimali: Yes, including posters.

Document No. 16

Answers dated 22-11-1956, of Maulana Azad, to the questions asked in the Rajya Sabha

STUDY OF HINDI IN UNIVERSITIES

Shri Deokinandan Narayan: Will the Minister of **Education** be pleased to state:

(a) the names of the universities that have adopted Hindi as the medium of instruction; and

(b) the universities that have adopted Hindi as an optional subject for degree examinations?

The Minister of Education (Maulana Abul Kalam Azad): (a) A statement giving the requisite information as far as available in this Ministry is laid on the Table of the Sabha.

(b) Information is being collected and will be laid on the Table of the Sabha.

STATEMENT

Adoption of Hindi as the medium of instruction in universities

S.N.D.T. Women's University– Since the inception of this University the media of instruction are Gujarati, Marathi and Hindi.

Agra University.– At present, teachers in the affiliated Colleges of the University have got the option to give instruction through the medium of Hindi or English.

Karnatak University–From June 1955, the University has allowed the affiliated colleges to adopt the regional language and /or Hindi as optional medium of instruction in the First Year Courses in Arts, Science, Commerce and Agriculture. It is also proposed to introduce this option regarding the medium of instruction progressively in the higher classes.

Allahabad University– Only at the undergraduate stage, the optional medium of instruction is both Hindi and English.

Lucknow University–Hindi is the medium of instruction in degree classes (B.A., B.Com., LL.B. and B.Sc).

Banaras Hindu University–'Hindi is used as an additional medium of instruction up to B.A., B.Com., B.Ed. and LL.B. classes.

Saugor University– The University has introduced 'Hindi' as the additional medium of instruction and Examination up to the degree classes except in the case of examinations for Engineering, Veterinary Science and Post-graduate classes.

Bihar University–Hindi is the sole medium of instruction for all the non-language subjects for I.A., I.Sc., I.Com., B.A., B.Sc., and B. Com. examinations.

Nagpur University.– This University has made compulsory the regional language *viz*. Hindi and Marathi as the medium of instruction for the Intermediate courses in Arts and Science. For the B.A. Courses the candidates have the option to offer either English or Hindi or Marathi as their medium.

Document No. 17

Answers of Dr. Shrimali (on behalf of Maulana Azad) to the questions asked in the Rajya Sabha on 28-11-1956

RURAL UNIVERSITY IN KERALA

Shri N.C. Sekhar: Will the Minister of **Education** be pleased to state:

(a) whether it is a fact that Government propose to start a rural university in Kerala; if so, when; and

(b) where it will be located?

Dr. K.L. Shrimali: (a) No, Sir.

(b) Does not arise.

Shri N.C. Sekhar: May I know whether the Government will take steps to establish a rural university in Kerala?

Dr. K.L. Shrimali: The Ministry of Education has no such proposal.

Shri Kishen Chand: What is meant by a rural university? Does it mean one situated in a rural area, or is there something fundamentally different about the scheme of education?

Dr. K.L. Shrimali: I would refer the hon. Member to the report of the University Education Commission which for the first time had mentioned the term 'rural university'.

Shri N.C. Sekhar: Am I to understand that there are no such universities anywhere in India?

Dr. K.L. Shrimali: As far as I am aware, there is none.

Dr. Shrimati Seeta Parmananad: Is there any rural university in Amraoti?

Dr. K.L. Shrimali: No, Sir.

Document No. 18

Answers[1] dated 28-11-1956, of Dr. M.M. Das, to the Questions asked in the Rajya Sabha

DEVELOPMENT OF KERALA KALA MANDALAM INTO A COLLEGE FOR STUDY OF INDIAN ARTS

Shri N.C. Sekhar: Will the Minister of **Education** be pleased to state:

(a) whether there is any scheme for developing Kerala Kalamandalam, at Cheruthuruthy in Kerala into a college for the study of Indian Arts;

(b) if so, what are the details of the scheme; and

(c) when it will be implemented?

Dr. Mono Mohan Das: (a) The Scheme submitted, on behalf of the Kerala Kalamandalam, has been referred to the Sangeet Natak Akadami, and is now under the consideration by that body.

(b) and (c) Do not arise.

---

1. On behalf of Maulana Azad.

Document No. 19

Answers dated 28-11-1956, of Dr. Shrimali[1], to the questions asked in the Rajya Sabha

FINANCIAL ASSISTANCE TO ORPHANAGES

Shri M. Valiulla: Will the Minister of **Education** be pleased to state:

(a) the number of orphanages (i) which were supported financially, and (ii) for which financial assistance was refused by the Central Social Welfare Board during the year 1955-56; and

(b) the number of inmates in both categories of orphanages during the same period?

Dr.K.L. Shrimali: (a) (i) Fifty-nine.

(ii) Twelve.

(b) The information is being collected and will be laid on the Table of the Sabha as soon as possible.

Shri M. Valiulla: May I know whether there has been any survey made of the total number of orphans in the country who need help?

Dr. K.L. Shrimali: I do not think any systematic survey has been made.

Shri M. Valiulla: What kind of survey has been made, if there has been no systematic survey?

Dr. K.L. Shrimali: I shall need notice.

Shri M. Valiulla: What is the test on the basis of which help is rendered, whether it is per head or institution – is it the kind of life the orphans are leading in the institutions?

Dr. K.L. Shrimali: The procedure with regard to these grants is that the institutions make their applications to the State Boards, and then they are scrutinised by the Central Social Welfare Board, and grants are given taking into account various factors including the number of children, the kind of institution and so on.

---

1. On behalf of Maulana Azad.

Shri M.Valiulla: May I know the amount spent on them by the Social Welfare Board?

Dr. K.L. Shrimali: I do not have the break-up.

Prof. Humayun Kabir: Will the hon. Minister be pleased to state which of the 12 institutions which were refused assistance in 1955 in U.P. received assistance earlier?

Dr. K.L. Shrimali: I have no information whether any of these institutions received any grants earlier, but most of these institutions were refused grants because they were not recommended by the State Boards.

Shrimati Savitry Devi Nigam: May I know whether the grants are given only to registered institutions or whether they are given to all institutions whether registered or not?

Dr. K.L. Shrimali: Grants are usually given to *bona fide* registered institutions.

Shri V.K. Dhage: Is it a fact that grants are not forthcoming in time because the audited accounts that are sent by the institutions are not accepted by the Social Welfare Board?

Dr. K.L. Shrimali: Usually the audited accounts come after the grants have been utilised, and the Board naturally has to look into the accounts before further grants are given.

Shri V.K. Dhage: May I know whether there is any *proforma* accounts in which the accounts are to be submitted by the various institutions?

Dr. K.L. Shrimali: Yes, Sir, there is a *proforma*.

Dr. Shrimati Seeta Parmanand: May I know in which States these 12 institutions which have been refused grants are situated?

Dr. K.L. Shrimali: Five in Bombay, six in Madras and one in U.P.

Shri V.K. Dhage: Is it a fact that the institutions have written to the Board saying that there are no such forms?

Dr. K.L. Shrimali: I should have notice to answer that question.

Shri Maheswar Naik: May I know whether there are orphanages run exclusively by the Board or the Central Government?

Dr. K.L. Shrimali: The Social Welfare Board do not run directly any such institution. They only give financial assistance.

Shri M. Valiulla: Is it not a fact that the Board has established some orphanages?

Dr. K.L. Shrimali: As far as I am aware, they are not running any orphanages directly. They only give financial assistance.

Pandit S.S.N. Tankha: Which is the institution in U.P. which has been refused grant, and on what grounds has it been refused?

Dr. K.L. Shrimali: The orphanages which has been refused grants is the Vish Orphanage, Eastern Kutchery Road, Meerut. Their application was rejected by the State Board.

Shrimati Savitry Devi Nigam: Is it a fact that the Board is going to run 390 homes for orphans in the various States?

Dr. K.L. Shrimali: I am afraid I cannot give that information just now.

Shri V.K. Dhage: Is it not a fact that these institutions have to face great hardship because the audited accounts are not accepted and grants are not forthcoming in time?

Dr. K.L. Shrimali: If the hon. Member has got any specific objection, he may kindly draw my attention to it and I would certainly look into it. I cannot make a general statement here.

Pandit S.S.N. Tankha: I want to know on what grounds grant was refused to the orphanage in U.P.?

Dr. K.L. Shrimali: I ask for notice.

Document No. 20

Answers dated 28-11-1956, of Dr. M.M. Das (on behalf of Maulana Azad), to the questions asked in the Rajya Sabha

SANDWICH SCHEME OF TRAINING IN MECHANICAL ENGINEERING

Shri M. Govinda Reddy: Will the Minister of **Education** be pleased to state:

(a) what is the "Sandwich" scheme of training in Mechanical Engineering; and

(b) when this scheme is likely to be brought into force?

Dr. Mono Mohan Das: (a) The "Sandwich" scheme is an integrated course of technical studies and practical training which are provided in alternative layers within the overall period of the course itself for a degree or diploma in engineering. The object is to equip the candidates with sufficient practical experience during the course, for gainful employment in industry:

(b) The course will be organised in certain selected centres as soon as the necessary arrangements have been completed.

Shri M. Govinda Reddy: May I know the duration of the course–both the practical course as well as the theoretical course?

Dr. Mono Mohan Das: As I have said, the Sandwich course is an integration of both these systems, theoretical teaching and practical training combined in alternative layers. The duration of the course has to be increased a bit. For example, at present for the under-graduate course or the supervisor's course, that is, the diploma and certificate course, three years theoretical training is necessary and after the boy passes this theoretical examination, he generally takes one or two years' practical training. In the integrated course, there will be four years in total.

Shri M. Govinda Reddy: May I know whether separate training institutions will be established for this purpose or whether these candidates are going to be trained in any existing industrial institution?

Dr. Mono Mohan Das: So far as under-graduate or diploma or certificate courses are concerned, there is a proposal to establish a few more institutions but we have to introduce this course in the existing institutions also.

Shri M. Govinda Reddy: May I know whether selection has been made of the existing concerns where these courses are to be undergone?

Dr. Mono Mohan Das: No, it is too premature.

Shri M. Govinda Reddy: May I know the target of the number of trainees, if the Government have fixed the same?

Dr. Mono Mohan Das: The present position is that so far as undergraduate or supervisory courses are concerned that is the diploma and certificate courses are concerned, we have asked the regional committees of the All India Council for Technical Education to prepare a detailed scheme to find out suitable institutions which are existing and also to suggest the location where future institutions may be set up; and so far as the degree course is concerned, it has been decided that this course should be introduced in the Kharagpur Higher Technological Institute for a limited number of students at present.

Shri M. Govinda Reddy: May I know whether stipends will be given to the candidates?

Dr. Mono Mohan Das: Yes, stipends will be given.

Replies to supply. questions asked by Shri Nawab Singh Chauhan in Hindi

Dr. Mono Mohan Das: 1– That information is not at present at my disposal but in America this particular type of course is also called 'Co-operative course'.

2– That is indeed a very important question but I would ask the hon. Member to take a little more trouble and give notice.

Prof. Humayun Kabir: Is it not a fact that there are some such courses actually in operation in the Sheffield University in the United Kingdom?

Dr. Mono Mohan Das: I don't know whether actually there is a course in that university.

Document No. 21

Answers[1] of Dr. Shrimati, to the questions, asked in the Rajya Sabha on 5-12-1956

PUBLIC LIBRARIES IN DELHI

Shri M. Valiulla: Will the Minister of **Education** be pleased to state:

(a) what is the number of public libraries in Delhi at present; and

(b) how many of them are given assistance by Government?

Dr. K.L. Shrimali: (a) Three

(b) All.

Shri M. Valiulla: May I know whether the grant is given to them because they publish some books or is it merely to purchase books or what is the other scheme for which grant is given to those libraries?

Dr. K.L. Shrimali: Grants are given for the maintenance as well as for the purchase of books and for the library as a whole to discharge its functions properly. The hon. Member perhaps wanted to know the amounts given.

Shri M. Valiulla: I wanted to know whether it is given also because the libraries publish some books for adult education.

Dr. K.L. Shrimali: I don't have the details just now but grants are given for the maintenance and upkeep of the libraries.

Shri M. Valiulla: Which are the libraries and what is the amount given?

Shri K.L. Shrimali: The three libraries are, the Delhi Public Library, Delhi, the Government Library, Najafgarh, the Government Library, Mehrauli. The assistance given to these libraries in 1955-56 out of the Government funds was Rs. 2,10,000, Rs. 18,182 and Rs. 4,210.

Shri M. Valiulla: What is the amount given to the rest of India for libraries?

Mr. Deputy Chairman: Your question is only about Delhi.

---

1. On behalf of Maulana Azad.

Shri M. Valiulla: Anyway I want the percentage.

Shri H.C. Dasappa: It is a question of policy. We would like to know that.

Mr. Deputy Chairman: You may put a separate question.

Shri H.C. Dasappa: May I know whether these grants are given only to the Delhi libraries or are there other libraries which are getting grants and if so, how much?

Mr. Deputy Chairman: You can add but not the whole of India.

Shri H.C. Dasappa: Let the first question be answered.

Mr. Deputy Chairman: You cannot travel widely like that.

Shri H.C. Dasappa: May I know whether only the Delhi libraries are given grants?

Mr. Deputy Chairman: Anything as regards Delhi libraries will be admissible, not others.

Shri H.C. Dasappa: The question arises naturally from the answers.

Mr. Deputy Chairman: That is not the question he answered.

Shri K.S. Hegde: What is the percentage of grants given to the Delhi libraries in relation to that of other libraries?

Dr. K.L. Shrimali: I cannot give that answer but the Government of India has a scheme under which they give grants to the State Governments for the development of libraries.

Shri H.C. Dasappa: Are these Government libraries, State Government libraries or Union Government libraries?

Dr. K.L. Shrimali: They are Delhi libraries.

Shri H.C. Dasappa: Is it State Government library or Union Government library?

Mr. Deputy Chairman: Now it is Union Government's.

Document No. 22

Answers dated 5-12-1956, of Dr. Shrimali (on behalf of Maulana Azad), to the questions asked in Rajya Sabha

AUDIO-VISUAL EDUCATION SCHEME

Shri M. Valiulla: Will the Minister of **Education** be pleased to state:

(a) whether any training is given to the Audio-Visual Education personnel under the Audio-Visual Education Scheme;

(b) if so, where is it given and at what cost; and

(c) who bears the cost?

Dr. K.L. Shrimali: (a) Yes, Sir.

(b) In Teachers Training Institutions and seminars. The cost depends upon the Teachers' Training Institution and on the scope and duration of the seminar.

(c) The cost in the Teachers' Training Institution is borne by the concerned administration. As for the seminars, Government of India bears the entire cost of those organised by them and 50 per cent of those organised by State Governments.

Shri M. Valiulla: May I know the number of trainees that are undergoing training in this?

Dr. K.L. Shrimali: As I said, there is no regular institution but there were seminars which were organised at Delhi and Mysore, the seminar which was held at Delhi had 30 trainees and there was another seminar of 25 days' duration held at Lucknow in which there were 18 trainees from outside India and 25 trainees from India. As regards Teachers' Training Institutes, I cannot give the number.

Shri M. Valiulla: What is the duration of the training?

Dr. K.L. Shrimali: It varies, as I said. The seminars which were held at Delhi and Mysore had three months duration. Then there was another seminar held at Lucknow which had 25 days' duration.

Shri M. Valiulla: May I know if any foreign equipment has been received for this purpose?

Dr. K.L. Shrimali: I shall need notice to answer that.

Shri M. Valiulla: May I know now that we are going to give training through audio-visual education scheme whether it will replace the present method of education or it will be supplementary to that?

Dr. K.L. Shrimali: I don't know what the hon. Member means by the present method of education. All these methods are the present methods of education. Audio-visual education is well known to be a better means and a very healthy means of educating children.

Shri M. Valiulla: Audio-visual education means education through the eyes and ears and I think this is not very common in India till now.

Dr. K.L. Shrimali: It is true that it is not very common but this method has always been used.

Document No. 23

Answers[1] dated 5-12-1956, of Dr. M.M. Das, to the questions asked in the Rajya Sabha

TRAINING FACILITIES OFFERED BY LONDON TRANSPORT AUTHORITY, U.K.

Shri Nawab Singh: Chauhan: Will the Minister of **Education** be pleased to state:

(a) whether it is fact that the London Transport Authority, United Kingdom have offered to train six Indian nationals in Traffic Control and Engineering;

(b) if so, whether their offer has been accepted; and

(c) if the answer to part (b) above be in the affirmative, how the candidates will be selected, what are the qualifications prescribed for them and who will bear the expenses?

Dr. Mono Mohan Das: (a) and (b) Yes, Sir.

(c) A statement is laid on the Table of the House.

STATEMENT

Mode of Selection–Candidates have been selected by a duly constituted Selection Committee.

Qualifications–(a) at least a Bachelor's degree with Economics as one of the subjects or a degree or a diploma in Mechanical Engineering; and

(b) at least 5 years' practical experience in the line.

Cost of Training–The cost of passage from India to the United Kingdom and back and maintenance for the entire period of their stay abroad is to be met either by the candidates themselves or their sponsors. The Government of India have no financial responsibility in this regard.

Reply to supply. question asked in Hindi by Shri Nawab Singh Chauhan

Dr. Mono Mohan Das: I have got the names of three candidates who wer selected, but I do not have here the names of the others, nor the details of those who were not selected.

1. On behalf of Maulana Azad.

Further reply to Supply. question asked in Hindi by Shri Nawab Singh Chauhan

Dr. Mono Mohan Das: They are all employees serving somewhere, either under the State Governments or under the Transport Ministry, or the Railway Ministry or the Defence Ministry.

Reply to Supply. question asked in Hindi by Shri Nawab Singh Chauhan

Dr. Mono Mohan Das: Does the hon. Member want to know whether we have any plans to set up a training institute here?

Shri Nawab Singh Chauhan: Yes.

Dr. Mono Mohan Das: None at present.

Shri M. Valiulla: Will these three people be enough to meet the needs in India? Will they not be allowed to train others? Will they not be used to train others in India?

Dr. Mono Mohan Das: These scholarships were offered by the London Transport Authority only last year, and some of our State Governments and other transport authorities have taken advantage of them and up till now only three students have gone there. We do not think that this is of such importance that every transport officer should be trained like this.

Document No. 24

NOTIFICATION PUBLISHING THE UNIVERSITY GRANTS COMMISSION (DISQUALIFICATION, RETIREMENT AND CONDITIONS OF SERVICE OF MEMBERS) RULES, 1956

Dr. K.L. Shrimali: Sir, I beg to lay on the Table[1], under sub-section (3) of section 25 of the University Grants Commission Act, 1956, a copy of the Ministry of Education Notification No. F. 24-18/56'/A-I, dated the 1st November, 1956, publishing the University Grants Commission.

(Disqualification, Retirement and Conditions of Service of Members) Rules, 1956. [Placed in Library, *see* No. S-40/56.]

1. On behalf of Maulana Azad in the Rajya Sabha on Dec. 11, 1956.

Document No. 25

ELECTION TO THE SAMSAD (COURT) OF VISVA-BHARATI

Dr. K.L.Shrimali: Sir, I beg to move[1] the following motion:

"That in pursuance of clause (xii) of sub-section (1) of section 19 of the Visva-Bharati Act, 1951, read with clause (5) of Statute II of the First Statutes of the University, this House do proceed to elect, in such manner as the Chairman may direct, one member from among themselves to be a member of the Samsad (Court) of Visva-Bharati *vice* Prof. Satyendranath Bose, who has since been appointed as the Upacharya of the Visva-Bharati."

Mr. Chairman: The question is:

"That in pursuance of clause (xii) of sub-section (1) of section 19 of the Visva-Bharati Act, 1951, read with clause (5) of Statute II of the First Statutes of the University, this House do proceed to elect, in such manner as the Chairman may direct, one member from among themselves to be a member of the Samsad (Court) of Visva-Bharati *vice* Prof. Satyendranath Bose, who has since been appointed as the Upacharya of the Visva-Bharati."

The motion was adopted.

Mr. Chairman: I have to inform Members that the following dates have been fixed for receiving nominations and for holding elections, if necessary, to the Samsad (Court) of Visva-Bharati.

Last date and time for information	13th December 1956, 3 p.M.
Date and time of election if neccess-sary.	14th December 1956, between 3 and 5 P.M.
Place of election	Room No. 29, Ground Floor, Parliament House.
Method of election	Proportional representation by means of the single transferable vote.

1. On behalf of Maulana Abul Kalam Azad the Minister of Education on Dec. 11, 1956.

Document No. 26

Written answers of Maulana Azad to the questions asked in the Rajya Sabha on 18-12-1956

EROSIVE THREAT TO THE HOUSE OF SANT TULSIDAS

Maulana M. Faruqi: Will the Minister of **Education** be pleased to state:

(a) whether the house of the poet Sant Tulsidas is considered as a monument of national importance;

(b) whether Government are aware that the house is threatened by erosion by the Jamuna; and

(c) if so, what action has been taken to save the house from such erosion?

The Minister of Education and Natural Resources and Scientific Research (Maulana Abul Kalam Azad): (a) There is no house as such now in existence which can be called "the house of the poet Sant Tulsidas". The house referred to in the question is probably the small temple and *ashram* which were constructed by the local people only fifty years back.

(b) Yes. In 1952, the Government of Uttar Pradesh reported that the temple and *ashram* which had been erected at the place where Sant Tulsidas was commonly believed to have been born were threatened by the erosive action of the Jamuna.

(c) We have informed the Uttar Pradesh Government that they themselves should take steps to save the building from the erosive action of the Jamuna.

Document No. 27

Answers dated 18-12-1956, of Maulana Azad, to the questions asked in the Rajya Sabha

CENTRAL ASSISTANCE TO STATES FOR LIBRARIES

Shri Ram Sahai: Will the Minister of **Education** be pleased to state:

(a) the number of libraries in each State run by the Central Government;

(b) the principles governing the grant of Central assistance to the States for development of libraries; and

(c) whether any aid has been given to the States this year for this purpose and if so, what is the amount given to each State?

The Minister of Education and Natural Resources and Scientific Research (Maulana Abul Kalam Azad): (a) One in west Bengal.

(b) and (c) A statement is laid on the Table of the House.

STATEMENT

(b) Grants are sanctioned to various State Governments for the development of libraries on the basis of Library Schemes formulated by them and approved by the Planning Commission. The Central Government shares 66 per cent of the non-recurring and 60 per cent of the recurring expenditure for Central, State and District Libraries and 50 per cent of the expenditure both recurring and non-recurring for libraries below district level during the current financial year.

(c) Yes, Sir. The Central aid given so far to each State for the purpose during the current financial year is tabulated below:

Name of the State	Amount of Central grant sanctioned
	Rs.
Andhra . . .	34,500
Assam . . .	8,100
Bihar . . .	80,750
Bombay . . .	6,000

Jammu and Kashmir .	..
Kerala . .	..
Madhya Pradesh . .	1,40,000
Madras . . .	..
Mysore . . .	3,000
Orissa . . .	50,000
Punjab . . .	58,500
Rajasthan . . .	..
Uttar Pradesh . . .	1,54,500
West Bengal . . .	45,000
Total	5,80,350

Document No. 28

Answers dated 18-12-1956, of the Dr. M.M. Das (on behalf of Maulana Azad) to the questions asked in the Rajya Sabha in Connection with the Sangeet Natak Akadami

Shri S.N. Mazumdar: May I know, what is the procedure adopted in this matter, that is, whether it is the procedure to ask the permission of the organisers, in this case, the Sangeet Natak Akadami, or the artistes?

Dr. Mono Mohan Das: There is no hard and fast rule about these matters. Generally the artistes do not object at all to their records being taken by the All India Radio and relayed again. So far as this particular case is concerned, the artistes were very famous – one of them, Wilayat Khan and among others, Doogar brothers. From the very beginning they objected to any record being made of their performance.

Shri S.N. Mazumdar: Secondly, May I know whether the permission of the Sangeet Natak Akadami was asked for? If not, how can the question of refusal come?

Dr. Mono Mohan Das: Permission of the Sangeet Natak Akadami was asked by the All India Radio? No, Sir, So far as I know, no pemission was asked for.

Shri S.N. Mazumdar: I have another question. May I know how the activities of the song, dance and drama division under the Ministry of Information and Broadcasting and the activities of the Sangeet Natak Akadami are being co-ordinated? Or, is there a conflict between these two?

Dr. Mono Mohan Das: The Sangeet Natak Akadami has nothing to do with the Information and Broadcasting Ministry. It is one of the three Akadamis which are administered by the Education Ministry. So, if there is to be any co-ordination, it should be between the Ministry of Education and the Akadami and not with the Information and Broadcasting Ministry.

Shri S.N. Mazumdar: What I wanted to know was whether there is any sort of a private war between these two units.

Dr. Mono Mohan Das: How that question arises?

Document No. 29

Answers dated 18-12-1956, of Dr. M.M. Das[1], to the questions asked in Rajya Sabha

TRAINING IN DRAMATICS

Shri B.V. (Mama) Warerkar: Will the Minister of **Education** be pleased to state:

(a) the number of institutions in the country which impart training in dramatics to promising artistes;

(b) the number of students undergoing training in each of these institutions at present; and

(c) whether any scholars have been granted scholarships for receiving training in dramatics in foreign countries and if so, how many and to which countries they have been sent?

Dr. Mono Mohan Das: (a) and (b) Information is being collected and will be laid on the Table of the Sabha in due course.

(c) Five have been permitted to go to the United Kingdom for training in acting, production, stagecraft, etc., under the Government of India scheme of scholarships to young workers in different cultural fields.

Shri B.V. (Mama) Warerkar: May I know, Sir, whether these scholarships are intended for training in Indian dramatics and can that instruction be taken in England.

Dr. Mono Mohan Das: So far as these scholarships are concerned, their monthly amount is Rs. 250 only, which is insufficient for maintaining them in any foreign country. But in these particular cases these scholars wanted that they should be permitted to go to England and take training there and no extra money should be given by the Government of India.

Mr. Chairman: The question is not that. Whether they can be given training in Indian stage-craft, production, etc. in England – that is the question.

---

1. On behalf of Maulana Azad.

Shri B.V. (Mama) Warerkar: In fact, there are so many institutions in India which can impart training in this respect. Why did they want to go to foreign countries?

Dr. Mono Mohan Das: Perhaps they thought that the training would be better there.

Shri M. Valiulla: Who are these people that were sent there; what are their qualifications in each case?

Dr. Mono Mohan Das: One was Shrimati Gurunan Soni. She is studying at the Guildhall School of Music and Drama, London. Another was Shri Habib Ahmed Khan Tanvir. He joined the Royal Academy of Dramatic Art, London, on 18th May 1955. Another was Shri Shivendra Kumar Sinha who joined the Royal Academy of Dramatic Art, London. There are two others. One was Shri Sushil Kumar Anand. He joined the Bristol Old Vic. Theatre School, Bristol, England. Another was Kumari Madhur Bahadur. She joined the Royal Academy of Dramatic Arts, London.

Shri B.B. Sharma: May I know the States from which the scholars come?

Dr. Mono Mohan Das: That information is not with me now.

Shri J.V.K. Vallabharao: Did the Government of India pay the passage money?

Dr. Mono Mohan Das: There is no provisin for giving any passage money to the scholars. It was met by the scholars themselves.

Shri B.B. Sharma: Sir, My question has not been answered. From what States these scholars come?

Dr. Mono Mohan Das: That particular information is not at my disposal.

Shri B.V. (Mama) Warerkar: What are the qualifications of these students who have been sent to the foreign countries?

Dr. Mono Mohan Das: I have not that information at my disposal. If the hon. Member wants it, he may give notice.

Document No. 30

Answers dated 18-12-1956 (on behalf of Maulana Azad), by Dr. K.L. Shrimali, to the questions asked in Rajya Sabha

NATIONAL BOOK TRUST

Shri B.V. (Mama) Warerkar: Will the Minister of **Education** be pleased to state:

(a) whether the National Book Trust has started functioning;

(b) if so, what work has so far been done by the Trust; and

(c) what expenditure has been incurred on that account?

Dr. K.L. Shrimali: (a) No. Sir.

(b) and (c) The questions do not arise.

Shri B.V. (Mama) Warerkar: When will the Trust begin in this respect?

Dr. K.L. Shrimali: About what?

Shri B.V. (Mama) Warerkar: When will the Trust begin working?

Dr. K.L. Shrimali: Shortly.

Document No. 31

Oral answers dated 18-12-1956 of Dr. K.L. Shrimali (on behalf of Maulana Azad), to the questions asked in the Rajya Sabha

SURVEYS OF STUDENTS' CONDITIONS

Shri J.V. K. Vallabha Rao: Will the Minister of Education be pleased to state;

(a) whether Government are aware of any institutions, organisations or universities in India undertaking surveys of conditions of students through their educational institutions:

(b) if so, what are the names of such bodies;

(c) whether any reports have been received by Government from them; and

(d) if so whether a copy of these reports will be laid on the Table of the House?

Dr. K.L. Shrimali: (a) A statement is laid on the table of the House.

(b) (1) Calcutta University, Calcutta, (2) Merrut College, Meerut.

(c) A copy of the report has been received from the University of Calcutta only.

(d) The copies of the report received from Calcutta University have been placed in the Parliament Library.

Document No. 32

Answers dated 18-12-1956 (on behalf of Maulana Azad), by Dr. M.M. Das, to the questions asked in the Rajya Sabha

RELICES OF NAWAB TIPU SULTAN LYING IN U.K.

Shri Nawab Singh Chauhan: Will the Minister of **Education** be pleased to state whether it is a fact that some relics of Nawab Tipu Sultan of Mysore are lying in the United Kingdom; and if so what steps Government have taken to get them back?

Dr. Mono Mohan Das: Yes, Sir. There were some relics of Tipu Sultan in the United Kingdom, in the possession of the present Duke of Wellington which have now been handed over to the Indian High Commissioner in the United Kingdom in exchange for a portrait of General Sir Arthur Wellesley in the old Government House, Madras.

Reply to supply. Question asked in Hindi by Shri Nawab Singh Chauhan

Dr. Mono Mohan Das: (1) Personal clothing consisting of (a) an embroidered coat in a damaged condition, (b) a pair of silk brocade trousers, and (c) a hat; (2) a gold chronometer watch by Elliott of London in mahogany case; (3) a small portrait of Tipu Sultan by an Indian artist: and (4) 18 drawings of contemporary Indian sitters.

Further reply to question asked by Shri Nawab Singh Chauhan in Hindi

Dr. Mono Mohan Das: In the original reply I have stated that these relics have been handed over to the Indian High Commissioner in the U.K.

Shri Nawah Singh Chauhan: When are these expected to reach here?

Dr. Mono Mohan Das: It is now at the disposal of the Indian High Commissioner in the U.K. It will take some time.

Shri Jaswant Singh: What is the guarantee that they are genuine relics of Tipu Sultan? Have Government verified it in any way?

Dr. Mono Mohan Das: That information is not at my disposal.

Document No. 33

Answers dated 18-12-1956, of Dr. Shrimati (on behalf of Maulana Azad), to the questions asked in the Rajya Sabha

HOSTEL ACCOMMODATION FOR STUDENTS

Shri M. Valiulia : Will the Minister of **Education** be pleased to state:

(a) the extent of hostel accommodation available for high school and college students at present; and

(b) what accommodation will be available at the end of the Second Plan period?

(a) A Statement giving the requisite information in so far as it is available is laid on the Table of the Sabha.

(b) No estimates have been prepared in this regard so far.

STATEMENT

Figures for 1954-55

Number of students of high and higher secondary schools residing in approved hostels.	1,52,783, 42,97,845	out of
Number of university and college students hostels.	1,12,290 6,18,230	out of
Total	2,65,073 49,16,075	out of

Shri M. Valiulla: May I know whether any amount has been allotted for the purpose of hostel construction in the Second Five Year Plan and, if so, on what basis it has been allotted?

Dr. K.L. Shrimati: Yes, Sir, it has been allotted. It is on the basis of the total amount available for university education and on the basis of the requests that have been received from the universities.

Shri M. Valiulla: I wanted to know in how many years, in how many Plan periods, it will be possible for the Government to see that hostel accommodation is constructed for all students.

Dr. K.L. Shrimali: I could not exactly say, but in the Second Five Year Plan we have made provision for Rs. 2.5. crores for hostel constructions. We propose to give loans to the universities for this purpose and the Ministry of Education has also a proposal to sanction loans of about Rs. 2 crores for the constructions of hostels for affiliated colleges, higher secondary schools, and basic and social education institutions.

Shri M. Valiulla: In the statement it is said that the number of university and college students residing in approved hostels is 1,12,290 out of nearly 6 lakh students. May I know how many of them actually want hostel accommodation?

Dr. K.L. Shrimali: I do not have the total estimate, but the number varies from time to time.

Shri B.P. Basappa Shetty: May I know whether there is any proposal under contemplation by the Government to convert all communal hostels into general hostels?

Dr. K.L. Shrimali: To convert communal hostels into general hostels? Government has no such proposal.

Shri B.P. Basappa Shetty: Are there not communal hostels like Lingayat Hostels, Brahmin Hostels, and so on?

Dr. K.L.Shrimali: May be; I do not have the information at my disposal just now.

Shri Maheswar Naik: May we have an idea of the actual student population which needs to be provided with hostel accommodation?

Dr. K.L. Shrimali: I said that statistics had not been collected. We are going to collect statistics on that subject.

Shri Jaspat Roy Kapoor: May I know whether, while granting aid or assistance to universities for the construction of hostels, it is that policy of the Government to see that aid is not granted to any hostel which bears a caste or communal name?

Dr. K.L. Shrimali: Government grants loans – no grants are given – to the universities, and universities, as far as I know, are not communal in their nature.

Shri Jaspat Roy Kapoor: My point was whether, while granting loans to the universities, for the constructions of hostels it is the policy of the Government or not to lay it down as a condition to the universities that such loans as they get from the Government should not be utilised for the constructions of hostels that bear a caste or communal name.

Dr. K.L. Shrimali: Loans are given to the universities, and universities, as far as I know, in India are not communal in their character.

Shri Jaspat Roy Kapoor: Nobody suggests that.

Dr. K.L. Shrimali: We only give loans to the universities for the construction of hostels for students to reside there. It is obviously the policy of the Government not to encourage casteism or communalism in the country.

Shrimati T. Nallamuthu Ramamurti: Is it not a fact that hostels under Government management or under the aegis of universities are run only on the basis of food being vegetarian or non-vegetarian or cosmopolitan, etc.? At least, that is what prevails in Madras.

Dr. K.L. Shrimali: I think. Sir, we are going beside the point. The question was with regard to the loans for hostels and I do not think the Government of India can dictate as to whether they should be vegetarian or non-vegetarain. It is for the universities to decide about this matter.

Document No. 34

Replies of Dr. Shrimali (On behalf of Maulana Azad), to the questions asked in the Lok Sabha on March 26, 1957

SCHOLARSHIPS TO SCHEDULED CASTES AND OTHER BACKWARD CLASSES STUDENTS

Dr. Rama Rao: Will the Minister of **Education** be pleased to state:

(a) the amount disbursed as scholarships to Backward Classes students upto the 28th February, 1957 in 1956-57;

(b) the amount disbursed to the above categories in 1955-56;

(c) the amount disbursed as scholarships to Scheduled Castes students upto the 28th February, 1957 in 1956-57; and

(d) the total amount sanctioned for Scheduled Castes students in 1956-57?

Dr. K.L. ShrimaliL (a) to (d) A Statement is laid on the Table of the Lok Sabha. [See Appendix II, Annexure No.20.]

Dr. Rama Rao: May I know whether Government have received any suggestions for increasing the amounts allotted for these scholarships.

Dr. K.L. Shrimali: The amount was already increased last year, and as the need arises, the Government will certainly take it into consideration.

Dr. Rama Rao: May I know whether Government's attention has been drawn particularly to other backward classes where the scholarship amount is quite inadequate?

Dr. K.L. Shrimali: It is not possible to include students under other backward classes or students of all categories, but the most intelligent students do get the advantage.

Shri Veeraswamy: May I know whether it is not a fact that the Scheduled Caste students are being sanctioned scholarship amounts at a lower rate than backward class students, and if so, may I know the reason therefore?

Dr. K.L. Shrimali: If the hon. Member has any instances in view, he may kindly let me know and I will look into the matter.

Shri Kelappan: May I know whether the total amount sanctioned for the years 1955-56 and 1956-57 has been disbursed. If not, may I know the reasons therefor?

Dr. K.L. Shrimali: Information on both these points is given in the statement and if the hon. Member will kindly go through it, he will have it.

Shri Achutan: What was the criterion adopted in regard to students coming from other backward classes for awarding scholarships? Was there any distinction between State and State? What was the policy of the Government with regard to the allotment of scholarships to other backward classes? Is it decreasing year after year as is seen from the statement because the amount for 1955-56 is Rs. 73,53,000 approximately while the amount for 1956-57 has come down to Rs. 73,18,000 approximately?

Dr. K.L. Shrimali: With regard to other backward classes men candidates securing first class with 60 per cent. and above marks in the Matriculation or Intermediate examination or 50 per cent. and above in Degree examination, and women candidates securing 5 per cent. less marks in each were awarded scholarships last year. That was the basis.

Shri Keshavaiengar: May we know the reasons for the inordinate delay in sanctioning the scholarships which causes very great hardships to the students?

Dr. K.L. Shrimali: There has been no delay except in a few cases. The reason was that the amount which was allotted was exhausted and we had to request the Finance Ministry to allot additional funds. Government were anxious to cover all eligible students, and it was with a view to help the students that certain delays did occur.

Shri Jangde: Is it not a fact that in spite of the request from so many Members of Parliament, stipends are not paid in monthly instalments and the students who are receiving stipends are not paid even in the month of April?

Dr. K.L. Shrimali: That is not a correct statement. An *ad hoc* amount totalling to about Rs. 23 lakhs was placed at the disposal of 1400 institutions in the months of April and May 1956 for disbursement during the first four months of the academic session, to eligible Scheduled Caste and Scheduled Tribe candidates, and that amount was to be adjusted later. So there has been no delay except in the cases about which I have already mentioned.

Shri B.S. Murthy: May I know the increase in the amount this year in respect of Scheduled Caste students and also backward class students as compared with last year?

Dr. K.L. Shrimali: If the hon. Member will kindly look into the statement, he will find that it gives a rough idea about it.

Document No. 35

Answers dated 26-3-1957, of Dr. Shrimali (on behalf of Maulana Azad), to the questions asked in the Lok Sabha

OSMANIA UNIVERSITY

Dr. Rama Rao: Will the Minister of **Education** be pleased to state:

(a) whether Government have received any representation from the Andhra Government against the Centre's proposal to take over the Osmania University; and

(b) the stage at which the proposal is at present?

Dr. K.L. Shrimali: (a) No, Sir.

(b) Does not arise.

Dr. Rama Rao: Is the Government aware of the strong public opinion in the Andhra Pradesh against the Centre taking away one of their few universities?

Dr. K.L. Shrimali: The Government will take into account all the facts before they take a final decision.

Dr. Rama Rao: How long will the Government keep this Democles' sword hanging?

Dr. K.L. Shrimali: There is no question of any sword hanging. The Government will negotiate with the Andhra Government. All the State interests as well as the national interests will be taken into account.

Shri Ramachandra Reddi: What were the reactions of the Inter-Universities Board and the University Grants Commission in this regard?

Dr. K.L. Shrimali: The University Grants Commission has not been consulted. As I said the Government of India will negotiate this matter with the Andhra Government.

Shri B.S. Murthy: May I know the reasons forwarded by the Andhra State for the non-acceptance of the offer made by the Central Government?

Dr. K.L. Shrimali: The question of the Andhra Government not accepting this proposal has not yet arisen. The matter was between the

Hyderabad Government and the Central Government before the State's reorganisation took place. After that, the Osmania University has gone to the Andhra Government. Now, the Central Government will take up this matter with the Andhra Government.

Dr. Rama Rao: If the Central Government is anxious to have a Hindi institution in the South, why not it starts a new university instead of taking away this well-equipped university of the Andhra Pradesh?

Dr. K.L. Shrimali: As early as 1951, the Government decided to make this Osmani University a Central University with Hindi as the principal medium of instruction. We are working at this proposal and will certainily consult the Andhra Government before taking up a final decision in the matter.

Shri B.S. Murthy: Is it not a fact that the Andhra Government refused to hand over this institution to the Centre but wanted more money to have a plan of teaching in Hindi at Hyderabad?

Dr. K.L. Shrimali: As long as the matter is under negotiation by the Government of India, there cannot be any final refusal from any State.

Document No. 36

Maulana Azad and Demands for Grants of Education Ministry for 1957-58

(Lok Sabha, July 25, 1957)

MINISTRY OF EDUCATION AND SCIENTIFIC RESEARCH

Mr. Speaker: The House will now take up discussion of the Demands for Grants Nos. 13, 14, 15, 16, 17, 18, 19, 20, 21, 22 and 107 relating to the Ministry of Education and Scientific Research. As the House is aware, 4 hours have been allotted for the Demands of this Ministry.

There are a number of cut motions to these various Demands. Hon. Members may hand over at the Table within 15 minutes the numbers of the selected cut motions which they propose to move. I shall treat them as moved, if the members in whose names those cut motions stand are present in the House and the motions are otherwise in order.

DEMAND NO. 13–MINISTRY OF EDUCATION AND SCIENTIFIC RESEARCH

Mr. Speaker: Motion moved:

> "That a sum not exceeding Rs. 65,24,000 including the sums already voted on account for the relevant services be granted to the President to defray the charges which will come in course of payment during the year ending the 31st day of March, 1958, in respect of 'Ministry of Education and Scientific Research'."

DEMAND NO. 14–ARCHAEOLOGY

Mr. Speaker: Motion moved:

> "That a sum not exceeding Rs. 56,54,000 be granted to the President to complete the sum necessary to defray the charges which will come in course of payment during the year ending the 31st day of March, 1958, in respect of Archaeology'."

DEMAND NO. 15–SURVEY OF INDIA

Mr. Speaker: Motion moved:

> "That a sum not exceedings Rs. 96,16,000 be granted to the

President to complete the sum necessary to defray the charges which will come in course of payment during the year ending the 31st day of March, 1958, in respect of `Survey of India'."

DEMAND NO. 16–BOTANICAL SURVEY

Mr. Speaker: Motion moved:

"That a sum not exceeding Rs. 6,22,000 be granted to the President to complete the sum necesary to defray the charges which will come in course of payment during the year ending the 31st day of March, 1958, in respect of `Botanical Survey'."

DEMAND NO. 17–ZOOLOGICAL SURVEY

Mr. Speaker: Motion moved:

"That a sum not exceeding Rs. 5,97,000 be granted to the President to complete the sum necessary to defray the charges which will come in course of payment during the year ending the 31st day of March, 1958, in respect of `Zoological Survey'."

DEMAND NO. 18–GEOLOGICAL SURVEY

Mr. Speaker: Motion moved:

"That a sum not exceeding Rs. 55,62,000 be granted to the President to complete the sum necessary to defray the charges which will come in course of payment during the year ending the 31st day of March, 1958, in respect of `Geological Survey'."

DEMAND NO. 19–SCIENTIFIC RESEARCH

Mr. Speaker: Motion moved:

"That a sum not exceeding Rs. 2,07,78,000 be granted to the President to complete the sum necessary to defray the charges which will come in course of payment during the year ending the 31st day of March, 1958, in respect of `Scientific Research'."

DEMAND NO. 20–OTHER SCIENTIFIC DEPARTMENTS

Mr. Speaker: Motion moved:

"That a sum not exceeding Rs. 1,61,14,000 be granted to the President to complete the sum necessary to defray the charges which will come in course of payment during the year ending 31st day of March, 1958, in respect of 'Other Scientific Departments'."

DEMAND NO. 21–EDUCATION

Mr. Speaker: Motion moved:

"That a sum not exceeding Rs. 15,08,86,000 be granted to the President to complete the sum necessary to defray the charges which will come in course of payment during the year ending the 31st day of March, 1958, in respect of 'Education'."

DEMAND NO. 22–MISCELLANEOUS DEPARTMENTS AND EXPENDITURE UNDER THE MINISTRY OF EDUCATION AND SCIENTIFIC RESEARCH

Mr. Speaker: Motion moved:

"That a sum not exceeding Rs. 1,95,54,000 including the sums already voted on account for the relevant services be granted to the President to defray the charges which will come in course of payment during the year ending the 31st day of March, 1958, in respect of 'Miscellaneous Departments and Expenditure under the Ministry of Education and Scientific Research'."

DEMAND NO. 107–CAPITAL OULAY OF THE MINISTRY OF EDUCATION AND SCIENTIFIC RESEARCH

Mr. Speaker: Motion moved:

"That a sum not exceeding Rs. 1,83,17,000 including the sums already voted on account for the relevant services be granted to the President to defray the charges which will come in course of payment during the year ending the 31st day of March, 1958, in respect of 'Capital Outlay of the Ministry of Education and Scientific Research'."

Does the hon. Minster wish to say anything to start with?

The Minister of State in the Minstry of Education and Scientific Research (Dr. K.L. Shrimali): I shall reply at the end of the debate.

Mr. Speaker: Who begins on this side?

Some Hon. Members *rose* –

Mr. Speaker: Two names have been given to me. If I have to call–Shri H.N. Mukherjee first.

Shrimati Renu Chakravarty (Bashirhat): He will take his chance next.

Mr. Speaker: No question of chance.

Shrimati Renu Chakravartty: How is it....

Mr. Speaker: Order, order. I feel embarrassed so far as these matters are concerned. An important person is left behind and some other person begins. Of course, all of them are important. I have nothing to say against them. Some are inescapable. If they stand, they have to be called. They contribute to the debate from their experience. That is why they are actually chosen as Deputy Leaders. To keep them behind and to put some other person and then say, I have not been called, is not correct. I have already told the hon. Lady Member. When she says, let so and so be called first and then Shri H.N. Mukerjee, I say, four hours have been allotted for this, I may not be able to allow more than one Member. If still she says that the other Member would begin, I say, there would not be any chance so far as that matter is concerned. I do not want inconvenience to Shri H.N. Mukherjee. If he wants to speak, I would like to call him first. The other hon. Member may take his chance.

Shrimati Renu Chakravartty: That is left to you.

Mr. Speaker: Shri H.N. Mukerjee is not here.

Shri Vasudevan Nair: (Thiruvella): Sir, I am very glad that you have given a ruling, so to say, on the importance of Members.

Mr. Speaker: No question of ruling. Time is limited. I cannot expand it.

Shri Vasudevan Nair: While trying to make certain observations about the activities of the Ministry of Education and Scientific Research, I am fully conscious of the several limitations and checks that are before me. I am referring to the fact that Education is mainly a State subject.

I was trying to go through the debate that took place last year on the Ministry of Education. I read through the speech made by our Deputy Minister in reply to the several criticisms made. He advanced two arguments in reply to the criticisms that enough advance was not made on this front. One of his arguments was that we have very little funds. We all agree with the Minister. We all understand his difficulties. Our Education Minister and our Education Ministry asked for Rs. 1000 crores in the Second Plan, but, mercilessly, our Planning Commission and other authorities concerned gave only Rs. 307 crores. So, it is quite natural that there is a severe check on the advance of education in our country.

The second argument put forward by the hon. Deputy Minister a year ago was that mainly this is a State subject, that we have very little to do with this and that the Central Government has very little physical control, so to say, over the educational institutions in this vast country. That is also true.

But, in that speech, the hon. Minister claimed two things. He claimed that the Government of India has given grants to the State Governments and to the various educational institutions in this country. Secondly, he said, the Government of India is furnishing leadership in educational planning. Naturally, the Government of India is expected to give leadership in educational planning. I want to refer to that question in some detail. It is true, we have made a certain advance. I do not wish to decry the activities of the Education Ministry as such *in toto*. The number of our institutions, elementary schools, secondary schools, Universities, Colleges and even Technical institutions has increased substantially, I admit. There is an advance.

But, when we look at this question, we should also take into consideration the target that was fixed. For instance, the Constitution itself directed the Government, that within the course of 10 years, we should achieve the aim of universal compulsory education up to the age of 14. But now, that is the position. It is really deplorable. The Planning Commission itself has accepted defeat. It is said on page 155 of the Summary of the Second Five Year Plan,

> "The country is still far from fulfilling the directive of the Constitution. But, it is necessary to make every possible effort to reach it within the next 10 or 15 years."

It is really a very deplorable situation. I do not want to blame anybody in particular. Why should I blame the Minister for it because even a year ago, our hon. Deputy Minister himself has expressed his deep concern over the situation.

Shri B.S. Murthy: He is not Deputy Minister now.

Shri Vasudevan Nair: I correct myself. I am not a Member of the ruling party.

Shri B.S. Murthy: That is why you must be more careful.

Shri Vasudevan Nair: I thank you.

Compared to the target that was fixed not only in the Constitution, but also by the Planning Commission, our achievement has not come up to the mark. That is my main point.

Another important question has to be looked into by the Govt. especially as people who give leadership in educational planning. The Government of India ought to look into the question of changing the content of our education. That is a very important matter. We all know the history of our education. We all wanted to have a new content for our education, a democratic, national popular content if I can put it that way. On that question, I think, the lag is the greatest. The number has increased, but the content, I am afraid remains almost the same. There also I should like to quote an authority on education. He is none else than Dr. V.K.R.V. Rao, Vice-Chancellor of the Delhi University. In his article "Our Universities" in the June issue of *Education Quarterly*, a publication of the Ministry itself, after discussing the degenerate situation of our university education, he concludes thus:

> "I believe therefore that our universiteis should take positive and purposive action to stimulate in our student world the consciousness of Indian culture, its traditions and its values, and at the same time an equal consciousness of the poverty and misery that clogs the lives of so many of our fellow citizens. Once we get a true understanding of Indian culture and develop a living consciousness of our social responsibilities, character follows automatically."

It is a very important pronouncement of a very important personality in the field of education, and I hope our Government and the Education Ministry will give their attention to this problem. I do not wish to deal with this question in any more detail.

With regard to giving leadership in educational planning, I wish to remind the Minister that there is a great lag in the matter of technical education also. As I understand it, in the Second Plan we want to have a re-orientation in our educational system as a whole. We want to have more of technical education, more technical institutes, engineering colleges, a large number of them, but what is the position? If there was some kind of leadership in planning from the Government of India, I think there would have been some change in our State also. But what is the situation there? It is really an alarming situation.

In that small State there are nearly 45 colleges and I believe nearly half a lakh of students are studying in those 45 colleges. I would submit that out of these 45 colleges there is only one engineering college worth the name issuing a degree in the engineering course. I admit there are one or two more institutes where students are coached and given diplomas.

Every year private managements, individuals, certain associations and missionaries come forward and start colleges, and I may submit many of them make plenty of money out of this business, but they are not prepared to start technical institutions because it is an expensive affair. It is not as good business as the running of arts colleges. So, what being done is manufacturing of graduates, graduates who have only general knowledge about general questions. During the last five or ten years we have failed to give a turn to our education in such a way that large number of technical personnel come out of our own colleges so that we can mainly depend on our own young people. That is our experience. I do not know the situation in many other States.

So, the question of giving leadership in educational planning should be more carefully examined. My submission is there is no well-defined, concerted effort in this direction. There is only some hapazhard development. That will not do. That will only create problems, because in our State we have got the question of unemployment for large numbers of educated young men. So, my request to the Ministry is that there should be a more concerted, well-planned, all-India attempt to give this kind of technical bias to our education as a whole.

[PANDIT THAKUR DAS BHARGAVA in the chair]

Now I come to another very important question. Going through the amounts allotted under various heads I find that a large amount of money is set apart for distribution to States. That is necessary. The Centre is giving generous help to increase the salary of our secondary teachers and elementary teachers. Their condition has improved. I am coming to that question later. But the question of the distribution of the grants to the States has to be re-examined, I want the Ministry to examine it and lay down some definite principles.

In answer to a question in this very House, I think in the last session, the hon. Minister stated that out of Rs. 350 lakhs distributed to the various States to help the development of secondary education, our State, Kerala, was given Rs. 19 lakhs. We are thankful for that, but my point is: in dividing this amount, in allotting these grants, what is the principle adopted by the Government? It may be that the applications from the various States are taken into consideration. But my point is that the development in the various States is of differing character. For example, Kerala is perhaps the only State where almost cent per cent of our people are literate, where there are nearly 16 to 17 lakh students of the age group of between 6 and 11 going to school, where we have got more than 9,000 schools. There is this development, but this development should not become a curse for us. An undeveloped State will have its own problems. I am glad that the Government of India helps those States which are backward. They should be helped to come up very soon. But, at the same time, the problems of those States which are developed to a certain extent also should be understood and allotment should be made to such States considering their problems also. I do not know whether there is any well-defined policy with regard to this question of distribution of grants to the States.

Now I come to the very important question of our teachers.

Mr. Chairman: The hon. Member has exceeded his time.

Shri Vasudevan Nair: I am the only speaker from our group.

Mr. Chairman: Already he has taken about 20 minutes.

Shri Vasudevan Nair: I may be allowed some more time.

Mr. Chairman: Two minutes more.

Shri Vasudevan Nair: I will finish as soon as possible, but I may be allowed five minutes more.

Mr. Chairman: If the point he takes up is a long one, I am afraid I will not be able to allow it. After all, 20 minutes is not a small amount of time. He can take one or two minutes and finish.

Shri Vasudevan Nair: The question of our teachers is still a very serious one. Of course, the old position is no more. Being the son of a teacher, I can understand the difficulties of the life of teacher. I remember my father telling me that he started his job at a salary of Rs. 4 per month. That was long ago, but I remember that always. Now, in our State a primary school teacher gets a starting of Rs. 40 plus dearness allowance. That is a big advance from the old days, but still we should pay some more attention to him. In the report of the Planning Commission it is said that the teacher is the pivot of the entire educational system. Good words are spoken about the teacher always by everybody, but some more attention has to be given to him.

Another very important point I have to bring to the attention of the Ministry is the question of teachers working in private schools, management schools, – in our State nearly half the schools are management schools – at present there is no rule governing the service conditions of the teacher, when he will be sent away from the school, the question of provident fund, the question of leave etc. There is a kind of servant and master relationship between the teacher and the management.

I would suggest to Government to look into this matter, and if possible, to appoint some kind of a committee or commission to go into the service conditions, the life, salary and other problems of our primary school and secondary school teachers, and to lay down some uniform all-India standards with regard to these.

I hope the Ministry will give consideration to these suggestions and evolve a well-defined policy on these matters.

Shri V.P. Nayar (Quilon): I want to raise a point on which I seek your ruling. It is customary that when Demands for Grants are under discussion, the senior Minster incharge of the Ministry is present in the House. But I do not find the Minister here, and although his very able Deputies are here, I want to know what prevents the Minister from making at least a very rare appearance in this House on such a very important occasion as this.

Dr. K.L. Shrimali: I am in full charge of this subject, but the Minister will be here, I expect, during the course of the debate.

Shri Sarjov Pande *rose* to complain....

Mr. Chairman: The hon. Member may resume his seat. This kind of complaint has been raised many a time, and is bound to be raised many a time.

Mr. Chairman Spoke in Hindi (material not included).

Shri V.P. Nayar: He could not have meant all this.

Shri Punnoose (Ambalapuzha): He only wanted to speak on these Demands for Grants.

Seth Govind Das from Jabbalpore delivered speech in Hindi.[1]

Shri B.S. Murthy: Mr. Chairman, I have been very closely following the speech made just now by my predecessor, but I was not able to understand much. And, what little I could understand, from that I thought that he has been telling the Education Ministry that as far as possible English names should be avoided and suitable Hindi or sanskritised Hindi names should be used.

In this connection, I have already said what we in the South mean by this Hindiisation of English names. The new name for a wireless office is *Vithanthu Karyalaya*. In the south, *Vithanthu* means a widow.

Seth Govind Das: Have a Tamil word, or a Telugu word or a Malayalam word; I have no objection.

---

1. Not included.

Shri B.S. Murthy: I am illustrating how we should not run a race madly for the use of Hindi words for replacing English by Hindi and what it has meant to the public. This should not be done. I am anxious that English should be replaced as soon as possible. But, this does not mean that we should accept anything and everything. For instance, the word 'Republic'. What is the harm in using the word? Instead of that you want to have *Sarvatantra Swatantra Ganatantra*. That ordinary man in the street will be confused. He does not understand what this *Swatantra Ganatantra* is.

Shri Shree Narayan Das (Darbhanga): Have you any conception of the man in the street?

Shri B.S. Murthy: I do not conceive about it; if he conceives about it, let him answer it.

I am only saying, please do not run a mad, a fanatical race. Then, take the word, *Vyavasaya*. I hope the hon. Member will understand the difficulty in.....

Shri Shree Narayan Das: I did not say anything. When he said the man in the street will easily understand the import of the English word republic I asked him whether he had any conception of the man in the street.

shri B.S. Murthy: If I do not understnad the man in the street I who represent the lot of them, the hon. Member who has jus tinterrupted me does not know.

Vyavasaya is the word. In Andhra it means agriculture. Nothing more; nothing less. Further south, it means business. If you are going to say *Vyavasaya* as agriculture and all that and if you are trying to give suitable words for certain technical and other words in English, we must do it very carefully. We should use as many as possible and leave the rest to posterity. Do not make it confused. That is my humble submission. If I do not know the man in the street, I shall be a humble disciple of my friend Shri Shree Narayan Das. Let him lead me to where the common man, the man in the street is. Or, if he really wants to know the man in the street, let him follow me. I will lead him to the cheris where the people do not know a single Hindi word or what Hindi or Sanskrit is, much less sanskritised Hindi.

This Demand came rightly after the Defence Demands. The best defence of a country is an educated enlightened population conscious of its rights and also of its responsibilities. Therefore, it must be the duty of the State to see that democracy is successful and proper facilities are provided for all people in every nook and corner of the country.

It is said that democracy without education is a mansion without illumination. The Englishman has left the country with illiteracy, poverty, fanaticism, casteism and others as legacies to these 360 million people. It is a tremendous and stupendous task for our Government and our nation to eradicate illiteracy and educate our people. But, having taken to the democratic type of life, it is the bounden duty of the country and the nation to educate itself, because democracy is nothing but Government by discussion. If you want to place everything before the public, the representatives of the people and get decisions from their discussions, the people must be not only educated properly but they must be enlightened. I think it is Carlyle who said that a man is strong who has advancement or who has culture whose brain is quicker, whose blood is warmer and whose heart is softer. Therefore, these are the ideals which the Ministry of Education should place before it in order to impart education to our people. As the time is short and the subject is vast – and I am terribly afraid of you in the Chair – I do not want to exceed even a single minute, even a single second. Therefore, I would confine myself to certain remarks about this subject.

We see indiscipline among the student world in India. There are a number of strikes and demonstrations and so on. They indicate that there is a new wave of life that has overtaken the student life in India. It it not enough to say that this will be a passing phase and therefore, we must go on in our masterly inactivity and must not do anything. It will not be well for the country and the Government to ignore or bypass this. Indiscipline is a very grave disease which will eat into the vitals of the nation. Therefore, we must set before us the task of knowing the causes of indiscipline.

According to me, indiscipline among the students is responsible for certain things. It is because of two or three factors that the student is losing interests in his studies. Perhaps it is due to the large question of educated unemployed. He finds his brother or brother-in-law being unemployed after taking one or two degrees. He feels if this is the result, why should he study and join the ranks of educated unemployed. That may be one of the reasons.

Education is not attracting the youth today to concentrate his attention upon his subjects. Perhaps the teaching staff is unable to create sufficient enthusiasm in the student-folk. This cannot be denied because the Indian teacher is poorly paid and the respect he has got in our society is low especially the primary school teacher. Some time back, after reading the fifth class, he was given training and he was asked to handle infant standards. Sometimes, a man who is a lower trained teacher would be able to teach upto 5th standard. Then there is the higher grade training and then the secondary grade training and the BT or LT as the case may be. The Ministry should take early steps to see that highly qualified teaching staff is placed at the disposal of the primary schools. They should not be neglected because that is the basis on which we have to build the great mansion. Unless and until love for culture and enthusiasm for education are engendered in the tiny hearts of the young children, it is not possible for them to evince greater interest when they grow up.

Therefore, I say that the highly educated teaching staff with knowledge of child psychology with creative and enthusiastic missionary zeal to create a new nation which can hold aloft the beacon and gospel of Pancha Sheela and co-existence should be created. Therefore, I would like more money to be allotted for the primary schools. But, unfortunately, in the Second Plan the allotment is reduced.

For elementary education in the First Plan Rs. 93 crores were allotted, whereas in the Second Five Year Plan it is only Rs. 89 crores. It is a significant reduction which we cannot quite appreciate.

The country may be in need of technological personnel and, therefore, much more money may be spent on technical, collegiate and higher education. That does not mean that this fundamental part should be neglected. Until and unless we give a good start to the student who goes to the primary school in the village we cannot build up a new cadre of young and enthusiastic citizens to take up the future role which they will be called upon to take very soon.

It is a good augury that the Centre has come forward to bear 50 per cent. of the increased emoluments of primary teachers in the States. With that the Education Ministry should not feel that it has done everything, because in may State this concession is not being used. For instance, in Andhra State, I am told the Andhra Government wanted a loan and other financial assistance. The Centre must be able to give more money either as financial aid or loan for the States so as to make the primary school teachers most contented.

One more point, and that is regarding the wastage and stagnation at the primary school stage. After reading the report I can understand how the Government is also conscious about this fact. But, merely stating certain things is of no use, because 50 per cent. of the young children who get out of primary schools are not going to the secondary or higher middle schools. Therefore, Government must know what happens to these children. The education of girls, is much less satisfactory. Figures show that girls' education is going down and is not showing an increase. The stagnation question also must be clearly tackled before it becomes a menace.

In conclusion, I would appeal to the Ministry that the potentialities available in the community, in the villages and also among the teaching staff should completely be exploited to give India the much needed new type of education which will go a long way to create a citizen who will be a warrior of peace in this warring world.

The Lok Sabha then adjourned till Eleven of the Clock on Friday, the 26th July, 1957.

Document No. 37

Demands for Grants—*Contd.*[1]

MINISTRY OF EDUCATION AND SCIENTIFIC RESEARCH

Mr. Speaker: The list of Selected Cut Motions relating to the Demands of this Ministry has already been circulated to Members on the 25th July, 1957. I shall ask members to move these cut motions subject to their being otherwise admissible.

How much time would the hon. Minister require for reply?

The Minister of State in the Ministry of Education and Scientific Research (Dr. K.L. Shrimali): I will need at least half an hour.

Mr. Speaker: The debate should conclude at 3 p.m. today. So, I will call upon the Minister of Education and Scientific Research to reply to the debate at 2-30 p.m.

The cut motion numbers are as follows:

Demand No.	No. of cut motion
13	586, 651
14	587, 85, 588
18	240, 241
21	3, 590, 591, 86 to 88, 593, 594, 598, 606, 610 to 614.

Policy in regard to promotion of technical education

Shri Vasudevan Nair (Thiruvella): I beg to move:

"That the demand under the head 'Ministry of Education and Scientific Research' be reduced to Re. 1."

Inordinance delay in sanctioning the grant of house rent allowance and city allowance to employees of the Indian Association for the Cultivation of Science at Jadavpur in Calcutta.

Shri Sadhan Gupta (Calcutta-East): I beg to move:

"That the demand under the head 'Ministry of Education and Scientific Research' be reduced by Rs. 100."

---

1. Lok Sabha, July 26, 1957.

Discrimination in the case of certain areas and Provinces

Shri Vasudevan Nair: I beg to move:

"That the demand under the head 'Archaeology' be reduced to Re.1."

Centralisation of archaeology and neglect of Orissa ancient monuments

Shri Supakar (Sambalpur): I beg to move:

"That the demand under the head 'Archaeology' be reduced by Rs. 100."

Pepairs, maintenance and upkeep of monuments in Madras State

Shri Tangamani (Madurai): I beg to move:

"That the demand under the head 'Archaeology' be reduced by Rs. 100."

Failure to carry out proper Geological Survey in the Southern States of India

Shri Sampath (Namakhal): I beg to move:

"That the demand under the head 'Geological Survey' be reduced by Rs. 100."

Desirability of conducting archaeological exploration in eastern coasts of Tamilnad

Shri Sampath: I beg to move.

"That the demand under the head 'Geological Survey' be reduced by Rs. 100."

Educational policy of the Indian Government

Shri B. Dasgupta (Purulia): I beg to move:

"That the demand under the head 'Education' be reduced to Re.1."

Lack of any well defined principle in the distribution of grants to the States

Shri Vasudevan Nair: I beg to move:

"That the demand under the head 'Education' be reduced by Re. 1."

Encouraging Public Schools

Shri Vasudevan Nair: I beg to move:

"That the demand under the head 'Education' be reduced by Re. 1."

Necessity of introducing free and compulsory education in selected areas

Shri Supakar: I beg to move:

"That the demand under the head 'Education' be reduced by Rs. 100."

Policy regarding technical education

Shri Supakar: I beg to move:

"That the demand under the head 'Education' be reduced by Rs. 100."

National Book Trust

Shri Supakar: I beg to move:

"That the demand under the head 'Education' be reduced by Rs. 100."

Scheme for giving relief to educated unemployed

Shri Vasudevan Nair: I beg to move:

"That the demand under the head 'Education' be reduced by Rs. 100."

Question of a uniform pay scale for primary teachers

Shri Vasudevan Nair: I beg to move:

"That the demand under the head 'Education' be reduced by Rs. 100."

Problem of bettering the service conditions of teachers

Shri Vasudevan Nair: I beg to move:

"That the demand under the head 'Education' be reduced by Rs. 100."

More grants for Kerala State to convert some of the arts colleges into technical institutions

Shri Vasudevan Nair: I beg to move:

"That the demand under the head 'Education' be reduced by Rs. 100."

Inadequate grants sanctioned to Madras State for Primary Education

Shri Tangamnai: I beg to move:

"That the demand under the head 'Education' be reduced by Rs. 100."

Grants sanctioned to State Govenrments for enhancing primary teachers salaries

Shri Tangamnai: I beg to move:

"That the demand under the head 'Education' be reduced by Rs. 100."

Failure to provide education for handicapped and juvenile delinquents

Shri Tangamani: I beg to move:

"That the demand under the head 'Education' be reduced by Rs. 100."

Delay by Sahitya Akademi in bringing Tamil translation of Arabic Fable '1001 Nights'

Shri Tangamani: I beg to move:

"That the demand under the head 'Education' be reduced by Rs. 100."

Mr. Speaker: Now, the above Cut motions are before the House. Four hours have been allotted for this subject out of which we have spent one hour.

Shri Bimal Ghose (Barrackpore): So, this subject should close at 15.15 hours.

Mr. Speaker: 15 minutes does not matter.

After the Minister's reply the Cut Motions will be disposed of and the Demands put to vote.

Shri Thimmaiah (Kolar–Reserved–Sch. Castes): Mr. Speaker: Sir, I rise to support the Demands for Grants relating to the Ministry of Education and Scientific Research. I only want to make a few observations as far as this Ministry is concerned.

We have appointed many commissions to go into the question of secondary and higher education, whereas we have not yet entered into the field of primary education and enquired about the plight of the primary school teachers in this country. Their position is really miserable. It is high time that the Government gives due consideration to this matter, and enquires into the conditions under which the primary school teachers are working, and also their position in the society.

These primary school teachers, who work in the rural parts of the country, are in a miserable position. Their salary is not sufficient to maintain themselves in the rural parts. I know that the Ministry has recommended that 50 per cent of the enhanced salary will be given by the Central Government and the other 50 per cent may be paid by the State Governments. I do not know how far the State Governments have co-coperated with this proposal, and how many States have come forward to agree with this proposal.

Therefore, I submit that the Government should take a serious note of the position of the primary school teachers, make an effort to enquire into their pay structure and try to improve their pay scales as early as possible. These primary school teachers are the people who lay the foundation for the career of our young boys, and it is they who lay the foundation to make our young boys good citizens of the future. I would, therefore, request the Government kindly to look into this matter as early as possible.

Coming to the question of giving compulsory education, it is stated in the Constitution that it shall be the duty of the State to introduce compulsory education and give free education to all the people in this country. Even ten years after the Constitution came into existence we have not been able to implement that provision. At the same time, we are taxing the people for education and other things. There is no moral justification for taxing the people in this country without even giving them free elementary education. Therefore, whatever may be the financial difficulties, it is the moral duty of the Government to introduce compulsory education as early as possible in this country.

A vast majority of the people of this country are in a backward position so far as education is concerned. Literacy is very low in this country, and it is high time that the Government gives priority to this question of introducing compuslory education. If democracy has to be successful education is very essential. I would, therefore, once again, request the Government to introduce compulsory education as early as possible, especially in the rural parts of the country, where the people are illiterate and have no facilities even to get elementary education.

I now come to the question of scholarships for Scheduled Castes and Scheduled Tribes. No doubt, a large amount has been set apart for awarding scholarships to Scheduled Castes and Scheduled Tribes, but a vast number of students belong to the Backward Classes are going every year without scholarships. I admit that every student belonging to Scheduled Castes and Scheduled Tribes is getting scholarship, but a vast majority of these Backward Class students are not getting. Though the number of students is increasing every year, I do not think the amount of scholarship is being increased. I would, therefore, request the Government to see that the amount of scholarship allowed every year is increased in proportion to the increase in the number of students who apply for this scholarship.

I understand that though these scholarships are given to the students they are actually awarded at the fag end of the year, sometimes the scholarships are distributed after the examiantions, whereby the very purpose for which these scholarships are granted is not served. The students cannot have any benefit from these scholarships if they are given after the year is over. Therefore, I would request the hon. Minister to enquire why these amounts are delayed, why they are paid after the examinations are over. I want him to look into this matter, particularly, and set right things.

As far as discipline of students in this country is concerned, I think the standard is going down. I beg to submit that the Bhonsle National Discipline Scheme must be given due consideration by the Government. This National Discipline Scheme mut be introduced in every part of this country. There should be a proper organisation to see that it is introduced in every school and college in this country, so that the students may be kept in good discipline and they may grow as good citizens of the country. Sufficient financial aid must be given for the introduction of the scheme in all schools and colleges. I know the Minister has already got this scheme in his mind, because the ministry has sanctioned about Rs. 7 lakhs for the introduction of this National Discipline Scheme. I would request him to see that necessary amount is allotted, so that this scheme may be introduced throughout the country.

About this development of Hindi, I understand from the figures here that non-Hindi areas, where Hindi has not yet been developed, where Hindi is not the mother-tongue, have been given less amounts than areas where Hindi is the regional language. This is not correct. I submit that non-Hindi areas, particularly the south, should be given larger sums of money for the development of Hindi. There are various organisations working in these parts for the development of Hindi, and these organisations must be given sufficient sums of money to enable them to carry on their work. The Government should also ask for a report from them every year to see how far the money given has been well spent and how far Hindi has developed in those areas. I hope the Minister will take interest to see that proper encouragement is given to the southern parts of the country for the development of Hindi, because Hindi is not a regional language in those parts, and thus see that Hindi is spread throughout the country as early as possible.

Every year a dozen students belonging to the Scheduled Castes, Scheduled Tribes and Backward Classes are sent to foreign countries under the foreign scholarship scheme. I am at a loss to know whether they have made proper use of these scholarships, whether they have been successful in the examinations in foreign countries. I also do not know whether after their return they are given appointments here or not. I would request the Minister to tell us what their fate is after they return from foreign countries on completion of their education.

In this connection I would like to point out that only 12 students from these backward classes are sent every year. I submit that in all other schemes of foreign scholarships, no backward class students or Scheduled Caste students are generally selected to go abroad for education. Therefore, I request the Minister kindly to see that the number of students sent abroad among these three categories of backward classes may be increased and that every year that number must be doubled, so that a large number of students may have the benefit of foreign education from this country.

Lastly, I come to the educated unemployment scheme. I understand that this scheme is meant only to give some appointments to primary school teachers. I do not know how many of the Scheduled Castes people have been benefited by this educated unemployment. I request the hon. Minister to see that the educated unemployed among the Scheduled Castes people, are also benefited under this scheme, because I am aware that in my State no Scheduled Castes people have been benefited, as far as this scheme is concerned. So, I request the hon. Minister to see that these people are also benefited.

Shri Avasthi from Bilhore delived speech in Hindi[1]

Miss Manibehn Patel from Anand delivered speech in Hindi.[2]

The Minister of Education and Scientific Research (Maulana Azad): Is it compulsory in all the schools of the Delhi Municipal

1. Not included.
2. Not included.

Committee that children should come to the schools with socks and shoes on?

Miss Manibehn Patel continued his speech in Hindi (Material not included).

Dr. K.B. Menon (Badagara): Mr. Speaker, I have moved a cut motion in order to discuss the Government of India's policy on education. It may be more correct to say that the motion is to discuss the lack of policy on education on the part of the Government of India. Even the system of education for primary and secondary schools officially accepted by the Government namely, the basic system of education is implemented both by the Central Government and the State Governments in a half-hearted and halting manner. The new schools that are opened in many of the States are not basic schools. In some of the States, they are even going back on their basic system of education. I understand that the Delhi District Board has submitted a memorandum to the Government of India seeking permission to go back to the old system. A little misleading is the statement recently made by Sir J.C. Ghose, Education member of the Planning Commission, a statement made two weeks back in Poona, in which he says that perhaps the time has come to forget the artificial distinction between basic and non-basic system of schools. Personally, I welcome that statement, for, I feel that that is a very realistic appreciation of the existing situation that is obtaining here today.

Mr. Speaker: May I interrupt the hon. Member for a minute? I find the names of as many as 20 hon. Members here in my list. Some more are coming. I thought of calling the Minister to reply at 2.30 or 2.45. He wanted half an hour. So far as Private Members' Bills are concerned, I find, there are some Bills for introduction. That won't take more than two or three minutes. They can be introduced. For consideration, there are three Bills. Two hon. Members have sent intimation to the Secretary that they won't be present here. Therefore, those Bills won'be taken up. To Shri Jhulan Sinha's Bill, only one hour has been allotted. Thus, out of $2\frac{1}{2}$ hours allotted for Private Members' Bills, only $1\frac{1}{4}$ hours will be taken. If the House agrees, we can allot another $1\frac{1}{4}$ hours for this discussion.

Some Hon. Members: Yes.

Mr. Speaker: I think this is also an important discussion. I will extend it so that we shall push the Private Members' Bills by $1\frac{1}{4}$ hours. So far as introduction is concerned, at that time, I will give three or four minutes. That is an easy matter. I will take up consideration of Private Members' Bills last after this is disposed of. The Hon. Minister will be called at 3.45 to reply. Will that be all right?

Dr. K.L. Shrimali: I am in your hands.

Shri Jhulan Sinha (Siwan): If the introduction of the Bills also could be taken up at 4.15...

Mr. Speaker: Introduction, I will dispose of at 3.15.

Shri Jhulan Sinha: It will be convenient if the introduction could also be taken up at 4.15, simultaneously. I have a Bill for introduction also.

Mr. Speaker: All right. Private Members' Business will start at 4.15.

Dr. K.B. Menon: I was discussing the basic system of education. The system of education that is obtaining today in our country is by and large the system that we inherited from the British, a system that is neither typically British nor tolerably Indian. We were very critical about that system. But, when we became free, when we could devise a new system more suitable to the changing conditions of our infant democracy, we have failed to do so. We have, on the other hand, tinkered with the British system and in that tinkering, we have brought the educational system into confusion and chaos.

One reason for this confusion and chaos in education is the too early decentralisation of education. I am not against decentralisation of education. I accept the principle. But, I wish to submit that decentralisation pre-supposes a fairly high standard of development and efficiency in the States, which is not there. The result is that with every change in the Ministry in the States, which in some States is rather frequent, there is a change in the system and policy of education. Very often, since we are not much matured in politics. Politics also is injected to make the situation deteriorate. For example, the shift system that was scrapped after a few months trial in Madras was not done on the merits of the system, but because politics was injected into the issue. There are two Bills on the anvil in my State, Kerala, which in my opinion are ill-conceived and have roused considerable opposition.

Shri Punnoose (Ambalapuzha): On a point of order. Can an hon. Member raise something that is within the possession of a local legislature? There are certain Bills now in the Kerala legislature. Is it proper that the Member can discuss that specific matter in this House?

Shri Bimal Ghose: That was not what the hon. Member was saying. He was elaborating on the educational policy of the Government of India and incidentally referred as to how that policy is affected if a certain line is not taken by the States. That was his point of view.

Shri Punnoose: Point of view is all right. He specifically said that two Bills are on the anvil in Kerala State.

Shri Bimal Ghose: He was just referring to it.

Dr. K.B. Menon: May I just submit that I do not understand why the Communist Party should be so sensitive?

Shri Easwara Iyer (Trivandrum): It is not a question of sensitiveness. It is a matter under consideration by the State legislature.

Shri Punnoose: It is not being sensitive, only sensible.

Dr. K.B. Menon: When I state a point, I must be allowed to illustrate it by what is going on in the different States, and that is the reason why I referred to the Bill that is on the anvil in Kerala State.

Mr. Speaker: I can only say this much. If there is a Bill before a local legislature, is it not open to the public – I am not talking of this House – to criticise it?

An Hon. Member: Sure, sure.

Mr. Speaker: Any number of associations can hold meetings protesting against that Bill.

Shri Vasudevan Nair: And supporting the Bill also.

Mr. Speaker: If it is supporting, nobody will object. Supporting or opposing, it is open to the general public. As a matter of fact, it is inteded that it ought to be done. Now, the only difference is whether we in this House can do so. I will not allow the conduct of any Minister to be brought in question here or the conduct of a Governor, or the Government of any particular State. They are not here to explain. But when it is available to the public and it is a related matter – irrelevance I will not allow –over which this House also has concurrent jurisdiction, in some cases, joint over-all jurisdiction, and is spending a lot of money, there is no harm in referring to it without saying this party is wrong or that party is wrong. Whichever might be the party, if the people put them into office, they are entitled to be in saddle and carry on. We can only criticise the policy and not the persons involved in it.

Dr. K.B. Menon: Thank you, Sir.

I am against Government's monopoly on education. I feel that that end would be injecting totalitarianism into education. I am for lifting education above party politics.

There is I understand a public service recruitment board in Kashmir for the selection of students for the universities in India. I feel that this also would be an interference with the free flow of students into the various universities and that it is likely to interfere with the selection of students on the score of merit. I also feel that however carefully the selection of the personnel of the board may be, influences like such as sectionalism and communalism and politics are likely to interfere with such selection.

The second reason why there is chaos and confusion in education is that we have been rather unbalanced in our approach to the problem of languages. This problem has been underscored by the redistribution of States on the basis of language, and every State today naturally wants to have the local language as the medium of instruction in the primary and secondary schools. This is causing considerable inconvenience to those parents who are shifted or transferred from one State to another, especially the Central Government employees, and their children are stranded. There is also another handicap arising from it. Because English is slowed down in the primary and the secondary stages, students, when they go up to the university where the medium of instruction is English, are not able to follow lectures in English. I feel that 50 per cent. of the students in universities are not able to follow lectures in English.

I have so far stated the reasons for the confusion. I must now analyse the results of the confusion.

I submit that one disastrous consequence of this chaos and confusion in education has been the lowering of the quality of education, the quality of teaching and the quality of students that come out of our schools and universities. I am sure I would not be expected to quote chapter and verse in order to substantiate my statement, for I believe that it is generally accepted that the standard of students coming out of our high schools and universities today is below par. This has been voiced by many a public service commission, and some of them have even gone on record. I believe the public service commissions of Madras and U.P. have expressed their dissatisfaction on this issue. We have also heard it voiced on many platforms, at the convocation lectures by eminent educationist and eminent public men.

Another disastrous consequence has been the imbalance that it has brought about in the labour market by the increasing influx of education men into the labour field. In this connection I would like to invite the attention of the House to the report published by the Planning Commission, popularly known as Menon's report. In that report Mr. Menon points out that by 1960 there would be 20 lakhs of educated young men seeking employment. Analysing the figures, into which I have to time to go, he feels that by 1960-61 there would be only 5.5 lakhs of educated unemployed in this country. That certainly is not a very alarming figure, but I would like to point out the fallacy in that conclusion because he analyses men as those who have graduated from high schools and universities. I would like to submit that we have to extend the definition of educated to those persons also who have entered the portals of the high school, that is who have gone up to the ninth standard. If we also take into consideration the large dropouts during and in between the high school classes I am quite sure Mr. Menon's figures would not only be doubled, they may even be trebled or quadrupled. The position of the educated unemployed, particularly in those places where literacy is fairly high, as in Kerala for example, is rather alarming. It is alarming because when the educated adolescent and youngsters are made to walk the streets, they become the spearhead of anti-social activities.

I would like to conclude my short talk by making a few submissions to Government on this subject. The Constitution has placed a target before the Government, which is to be realised by 1960. I am sure that that target will not be realised in 1970 or even in 1980, unless we have a more dynamic programme which is implemented with greater vigour. My submission to Government is that there should be no student, boy or girl below the age of fourteen plus, outside schools, during a fixed period. The Central Government should also fix an annual quota which the State Government should fill every year. I am inclined even to suggest that if the State Governments plead financial difficulties to implement the programme, then the Centre should be in a position to subsidise the States, for it is so very important.

My second suggestion to Government is that fourteen plus should be the terminal age for general education. After fourteen plus, which will be about the ninth standard, or the fourth form, or the first year of the high school, I feel that the child should be given careful vocational guidance, when he or she may select technical subjects for study. If that is done, and if there is careful co-ordination and co-operation between the Education Department and the Departments of Industry and Labour, I am quite sure that instead of the child chasing the jobs, the jobs will be chasing the child. That may be too rosy a picture to paint, but I am perfectly sure that if Government have a plan, and if there is that co-ordination and co-operation which I suggested, it will not be difficult to implement.

There is just one other suggestion that I wish to make, and that is about the universities. There should be a certain uniformity of standards between the different universities, for it should be made easy for a student from one university to go to another university. As it is, each university thinks that its teaching is the best, and its standards are the highest. But if there is a classification of universities, and if there is a grading of universities by Government, I am quite sure that it will be easy for students from one university to go to another. This is necessary, especially at this stage, for a shuffling and reshuffling of students in different States in the various universities of India will help to create that unity which is so necessary at this stage of our development.

Mr. Speaker: In view of the fact that a large number of Members are desirous of taking part in the debate, hon. Members may confine their remarks to ten minutes each. Of course, in exceptional cases, one or two more minutes may be given.

I shall call hon. Members in the following order, so that they may be present in the House when their names are called. The order is as follows:–Shrimati Uma Nehru, Shri Ramakrishnan, Shrimati Subhadra Joshi, Shri Sampath of D.M.K.–those people have been complaining that they have not been given a chance, but they are not in their seats–Shri Dasgupta of the United Progressive Party, Shri Thanu Pillai, Shri Mulchand Dube, and Shri Sarjoo Pandey.

Shri M.K. Ghosh (Jamshedpur): May I have a chance to speak?

Mr. Speaker: I have not exhausted the number. Let these eight Members speak, and then we shall see.

Shri Shankaraiya (Mysore): Yesterday, some of us had sent some names.

Mr. Speaker: They are also here.

An Hon. Member: They are in the waiting list.

Mr. Speaker: If they do not get an opportunity on these Demands for Grants, they can speak on some others.

Shrimati Uma Nehru from Sitapur delivered speech in Hindi.[1]

Shri Ramakrishnan (Pollachi): Mr. Deputy-Speaker, Sir, I am a new Member of Parliament, and as Principal of an engineering college, I would like to confine my remarks to technical education.

In 1956, an assessment was made of the requirements of engineering personnel in the country, both for the public sector and for the private

1. Not included.

sector. I beg to submit that that assessment was very conservative in its estimate. Even though the estimate was only for 1,800 graduates and 8,000 diploma-holders, the Committee had recommended 2,045 graduates and 6,225 diploma-holders. But with the growing demand of the country, even this requirement will fall short of the demand. I request the Ministry to make periodical assessments and also try to enhance the supply of engineers to fulfil our Second Five Year Plan.

The Committee also went into the question of engineering colleges. There was a great imbalance in the location of engineering colleges. They have suggested 18 new colleges to be put up; they have also suggested the location would probably be confined to government colleges, and any private donors who are willing to put up colleges would be given ample chance to decide on their own locations. In this way, I believe many people would probably come forward with substantial amounts of donation to contribute to engineering education.

I would like to point out that for the existing engineering colleges, the grant that had been given was 2/3rd by the Central Government for non-recurring expenditure, 1/6th by the State and 1/6th by the donor. Since then, this has been revised to 50 per cent. by the State Government and 25 per cent. by the donor. If the previous proportion was maintained, namely, 2/3rd by the Central Government, 1/6th by the State Government and 1/6th by the donor, the chances of many donors coming forward to put up Engineering colleges would be brighter. There are many difficulties in putting up Engineering colleges. The main difficulty is, there is not enough personnel for teaching.

I would also like to point out in this connection that the pay-scales of the teaching personnel in the Engineering colleges are considerably lower compared to the pay-scales of people in government services or in the private sector. So, it is very unattractive especially for a competent engineer to go into the teaching profession. I beg to submit that the pay-scales may be raised and 50 per cent. of the increase in pay should be borne by the Central Government which has to give the incentive either to the State Governments or to the private donor. I may point out that a man goes into the teaching profession not just merely for the pay. There is also a dignity attached to the profession, especially so in Engineering colleges. If you see a Professor of the Massachussets Institute of Technology, you will find that he is an honoured man in his own profession and the Government even recognises him as such and he is put on a number of governmental committees to give advice to Government on different measures that are undertaken. Are our

Government also thinking of taking professors who are outstanding in their own fields in some governmental committees so that their advice can also be utilised usefully?

There is also a practice in these Universities not to maintain one as Professor unless he is an outstanding man in his own field. To that extent, the Professor has to make substantial contribution in the field in which he has specialised. He either conducts research in the college to which he is attached or he is a consultant to a number of big firms who pay him substantial amounts as consulting fee. Unfortunately, in this country, the professor has no touch with the industry as such and he is not called upon a consultant. I would suggest that colleges may be provided with facilities to do substantial industrial research so that they can utilise the knowledge to the best advantage also to the growth of our industry.

I would like to make an observation on the type of examinations that are conducted in Engineering colleges. I was asked to prepare a paper for the second year B.E. of the Madras University. I found the practice has been to select questions from published books and the students can very well judge what kind of questions are likely to be asked and they prepare only answers to those questions. So, in our Engineering colleges there is no initiative for the student. Apart from passing the examinations, he does not think of learning anything. So, I suggest that some revision of the examinations should be thought of. A proper assessment of the students can be made only by the teacher who teaches them. Sufficient assessment should be given to the classwork of the student. Oral examinations also should be instituted. The student can be asked to write a paper on any subject in his own field so that he can present the paper before a committee of Engineers or to his Professors. He can thus gain some confidence in the field in which he is trying to specialise.

I approve of the present policy of the Government of India in trying to meet the demands for engineers. They have enhanced by 20 per cent. the intake of all the Engineering colleges that are operating today. They have started now the pre-professional and made the course 5 years instead of 4 years. In actual practice, we found that the students who had been taken after the Intermediate examination were very raw. This has facilitated in giving a sort of orientation to the student before he actually joins the college. To that extent, I think, our Engineering colleges would turn out better engineers than we have done in the past.

I have heard many complaints that there has been a rapid expansion in the Engineering colleges and that we have watered down the courses so much so the quality has suffered. I do not agree with this. As far as my knowledge goes, the engineers that are being produced in this country are good men. The only defect in them is that they are worried more about examinations.

Shri V.P. Nayar (Quilon): Are they good men only or are they good engineers also?

Shri Ramakrishnan: Engineers. Their quality has not suffered at all.

I would like to suggest that all the equipment available in the Engineering colleges have not been fully utilised. Night classes can be conducted, especially in industrial areas. There are many young men who would like to take some course in the Engineering colleges to further their knowledge of engineering. I suggest facilities should be given to those and suitable courses may also be started so that they can also have the benefit. Here again, the question of personnel is involved. As I said before, if attractive pays are offered and if opportunities for widening their knowledge by providing facilities for carrying on research and chances of being appointed as consultants for big companies are also there, I am sure, we can attract enough personnel to the teaching profession.

Shrimati Subhadra Joshi from Ambala and Shrimati Laxmibai from Vikarabad delivered speeches in Hindi.[1]

Shri B. Dasgupta (Purulia): I thank you for giving me an opportunity for the first time to speak in this House. This is my first speech in this Parliament. I go direct to the programme of free and compulsory education and the adult illiteracy in our country.

There is a provision in our Constitution which says that the State shall endeavour to provide within a period of ten years from the commencement of the Constitution for free and compulsory education for all children until they complete the age of 14 years. The Constitution was adopted in December, 1949 and within 1960, there should have been arrangements for providing elementary education for every boy and girl between 6 and 14 years. But now we see that the Education Ministry and the Planning Commission are declaring that it will not be possible to implement this provision of the Constitution. Mr. J.C. Gosh of the Planning Commission declared on the 16th at Poona that it would not be possible to implement the provision of the Constitution within this period.

1. Not included.

Now, let us see the progress made towards this goal in the matter of free and compulsory education and adult literacy. We find that the percentage of the number of people from 6 to 14 years in the elementary stage of education in 1950-51 was 32 per cent. In 1955-56, they are expected to be 40 per cent. and the percentage for 1960-61 is expected to be 49 per cent and I think arrangements will be made for the remaining 51 per cent. The pace will take at least 3 or 4 more Five-Year Plans.

As regards adult literacy we find that only 16.6 per cent is literate or semi-literate in our country. This has been taken from the analysis of information on literacy and education of our census for 1951. We find that for at least 6 per cent of our children we shall have to provide opportunities for literacy. It is stated that there are difficulties in the way in the matter of getting teachers and provision of school houses and other paraphernalia. It is a tremendous task, no doubt, but it is not only India but many other countries which are faced with the problem.

I will cite two instances of two countries, namely, Russia and China. There they had a more difficult task to do than what we are facing today. At the time of the revolution in Russia not more than about 30 per cent could read and write. In southern parts, the entire population was illiterate; only about one-third of the school-going children attended elementary schools. They adopted certain scientific methods in the matter of liquidation of illiteracy in the country in 1919 which made it compulsory for all people between the ages of 8 to 15 to learn to read and write in their mother tongue or in the Russian language. They did not wait for school houses or finance or teachers or other paraphernalia. The whole nation including the teachers, engineers, students, workers and peasants came voluntarily with enthusiasm for this purpose. They taught their children in the open spaces; they did not wait for construction of school houses. They tried to teach their illiterates and their children in this way; and we know what followed afterwards. We find now that Russia has liquidated illiteracy. Not only has Russia liquidated illiteracy, but it is one of the foremost countries in the world regarding education and cultural progress.

Now I come to China. China was liberated long after us. But we find that China has outstripped us in the matter of education. Their problem of education and illiteracy was more acute than us. The condition of China was far worse than that of India at the time of liberation. But what do we find now? I shall cite only one or two instances. In Peking city in China, the school education is free. In

Peking city in China, the school education is free. In Peking city, the guardians of the pupils need not pay anything for their exercise books or writing materials. The charges for the hostels there are cheaper than us. The Government bears all the expenses of the poor students. The minimum pay of the teachers is something more than Rs. 150/-. They get free medical treatment. University education is almost free for students in Peking university and students do not even bear the cost of their books and papers. There they do not bother about school-houses and the like. The students are even given some pocket-money.

Mr. Deputy-Speaker: The hon. Member has taken up very big countries to discuss. The hon. Members' time is up.

Shri B. Dasgupta: Now I come to my own country. Regarding our state of education, we may take a broader outlook. Why should we bother about school-houses, finance and other things? There are easy ways of doing this. Let us call our villagers, give them some money and tell them 'you select your own teachers'. I find that 68 per cent. are illiterate in our country. We must have a broad base but I have no time now to go into aspect in greater detail.

Before I close, I would like to stress on one point for the consideration of the House, and that is about language. There is provision in the Constitution in the case of linguistic minorities. It is a vital point. After the reorganisation of States, some bengali-speaking portions in Bihar have remained outside Bengal. The educational policy of the Bihar Government regarding that portion is being carried on as before. The boys living in the Bengali-speaking portion, in parts of Manbhum which have been left in Bihar, are not having the freedom of being educated in their own mother tongue. I would like to invite any Member of this House to go and see the condition there. There are so many Bengali-speaking villages there and yet the students are compelled to take their lessons in Hindi. The primary schools are asked to keep their registers in Hindi; and the whole system of education is conducted in Hindi. Though there are proposals, resolutions, directions and safeguards in respect of the linguistic minorities, that they should be taught in their mother tongue, yet, in the practical field what is being done? They are being trampled as they had been trampled in the past. For the past 8 years we are crying hoarse against this aggression of Hindi on non-Hindi speaking people. But now it is time for us to consider this seriously. I put it before the House and I request the House to take note of this problem and to see that in India, wherever we live, we shall have free and equal opportunities of learning in our mother-tongue, in our own language.

Shri Thanu Pillai (Thirunelveli): Mr. Deputy-Speaker, in the first ten years of Independence, we have been experimenting on the education of children and too much of experimenting has taken place. There is no co-ordination in education. Within the same State, there is basic education, there is the old conventional education. Professors express doubts and difference of opinion whether basic education will produce proper students for university education. One reason which is stated for the modification of university education and introduction of pre-professional courses is that the quality of the products of basic schools, and even of the old High Schools, because of the language policy adopted by the States, has gone down. Whatever may be the truth or otherwise about it, the children are left in the lurch. They do not know which will be the right education for them to follow. To join the basic school or the other school, they are at a loss to know. On top of that, even between Universities, there is no co-ordination. One University says, you must have two years compulsory attendance after graduation for a Master's degree. Another University gives evening classes and night classes for the two degrees to be taken simultaneously. All the degrees are the same for appointment in Government. M.A., LL.B., B.A., or M.A. with two years attendance or non-attendance, there is no difference. There are certain Universities which are conservative; there are certain others which are very liberal, rather too liberal. Whether we should be conservative or liberal is a different matter. But, the quality should not deteriorate. We are not attempting co-ordination of any of these things though there is the University Grants Commission and other things. Universities have become autonomous bodies. They do not want any interference from Government. Autonomy sometimes degenerates into licence and there is no co-ordination between one University and another. We want co-ordination in every sphere. It is lacking in the fundamental sphere of education.

Then, I come to the propagation of Hindi. Hindi is going to be the official language in a few years, 15 years. The non-Hindi areas want more time. But, even after extending the period for another 15 years, if the present policy is to be continued, the non-Hindi areas will never be in a position to cope with the demands of Hindi areas or match with them, because, the Governments concerned are afraid of compelling the students to learn Hindi, but they are prepared to compel the administration, the officers, clerks and government servants to compulsorily learn Hindi. Here also, we are compelled to listen Hindi speeches whether we understand or not.

An Hon. Member: You understand Hindi very well.

Shri Thanu Pillai: The hon. Member cannot say whether I understand Hindi or not. I admit that I do not understand it even after five years. What I appeal is for the future generation. If you want India to continue united, if you want to introduce Hindi and expect Hindi to be the common language and still India to be united, if you continue this policy, the future generation of the non-Hindi areas will revolt and rebel because they cannot understand it. Why not we compel the students today? Children can learn 2 or 3 or 4 languages. In Delhi, boys from non-Hindi areas are learning Hindi. They are prize winners in Hindi. Why is the Government not making Hindi compulsory all over India even as a second language? There is such an uproar for university education to be imparted in the mother tongue. There are 14 mother tongues in our country. Each one is going to take a degree in Engineering or Law or Medicine in different languages. A doctor will attend on a patient with an interpreter and not by himself. That would be the fate of the country if this policy is pursued.

A sum of Rs. 276.00 is spent for the propagation of Hindi: Rs. 30,000 for non-Hindi areas. What for is this amount spent? It is such a niggardly sum when you think of the large number of non-Hindi people who are to be educated. If somebody want to give Hindi education in schools to the children, they want special fees to teach Hindi because they want to give a special pay to the Hindi teachers. Instead of spending money in Hindi areas, I would suggest this. The State Governments may not be able to find all the money because they are not able to match your grants and thereby they lose your grants. Therefore, Hindi education must be spread by compulsorily introducing Hindi in all the schools and by paying all the salaries of the Hindi teachers from the Centre and by giving Hindi scholarships for children who would not be entitled to scholarships otherwise. That would be an incentive for those boys to take up Hindi and learn Hindi.

Coming to scholarships to the backward classes and Scheduled castes, the provision was Rs. 1,50,00,000 last year. For renewal, adequate funds were not available. After much persuasion, Government was good enough to give Rs. 36,50,000. Now, the Budget papers show only Rs. $1\frac{1}{2}$ crores. I do not know whether they are increasing this amount. I remember to have read the figure Rs. 2 crores in some papers. Even that will not be sufficient to cover all the backward classes and Scheduled Castes scholarships.

Then I come to the allotment of scholarships. The allotment is on a population basis state-wise. Why should it be so? Other funds are not allotted on a population basis. The new projects, the new mines and the new grants for steel and iron works are not being divided on the population basis. Where there is raw material, there the money flows. We have got raw material, children to be educated. To boot we have abject poverty. We are a backward State economically. As I said, our backward class boys are expected to get 60 per cent. of the marks for getting a scholarship. In certain other states, a boy getting 40 per cent. gets a scholarship. In Madras and the southern States where there are a large number of people, they have to get 60 per cent. Some years ago it was 50 per cent. The parents borrow and send the children to school in the hope of getting a scholarship. At the end of the year, Government says, no scholarship. Either the boy has to leave the school half way or the parents have to go on borrowing for the education of the children or educate them somewhere else. This is a very difficult position for the people of our State. I submit that the Scheduled Caste boys, as at present, can get scholarships without any mark qualification. The marks for the backward class boys should not, under any circumstances, be more than 50 per cent.

Then about the forward community boys. The time has not yet come to remove the distinction between forward, backward and scheduled classes, but the time has come when the poor boys of the forward community should also get aid from the Government. I appealed two or three years ago to give a tax concession for contribution to scholarship for forward community boys. Even that period has gone now. With our new taxation proposals and the abuses that are thrown at us, even that amount of contribution will not be coming from anybody now, because we will be taxing for contribution also. That will be an excuse even if we do not do that. Therefore, I submit that the best boys who get more than 60 or 70 per cent. of marks, should be helped. Their talent should not be lost to the country if they are very poor and cannot continue their studies in colleges.

There is a merit scholarship for 400 boys, but that does not touch even the fringe of the problem. Even presidency first boys are not able to get the scholarship, and therefore they become lower division or upper division clerks, and they are a nuisance in all the departments because they are intelligent men doing very low jobs and getting a very low salary, and they are instigators of so many troubles. They are graduates and for want of a job they go in for this lower grade job and then they kick up a row saying: "I am a graduate, the other man who is my senior or superior is only a matriculate." So, lots of things are happening because of this educational policy and employment policy. Give free education to whoever is talented, and to catch up with the forward communities; give more aid to the backward communities, but do not deny aid to the forward community's deserving boys who are an asset and will be an asset to the nation.

Then when I compare the amount spent on the Social Welfare Board and the denial of scholarships to poor boys, it is really very painful. The Social Welfare Board gets Rs. 15 crores allotted for five years. There is a paper called *Yojana* which is also published by the Government and that says Rs. 10.5 crores for the Second Plan is allotted for rehabilitation of fallen women. You deny educational facilities, you deny economic facilities and then go on rehabilitating fallen women. Four hundred centres are to be started. Are we a nation of fallen women? I cannot understand this. And this paper, published by the Government of India, says : the write-up is very painful, it is something worse than Miss Mayo's Mother India –

> "Annas eight per client. Ten to twenty clients in an evening. It is the usual price of young womanhood when sold in the market in India. In common parlance the trade is known as prostitution which exists almost in every part of the country."

Is this the type of literature that should be sent out of the country for consumption by our people or by any people? And we are spending crores on this and denying the rightful claim of small boys to benefits of scholarships.

Dr. K.L. Shrimali: It is not published by the Ministry of Education.

Shri Thanu Pillai: Whatever Ministry it is, this *Yojana* is published by the Government of India. The Education Ministry does not take responsibility for *Yojana*, but somebody prints it. Whatever Ministry it is, the paper is there and it prints such things.

After spending that money, what is the conclusion which the author writes:

> "No matter how much we improve the basic economic and social conditions, women would always be available for this profession so long as the demand is there."

Is it for this that you want to spend Rs. 10.5 crores for five years? Our teachers are paid poorly, our children are denied funds for scholarships when here is such a lot of money available for other purposes. Then, the Social Welfare Board will take a long time, an hour or more, we cannot discuss it. I only want to say that the jeeps and women go ill together.

After this Shri Sarjor Pandey from Ramra and Shrimati Sushila Nayar from Jhansi delivered speeches in Hindi.[1]

Shri M.D. Mathur (Nagaur): Mr. Deputy-Speaker, Sir, a few days before I was pleading with the Railway Ministry for sympathetic consideration towards the under-developed areas. Today I plead the same with the Education Ministry, for sympathetic consideration of those backward areas which have not developed educationally in the last few centuries.

If you look to the development of education in India, you will find, that literacy in Kerala is more than 70 per cent. while in Assam and Rajasthan it is less than 10 per cent. We cannot deal with these two extremes with the same standard. Therefore, I would request the planners and the Ministry of Education that whenever they consider the question of allotment of grants, backward States must be given more sympathetic treatment and more funds should be placed at their disposal. Also the rigidity of the conditions of grants should be relaxed. In cases where matching grants are given, where the States have to contribute sometimes 50 per cent. or more, and where they are unable to do so, the people are deprived of the benefits of the State grants. Therefore, my humble submission is that to those States which are educationally backward, where literacy is below 10 per cent or 15 per cent. special consideration should be given.

Then, I would draw the attention of the Education Minister to the question of literacy in our country. This aspect of the problem has been completely ignored so much so that we stand exactly where we were. Our population has increased but the percentage of literacy has not increased except in one or two States. Adult education classes are run in a few places, but they do not serve the purpose.

Education has been considered as the second line of defence of the country. Yesterday and the day before we were discussing the Defence Demands and it is good that today we are discussing the Educational Grants immediately after it. We found that there was dissastisfaction when we were discussing the Defence Grants and the same dissatisfaction remains so far as Education is concerned. I want to submit that unless

1. Not included.

the people are made literate, the economic exploitation of the people shall continue. Unless the knowledge of the three 'R's are imparted to the people, unless the thumb impression practice is wiped out completely from the country, we cannot expect democracy to thrive successfully in India. Therefore, politically it is necessary to give prominence to the question of literacy. Economically it is also necessary; otherwise middlemen will exploit the poor villagers and the cultivators since they do not know how to read and write. They have to pay the money they take on loan a number of times because they are not literate. From these considerations, it is necessary that literacy should be given proper importance in the scheme of things.

The next point that I want to submit is the question of technical education in our country. Recently, we were circulated a Report of the Committee on Engineering Personnel from where we know that we are short of engineers and technical staff in our country. Russia produces about 70,000 engineers every year, as we were informed by the Prime Minister some time ago, and America produces 50,000 every year; but we have got 29,000 engineers, including big and small.

In recent years, technical and engineering colleges have increased. But, looking to our available resources the Ministry can very well say that it will not be possible for us to increase any more. My suggestion is this. These institutions should have double and, if possible, three shifts, because we can very conveniently run evening classes in these colleges and, instead of admitting 100 boys, we can easily take 200 boys. If this system is adopted, we can satisfy more students; as today only a fraction of the students are admitted and the rest are dissappointed. They have to get themselves admitted in the Arts or Law colleges and they have to leave the study of science or technical education. That is why my submission is that if more colleges are not possible, double shift should be adopted in technical colleges.

If we look at primary education, then, according to the Directive Principles of the Constitution, as so many hon. Members have pointed out, we ought to be able, by 1960 to give free and compulsory education to all the children up to the age of 14. But with the resources as they are, we will not be able to fulfil this Directive Principle even in 20 years' time. As has been rightly pointed out by one hon. Member, every time we expand our classes, the population of school-going children also increases and we are not able to cope with it. So, either we would have to revise the Directive Principles in our Constitution or we have to fall short of it or we will have to accelerate our pace in the matter.

The other difficulty is this. Wherever we have primary schools, the teachers are either matriculates or, sometimes, failed matriculates. They are poorly paid in the States and they do not like to go to the villages. When the teacher in a school is absent, then the school is absent. My experience is that 20 per cent. of these schools do not function properly. Therefore, it is necessary to consider the question of the salary of the teachers who are sent to the villages. You can imagine the state of mind of a man who is a mariculate and about 16 years of age when he goes to the village for teaching. He is there alone, sitting miles off in the desert or in the hilly areas, teaching school children. He is not feeling happy there; he has got limited resources. Therefore, he takes this job as a spring board for jumping into some other big job. Immediately he gets an offer from the Revenue Department, even as a patwari, he leaves. He thinks that the job of a patwari is more lucrative and has more amenities of life than the job of a school teacher. Unless the teacher's status is improved, however much you increase the number of schools, they will not work efficiently. The Ministry can easily say that it is the job of the States and that they are prepared to contribute 50 per cent. of the increase in salary. We know this reply well.

Look to the Budgets of the States. They are all deficit Budgets; they have no funds. Therefore, your offer is simply on paper. I would like the Minister, when he replies, to let us know how many States have taken full advantage of this offer and to what extent they have taken it. I know so many States......

Shri Ranga (Tenali): Not one State.

Shri M.D. Mathur: My hon. friend says, not even one. There may, possibly, be a few. But the purpose is not served.

Recently the Prime Minister of China said that the primary school teachers are engineers of the soul of the country. The engineers are paid so high to construct buildings. Then, the engineers who built the soul of the country should be paid better positively.

It is not because the teachers have formed some trade unions and they want more salaries that I am supporting them. I am supporting them because unless they are paid properly they will not come out to serve in the Education Department. You can say that you have raised the number of schools, say, by 500 or 600 in the financial year. But, we find that when 50 schools are opened, 50 others remain closed, because teachers are not available for 6 or 7 months after the month of July.

I would not like to take more time of the House because most of the Members have touched on so many problems. But, I would like to inform the Education Minister that unless and until a tempo is created we cannot achieve our object. An impression must be created in the common man that we want to wipe out illiteracy from our country, we want to eradicate it. The youth of the country and all the Members of Parliament should be called upon to observe "*Sikshadan* fortnight"— as the Ministry of Community Projects observed "*Shrmdan* fortnight" where in crores of rupees worth of labour was offered and buildings constructed. Every Member of Parliament should be requested to educate at least two people. So many employees of the State today want more salary. Why not you say, 'You will get your salary quite all right, but, you must also educate two men in one year or otherwise your promotion will not be given next time. If this is made compulsory, I think, thousands of people could be made literate. The States must take the responsibility for the refresher courses. But, so far as making the people literate is concerned, so far as the imparting of knowledge of the 3 R's is concerned, I think the private organisations and the educated middle-class should be invited and a tempo should be created. Unless you are not able to drive out illiteracy and this problem remains the democracy will not function efficiently and ultimately, because of this our political system would not work efficiently. We are all interested in this education programme. The arts colleges can wait. So far as technical education and the basic primary education are concerned, these are the basic demands of the country and I think the Ministry must give them proper attention.

After this Shri S.M. Banerjee from Kanpur delivered speech in Hindi.[1]

Shri Hem Barua (Gauhati): Mr. Deputy-Speaker, Sir, I would not be discussing the general policies of education pursued by the Government of India, but I would concentrate my discussion on a particular aspect of the policy that is pursued by the Government of India. It is, so far as the North-East Frontier Agency is concerned.

There has been trouble in the tribal areas of the North-East Frontier, and this trouble is not only political and economic but cultural and social as well. We know, these tribal people were isolated from the people of the plains by the British rule. The British Raj for obvious reasons instituted iron curtains between the people of the plains and the people of the hills. They had two nefarious regulations. One is the Inner Line Regulation passed in 1873, and the other is the Frontier Tracts

1. Not included.

Regulation passed in 1880. These have created a sort of separatist psychology amongst these people.

On the other hand, as soon as we became free it was the business, or it should have been the objective of the Government of India to create a new psychology amongst those people, and that psychology would be the psychology of a comprehensive Indian mind. Today what do we find amongst these people? We find that that comprehensive Indian mind is lacking among the tribal population inhabiting the North-East Frontier Agency, because of the fact that we have pursued the same bygone policy adopted by the British rulers, the policy of isolation. And, that was given a fillip to, when Professor Coupland, the British Constitutional Expert, came to this country prior to independence. He made a very sordid suggestion, a suggestion that the hills of Assam and the hills of Upper Burma must be bound together and a new colony instituted under the auspices of British rule.

That psychology is still there, and that is why we feel that the linguistic aspirations of the people inhabiting the NEFA area are to be met. But, somehow or other we are pursuing a most emasculated policy, and that is because of our bureaucrats, the administrators who have gone there all these years, who know nothing about the colourful life of the population there, the veins of the people there, the cultural standards of the people there and the aspirations of the people inhabiting the tribal areas – have their own steel-framed mind, and they suggest and commend certain things which go counter to the desires and aspirations of the people. That is the crux of the problem today.

I know, on the floor of the House I was just discussing the other day during Question Hour about certain memoranda submitted by the tribal people inhabiting this area. These people have been demanding that Assamese should be the medium of instruction in the schools but, somehow or other, Assamese is not the medium of instruction there, Hindi is being super-imposed. I want Hindi to develop, because Hindi is our national language, but not at the risk of super-imposing it on a people who want a different language, who have different aspirations and who, at the same time, say that Hindi is to be introduced as a compulsory subject in the later stages of educational life and not as a medium of instruction at the initial levels.

That is what Mahatma Gandhi has also said in his famous book called *Our Language Problem*. He has said that the medium of instruction must be in the mother tongue of the child. And, the medium of instruction should be in the mother tongue of the tribal population. We want these tribal dialects to develop into a language and not only as the medium of instruction at the elementary stage, we want this language to develop so as to be able to be the medium of instruction in the higher and secondary stages as well.

At the same time, these people have submitted more than one memorandum asking the Government of India to see that Assamese is used as the medium of instruction in the higher stages *i.e.* post-elementary stages because Assamese is the natural *lingua franca* of the People. There are different tribal groups. There are as many as 50 tribal groups living in the NEFA area. For some reasons these people have their own dialects, but in their inter-tribal communications, in the inter-tribal exchange of ideas they use only one language and that is Assamese. When these people inhabiting the tribal areas established contacts with the people of the plains, which they had been establishing since time immemorial before the British came and isolated them from the people of the plains, they used the Assamese language. Now there is a provision in our Constitution which provides for the ultimate integration of the NEFA region with the State of Assam. If that provision is given effect to, in that case, they must be taught in a language which they can understand.

Shri Ranga: Which Script would you like? Assamese?

Shri Hem Barua: I say like this. Naturally Assamese script may be used for the Assamese language. Hindi would be introduced at the higher stages, just as Hindi is introduced in the non-Hindi-speaking areas in the plains. Hindi should enjoy that position. That is what I say. At the same time, Assamese is their natural language.

I would quote from what Dr. Hutton, has said in his book called *The Sema Nagas* as follows:

> "Indeed the Assamese language as used in the Naga Hills is peculiarly well adapted for the reproduction of Naga idioms and as a vehicle of interpretation, it makes a far better *lingua franca* for the hills than Hindustani or English would, the substitution of which for Assamese has been occasionally suggested."

I want Hindi to occupy the same place as English is occupying today as far as we are concerned in those areas. I will quote another authority, W.C. Smith. In his book *The Ao Nagas,* he has siad:

> "In the neighbouring tribe, the Lohta Nagas, the Assamese language is used freely and this no doubt is largely due to the

fact that they raised cotton which is sold to the traders in the Assam Valley. In this way, their contacts have been more numerous. As a result of these contacts, the Assamese language is coming to be used by an increasing number of Nagas and the Assamese terms are creeping into their language."

I will quote another authority, J.P. Mills, He says:

"The Aos have probably received more admixture of actual Assamese blood than most Naga tribes, and during the Burmese invasions, many Assamese took refuge in the Ao country. The Lohta Nagas have long been in contact with the Assamese. Many villages even possess grants of land in the plains given by the Ahom Rajas."

Then, may I quote, Sir, another great authority on the tribal population of the north-east, Von Furer-Haimendorf. He says:

"If the tribesmen of the Subansiri region are to adapt themselves to their style of living and closer contacts with outside world, a measure of education is indispensable to make this process a success. Only literacy and a knowledge of Assamese can enable Dafalas or Apatanis to deal in equal terms with the people of the plains. There can be no doubt that acquisition of a working knowledge of colloquial Assamese must be the first choice among the Dafalas and South Kamal Miris."

My argument is this. The demand of this tribal population inhabiting the NEFA area – they live in 50 different groups–is for the Assamese language because of its historical association and because of the fact that Assamese is the natural *lingua franca* of the different tribal groups inhabiting the North-East Frontier Agency and also because that it is the natural language of the tribal population inhabiting the hills used in their contacts and communication with the people of the plains. That is why these tribal people have submitted that memorandum. As a matter of fact, I know that the memorandum, to which I made a reference on the floor of the House, was submitted to the Governor of Assam, who is incharge of the administration of the NEFA area, on the 22nd May by the tribal population of Ilargheflta demanding that Assamese should be the medium of instruction in the schools.

Another memorandum was submitted by the tribal people of the Lohit frontier division to the State Government. Recently on the 9th

June, there was a language day of the NEFA people organised by the Assam Sahitya Sabha and meetings were held demanding the introduction of Assamese as the medium of instruction. There were two speeches by two great tribal leaders, besides these by tribal students reading in the Basic training school at Marghita. The name of one is Ahang and the name of the other is Khongpai. These tribal leaders made speeches on the 9th June demanding Assamese to be the medium of instruction there in the NEFA regions.

Under these circumstances, I do not say that Hindi must not grow. Hindi is our national language and it must grow. As a matter of fact, since I came to New Delhi, the aspiration that is uppermost in my mind is that I should learn Hindi. The people in the non-Hindi-speaking areas should learn Hindi, but at the same time, they must learn it not at the expense of their own language nor at the expense of their own desires and aspirations. That is why I want this House to see that proper justice is done to the people inhabiting the NEFA region. India is a land of Einsteins and Adams and the Adams of India live in the north-east regions. So, we should see to it that the smouldering fire which was injected into them by the British and by Prof. Coupland, the British constitutional expert does not burst into a consuming flame and for that we should be able to satisfy the desires and aspirations of our people living in the tribal areas.

Shri Mohammed Imam (Chitaldrug): It should be a language which can be understood by everybody, irrespective of personal inclination.

Mr. Deputy-Speaker: The hon. Minister may speak in English or Hindi, as he likes.

Dr. K.L. Shrimali: I will start in English and end in Hindi.

Mr. Deputy-Speaker: There is half an hour in which he has to express what he want to say. Whether he wants to do it in two languages or one is his choice.

Dr. K.L. Shrimali: I should like to express my feelings of gratitude to the Members who have participated in the debate for their many constructive suggestions. It will not be possible for me to deal with all the points that have been raised by hon. Members; I would like to confine my remarks to the main issues that have been raised.

There has been a general dissatisfaction with our educational system. This is not a new thing. We had a legacy from the past and we have been dissatisfied with the whole educational system which we inherited from the British people. The Government has been making an attempt to reconstruct it. Whether the Government has been successful or has failed in the task of reconstruction has to be judged by this House. Before we pass judgment I would like the House to consider the criteria which we should lay down in passing that judgement. To my mind there are two criteria which should be laid down for making an appraisal of the national system of education of any country. In the first place, the system of education must be judged by the character and quality of the citizens. Does our educational system produce men with understanding? Do our people have faith in social ideas and social purpose? Do our peopole value spiritual and moral values more than material prosperity? These are some of the questions that we should ask ourselves in judging the system of education.

Now, Sir, I am prepared to admit that our educational system is far from being perfect. In fact, no country can claim that they have achieved perfection, as far as educational system is concerned. Education is a process of growth, a continuous growth and no finality can be achieved as far as education is concerned. The difficulty is that the results that we achieve sometimes are not perceptible. When we construct a bridge, or build a road, we see something concrete; when we put up a dam, it looks magnificent. Unfortunately, as regards the education of human personality is concerned it is a long drawn out process and the results are not either quick, or tangible.

Sir, the most important factor in the education of the child is the teacher. The house has rightly stressed that unless we improve the quality of our teachers, we shall not be able to improve our educational system. Education is an impact of the personality of the teacher on the child and unless we have men of character and ability and vision to make that impact, certainly we cannot have citizens of great vision and noble character.

The Ministry is fully aware of this weakness in our educational system and therefore in all its plans and programmes it has given the highest priority to the improving of the quality of the teachers. Even in a society like ours economic motive is a primary consideration, it is necessary that we should improve the salaries and emoluments of teachers and the Ministry has made a beginning, — it is a very small step, but a step in the right direction — by asking the State Governments to increase the salaries of teachers. We are giving assistance to State Governments, to increase the salaries of teachers at all levels, primary, secondary and university. At the primary and secondary stage we are giving assistance upto the extent of 15 per cent. of the increased expenditure. One hon. Member in the House pointed out that none of the States have taken advantage of this offer. This is not a correct statement. In 1956-57 we sanctioned Rs. 77,01,500. Four States could not take advantage of this offer, but most of them did.

Shri Harish Chanda Mathur: Which are the States which have not taken advantage?

Dr. K.L. Shrimali: The states which have not taken advantage are Andhra Pradesh, Mysore, Punjab and Jammu and Kashmir.

At the university level also we are giving assistance for raising the salaries of teachers. The Ministry, in addition to improving the quality of teachers, has taken various steps to reconstruct our educational system. We have arranged seminars for teachers, have made attempts to revise the curricula and text books, provided better educational facilities and have attempted to improve libraries and laboratories. Now it will take some time before all these steps that the Ministry has taken can make an impact on the educational system.

Education does not give results in one generation; it takes several years before tangible results can be shown. I can fully understand the feelings of hon. Members and the impatience which they have with regard to this question. But we have also to see that there are various influences which make an impact on the child. Home, surroundings, social institutions, the whole society in which the child moves and has his being influence the child and the school alone cannot change the personality of the child.

Sir, the second criterion that I would like to place before the House, the yardstick with which they should measure the educational system of the country is whether our educational system is geared to the changing needs of our society. We are living in a period of transition. Our society is undergoing transformation; the whole economy is changing. Now, have we been able to gear the whole educational system to meet the needs and requirements of the present society? If we have been able to do something in this direction we should be satisfied with what little we have done.

I would like to enumerate some of the steps which the Ministry has taken to gear the whole educational system to meet the requirements of our present society. It was said that in the field of technical education, there is a lag between the requirements of the society and the provision in the country. If we look at the development which has taken place during the last few years after independence in the field of technical education, I think we can look back with a feeling of satisfaction and also, if I may say so, with a feeling of pride. The policy of the Government was that there should be no State without its own facilities for the first degree and diploma courses in the basic branches of Engineering. I think all the States except Jammu and Kashmir have now provision for degree and diploma courses.

An Hon. Member: Why not Jammu and Kashmir?

Dr. K.L. Shrimali: That would come in course of time. That is the one State which has been left out so far.

In 1947 there was an annual admission of 2,900 students for the first degree course and 3,700 students for the diploma courses. Admissions have more than doubled in 10 years. We had 6,300 for the degree course and 8,800 for the diploma courses in 1956. The output of graduates increased from 1,300 in 1947 to over 4,000 in 1956 and diploma-holders from 1,450 to 4,200 during the same period which represents a three-fold increase. When all our schemes develop and reach maturity, the technical institutions in the whole country will be able to admit every year about 10,000 students for the degree course and 21,000 for the diploma courses by 1960-61.

We are not merely aiming at quantitative expansion. We are also trying to improve the quality of the training which is imparted at these institutions. We have made a comprehensive study of each State and we are now trying to improve the staff, personnel and other educational facilities inside these institutions. We have recently accepted a scheme for the expansion of the training capacity of some of the existing Engineering colleges and Polytechnics. The entire cost of the scheme is going to be Rs. 8.5 crores on the non-recurring side and Rs. 82 lakhs on the recurring side. Most of the expenditure is going to be met by the Central Government. In addition to these, we are giving loans for the construction of hostels, and improving the residential facilities in the institutions.

The House is aware that the Government was contemplating the setting up of four higher technological institutions in the country. We had already set up the Kharagpur Institute. We are setting up another in Bombay. In course of time, other institutions were to come. But, considering the urgency of the problem and the great need for supply of man-power for the industrial development that is going to take place in our country, it has been decided to set up all these institutions simultaneously.

Various other steps have been taken. The Institute of Science at Bangalore is being developed and it is now providing technological training in various subjects. Four Regional Schools of Printing are being set up in the four regions in addition to the one in Delhi. A School of Town and Country Planning has been established in Delhi.

Shri Ranga: Why concentrate in Delhi and a few cities only?

Dr. K.L. Shrimali: They are not concentrated.

Mr. Deputy-Speaker: The hon. Minister should read those that are outside.

An Hon. Member: First.

Dr. K.L. Shrimali: We have also decided to set up an Administrative Staff College for training new executives in business.

Shri Ranga: Also in Delhi?

Dr. K.L. Shrimali: That is in Hyderabad.

Shri Ranga: Again, one of the few cities.

Dr. K.L. Shrimali: That is the position with regard to technical education. Our young engineers who go out of these institutions and who are working in the factories in the various centres are enough proof that the technical institutions have been able to supply the man-power that is required for the development of our country.

I have had occasion to tell this House from time to time that steps have also been taken to re-organise our secondary education. Recently, we have set up the All India Council of Secondary Education which is trying to give technical assistance and guidance to the State Governments for the reorganization of education. Secondary Education is important. It is not only a preparation for the University, but it also aims at making education complete in itself and giving training to young people so that they might develop a sense of social responsibility and attain economic efficiency. The courses that are being provided in the multilateral schools will give various openings to the students. They need not follow the same beaten track, the academic course. They can choose courses according to their aptitudes and abilities. They may go to academic courses; or technical or vocational courses. In this way, we hope that the great rush to the Universities will be prevented. We expect that most of the students who go out of our Secondary schools will enter life with adequate preparation and with a full sense of social responsibility.

The most depressing feature of our educational system is elementary education. I am distressed as many other members are distressed that we are far from reaching the targets that we had laid down in the Constitution. The Report of the Planning Commission which this House has already accepted had said that by the end of the Second Five Year Plan, educational facilities will be provided for only 63 per cent. of the age group 6 –11 and 23 per cent. of the age group 11 – 14. There is no possibility now of achieving the target laid on the Constitution by the end of Second Plan. Here, again, we have to take into account the economic situation in the country. Education is dependent to a large extent on economic factors. It also helps in promoting economic development. But, unless we have adequate resources, we will have to remain satisfied with the progress that we have made.

Various suggestions have been made. Some have been made in a great spirit of enthusiasm, with all sincerity. But education costs money. We cannot have a system of free compulsory education for nothing. The country must find resources for us to provide a free system of education.

Shri B. Dasgupta: May I know whether it is on the basis of the shift system recommended by the Planning Commission that these targets were mentioned or without the shift system?

Dr. K.L. Shrimali: As far as I remember, the report of the discussions which the Planning Commission had at Poona has not reached us. I expect they have taken into account the shift system also.

I think it was Dr. Sushila Nayar who said that we should scrap university education in order to provide for elementary and secondary education.

Dr. Sushila Nayar: I said further spending of money on the arts colleges should be stopped and it should be spent on technical and elementary education. I did not say all college education should be stopped.

Dr. K.L. Shrimali: I am afraid I do not agree with the view which my hon. friend holds. University education and secondary education are as important as elementary education. If we stop university education, I do not know from where we are going to get our teachers.

Shri Ranga: From where are we going to get our know-how?

Dr. K.L. Shrimali: From where are we going to get leaders in the community? If a country cannot spend anything on university education....

Dr. Sushila Nayar: I had said: leave it to the private sector. I did not say there was no need in the country. I said the Government should concentrate on elementary education.

Dr. K.L. Shrimali: I quite agree that elementary education is the foundation of our democracy. We cannot call ourselves democratic and at the same time keep our children outside the educational institutions. We must move towards that direction, but it will be a wrong step to stop university education altogether.

It was pointed out by an hon. Member that there is a great disparity in the percentage of boys and girls attending elementary schools. The Ministry is taking special steps in this new plan to promote the education of girls. We are making special efforts and making certain recommendations to the State Governments which, if and when accepted, will go a long way in removing this disparity.

We are proposing to provide free accommodation for women teachers in rural areas and have also proposed that school mothers must be appointed in rural areas.

Shri Ranga: What do you mean by "school mothers"?

Dr. K.L. Shrimali: A person who would not only look after the children, but would also educate.

Shri D.C. Sharma: (Gurdaspur): That means a school teacher should be called school father.

Dr. K.L. Shrimali: Then we propose to organise condensed and special course of general education and teacher training for adult women. We also propose to award stipends to women teachers for teachers' training courses at under-graduate level, organise refresher courses for trained women teachers who need employment or who are already in employment. We also propose to award stipends for classes 8 to 11 provided the recipients undertake to take up teaching for a period of five years at least.

Then there are schemes for elementary school pupils—all for girls. We propose to award attendance scholarship to girls in elementary schools, and also exempt girls from tuition fees in all elementary schools.

Shri Ranga: Are there tuition fees in elementary schools now?

Dr. K.L. Shrimali: Wherever there are fees.

Shri Ranga: Where are they?

Dr. K.L. Shrimali: There are some States which are charging.

Shri Ranga: I thought it was free. It is free, is it not?

Dr. K.L. Shrimali: Not everywhere.

Mr. Deputy-Speaker: Not everywhere.

Dr. K.L. Shrimali: These are some of the schemes which we propose to take up to expand our elementary education for girls.

With regard to the propogation of Hindi, there have been arguments from both sides. As time passes, I feel that people will realise that the steps and the constructive approach that the Ministry has adopted with regard to the propogation of Hindi are the correct ones.

An Hon. Member: Very slow.

Dr. K.L. Shrimali: It is slow, but some work by its very nature has to be slow.

The work that has been done with regard to technological terms, about which Hon'ble Seth Govind Dasji said that the Ministry was not making satisfactory progress, is not a very easy work. It is not easy to construct a language. You have to give some thought and devote a lot of time before a word can be coined.

In the year 1952 we evolved nearly 2,000 words. Since then we have been making continuous progress. In 1953 we coined 3,623 words, in 1954, 15,692 words, in 1955, 23,145 words and in 1956, 30,354 words.

Shri Goray (Poona): But who is using those words?

Dr. K.L. Shrimali: The country will use them when they are ready.

Seth Govind Das: Are they all finalised?

Dr. K.L. Shrimali: Till 1956-57, 90,000 have been finalised in seven years or six years?

Dr. K.L. Shrimali: As I said, this is a work which cannot be done in haste, and we have to be very careful when we are constructing terminology. We are hoping to have 50,000 terms every year from now onwards, and we hope that by the time the administration takes to Hindi we will be ready as far as the terminology is concerned.

In addition to this, the Ministry has taken various steps and proposes to take various steps to propogate Hindi.

Shri Ranga: How?

Dr. K.L. Shrimali: We are preparing encyclopaedias and dictionaries, preparing manuals for using these technological terms. We propose to organise debates in the non-Hindi-speaking areas. We propose to organise lecture tours both in the Hindi-speaking and non-Hindi-speaking areas. And in this way the various steps that we are taking will help in promoting the official language.

Shri Ranga: How far are you encouraging the Hindi-knowing pandits hailing from non-Hindi-speaking areas in Central Government employment?

Dr. K.L. Shrimali: This is a different question that my hon. friend has raised.

Shri Ranga: Then, what is the encouragement that you are giving?

Dr. K.L. Shrimali: Shri Awasthi had suggested that there was no need for a Central Board of Terminology. It was after very great thought that the Central Board was appointed and if you only look at the different kinds of words that are being used, you will be convinced that this is the right step which the Government has taken.

After this the hon. Minister gave examples of the words "accredited" and "balance-sheet" used in Hindi in place of these words in different states.[1]

Shri Jhulan Sinha: It is already 4.20 p.m. We were told that non-official business would start at 4.15 p.m. May I know when it will be taken up?

Mr. Deputy-Speaker: We shall devote as much time as has been allotted to non-official business. We can push it ahead by another ten minutes. That does not matter.

Dr. Ram Subhag Singh (Sasaram): What are the terms that have been accepted by Government? The Minister has not stated them.

The Minister of Health (Shri Karmarkar): That will be decided.

Mr. Deputy-Speaker: Is there much more to be said by the Minister?

Dr. K.L. Shrimali: Yes, I shall take a few more minutes.

Dr. Ram Subhag Singh: They are not having any terminology now.

Dr. K.L. Shrimali: Then, I have got something to say about scientific research.

An Hon. Member: What was the word finally accepted by the Board?

Dr. Ram Subhag Singh: When the Minister has pointed out the different translations, he ought to give his substitute.

Mr. Deputy-Speaker: Government have not taken any decision yet.

Dr. K.L. Shrimali: Government have not finalised the whole terminology so far.

Dr. Ram Subhag Singh: They are not proceeding themselves; nor do they want that anybody else should proceed.

Dr. K.L. Shrimali: This is not fair. So far, nobody has raised any objection to the terminology which Government have prepared.

---

1. Not included.

Dr. Ram Subhag Singh: What is that terminology? The Minister should explain it.

Dr. K.L. Shrimali: I cannot say what word they are using for "accredited", because Government have not finalised all the terms.

Dr. Ram Subhag Singh: The Minister has given words from Calcutta, Patna and Bhopal, but it is very difficult for him to give the word which has been coined by the Delhi Secretariat which is so near. I cannot understand what the Minister is saying.

Mr. Deputy-Speaker: What the Minister wanted to explain was that because there was difference of opinion and there was need to have standard words, and different words were being used, there was the necessity of appointing a Central Board. But he has not seen whether any finality has been reached with regard to any of these words which, he has stated, are being used by the different State Governments.

Dr. Ram Subhag Singh: My point is very simple, namely that that body should not remain idle, but it should act.

Shri Sonavane (Sholapur--Reserved--Sch. Castes): Let the hon. Minister give us some examples of the different words which are used by the different States, and the words accepted by the Board as final or the words of their choice.

Mr. Deputy-Speaker: We shall have them on a different occasion, not today.

Dr. K.L. Shrimali: I would like to add a word with regard to the great work that is being done in our national laboratories. We have now 18 laboratories, and the research work that is being done there should find a place of pride in any country. We have passed through the formative period, and we are now making an attempt to gear up the whole research work to the programme of national development.

There are various practical problems that these laboratories are tackling, with regard to fuel, food, building construction, leather, drugs, mining, metallurgy, roads, glass and ceramics, electro-chemicals, electronics and salt industries. I have no doubt that the House would agree that we have laid solid foundations for the future scientific research in our country.

Shri Ranga: We do not know.

Pandit Thakur Das Bhargava (Hissar): Give us some specimens of the results.

Dr. Ram Subhag Singh: No results.

Shri Ranga: May we know whether any effort is being made by Government to have a committee of evaluation or something like that in order to see whether the reports that these various research institutes send to Governments approximate to their actual achievement?

Dr. K.L. Shrimali: The Council of Scientific and Industrial Research, under which all these laboratories function, evaluate the programme. The Prime Minister himself is the chairman of this Council, and the Council evaluate the programme from time to time.

Shri Ranga: Do they do it themselves, or does somebody else do it?

Dr. K.L. Shrimali: If you only look at the patents which have been leased out to industry for the last few years, you will understand that the laboratories have done useful work.

Shri Ranga: I am talking of the research institutes and laboratories and the evaluation of their programmes and achievements. Patents have nothing to do with them. (*Interruptions*).

Mr. Deputy-Speaker: Already, we have drawn very heavily on the non-official business. So, perhaps, we might proceed with this.

Pandit Thakur Das Bhargava: We do not know what those patents are.

Dr. K.L. Shrimali: There are various patents. Out of 450 patents prepared, 166 have been leased out to industry for commercial exploitation.

Shri Goray: What has happened to the solar cooker? What has happened to that great discovery?

Dr. K.L. Shrimali: I understand it is already in the market.

Shri M.K. Ghosh: It is out of market.

Dr. K.L. Shrimali: This is a brief review of the work that has been done by the Ministry. As I said in the beginning, we do not by any means think that we have reached perfection. We shall continue our endeavour to reconstruct our educational system, so that it may suit the genius and culture of our people.

Finally, I would like to say a word of appreciation of the thousands of teachers who are working in the field of education. Many of them are unknown, but still....

Shri D.C. Sharma: They want salary scales, not words of appreciation.

Dr. K.L. Shrimali: Along with salary scales, if there is a word of appreciation, it gives them encouragement. I wish to mention this on the floor of the House because they are doing national service. The country should recognise that our teachers are doing national work.

Shri Hem Barua: At starvation levels.

Dr. K.L. Shrimali: If I had more time, I would have liked to deal with the various activities of the Ministry and the work that has been done by the Ministry.

Pandit Thakur Das Bhargava: That may be circulated now.

Dr. K.L. Shrimali: The report has already been circulated....

Shri M.L. Dwivedi: He may circulate a detailed note.

Mr. Deputy-Speaker: Hon. Members may accept this much now.

Shri M.L. Dwivedi (Hamirpur): This is a brief one. So, he may circulate a detailed note.

Dr. K.L. Shrimali: I should also like to say a word of appreciation of the officers of the Ministry, whose photographs and names do not appear in the press.

Shri Ranga: Quite a lot are there.

Shri D.C. Sharma: No. They do appear.

Dr. K.L. Shrimali: They are a band of devoted workers.

Dr. Ram Subhag Singh: This is bad practice, that a Minister should come here and start praising his secretariat.

Shri Barrow (Nominated–Anglo-Indians): Lots of lip-service.

Mr. Deputy-Speaker: There is no harm in saying a few words in general.

Dr. Ram Subhag Singh: No Minister has done like that so far. But this practice is being newly introduced.

Mr. Deputy-Speaker: If appreciation of a particular person is made, that would be objectionable. But, so far as general remarks about the general body are concerned, I suppose there is no harm.

Have I the permission of the House to put all the cut motions to the vote of the House?

Shri Sadhan Gupta *rose–*

Mr. Deputy-Speaker: We have got the address by the Prime Minister also. So, perhaps, I might be allowed to proceed.

I shall now put all the cut motions to vote:

All the cut motions were put and negatived.

Mr.Deputy-Speaker: I shall now put the Demands for Grants to vote. They have to be put in two groups.

The question is:

"That the respective sums not exceeding the amounts

shown in the fourth column of the Order Paper including the sums already voted on account for the relevant services be granted to the President to defray the charges which will come in course of payment during the year ending the 31st day of March, 1958, in respect of Demands Nos. 13, 22 and 107."

The motion was adopted.

Mr. Deputy-Speaker: The question is:

"That the respective sums not exceeding the amounts shown in the fourth column of the Order Paper, be granted to the President, to complete the sums necessary to defray the charges which will come in course of payment during the year ending the 31st day of March, 1958, in respect of the following heads of Demands entered in the second column thereof;

Demands Nos. 14, 15, 16, 17, 18, 19, 20 and 21."

The motion was adopted.

[*The motions for Demands for Grants which were adopted by the Lok Sabha are reproduced below – Ed.*]

DEMAND NO. 13—MINISTRY OF EDUCATION AND SCIENTIFIC RESEARCH

"That a sum not exceeding Rs. 65,24,000 including the sums already voted on account for the relevant services be granted to the President to defray the charges which will come in course of payment during the year ending the 31st day of March, 1958, in respect of 'Ministry of Education and Scientific Research'."

DEMAND NO. 14—ARCHAEOLOGY

"That a sum not exceeding Rs. 56,54,000 be granted to the President to complete the sum necessary to defray the charges which will come in course of payment during the year ending the 31st day of March, 1958, in respect of 'Archaeology'."

DEMAND NO. 15—SURVEY OF INDIA

"That a sum not exceeding Rs. 96,16,000 be granted to the President to complete the sum necessary to defray the charges which will come in course of payment during the year ending the 31st day of March, 1958, in respect of 'Survey of India'."

DEMAND NO. 16—BOTANICAL SURVEY

"That a sum not exceeding Rs. 6,22,000 be granted to the President to complete the sum necessary to defray the charges which will come in course of payment during the year ending the 31st day of March, 1958, in respect of 'Botanical Survey'."

DEMAND NO. 17—ZOOLOGICAL SURVEY

"That a sum not exceeding Rs. 5,97,000 be granted to the President to complete the sum necessary to defray the charges which will come in course of payment during the year ending the 31st day of March, 1958, in respect of 'Zoological Survey'."

DEMAND NO. 18—GEOLOGICAL SURVEY

"That a sum not exceeding Rs. 55,62,000 be granted to the President to complete the sum necessary to defray the charges which will come in course of payment during the year ending the 31st day of March, 1958, in respect of 'Geological Survey'."

DEMAND NO. 19—SCIENTIFIC RESEARCH

"That a sum not exceeding Rs. 2,07,78,000 be granted to the President to complete the sum necessary to defray the charges which will come in course of payment during the year ending the 31st day of March, 1958, in respect of 'Scientific Research'."

DEMAND NO. 20—OTHER SCIENTIFIC DEPARTMENTS

"That a sum not exceeding Rs. 1,61,14,000 be granted to the President to complete the sum necessary to defray the charges which will come in course of payment during the year ending the 31st day of March, 1958, in respect of 'Other Scientific Departments'."

DEMAND NO. 21—EDUCATION

"That a sum not exceeding Rs. 15,08,86,000 be granted to the President to complete the sum necessary to defray the charges which will come in course of the payment during the year ending the 31st day of March, 1958, in respect of 'Education'."

DEMAND NO. 22—MISCELLANEOUS DEPARTMENTS AND EXPENDITURE UNDER THE MINISTRY OF EDUCATION AND SCIENTIFIC RESEARCH

"That a sum not exceeding Rs. 1,95,54,000 including the sums already voted on account for the relevant services be granted to the President to defray the charges which will come in course of payment during the year ending the 31st day of March, 1958, in respect of

'Miscellaneous Departments and Expenditure under the Ministry of Education and Scientific Research'."

DEMAND NO. 107—CAPITAL OUTLAY OF THE MINISTRY OF EDUCATION AND SCIENTIFIC RESEARCH

"That a sum not exceeding Rs. 1,83,17,000 including the sums already voted on account for the relevant services be granted to the President to defray the charges which will come in course of payment during the year ending the 31st day of March, 1958, in respect of 'Capital Outlay of the Ministry of Education and Scientific Research'."

Document No. 38

Answers (on behalf of Maulana Azad) by Dr. Shrimali to the questions asked in the Lok Sabha on November 13, 1957

INSTITUTE OF INDOLOGY

Shri B.S. Murthy:
Shri Shivananjappa:

Will the Minister of **Education and Scientific Research** be pleased to state:

(a) whether Government propose to set up an Institute of Indology;

(b) if so, where;

(c) the scope and functions of the Institute; and

(d) the annual estimated expenditure on it?

Dr. K.L. Shrimali: (a) Yes, Sir.

(b) In New Delhi.

(c) As regards the scope of the Institute, while a tentative scheme has been drawn up, it is proposed that the precise scope of the Institute may be worked out by the Director when one is appointed.

Its functions will be higher studies and research in all branches of Indology and allied subjects.

(d) Rs. 2,65,640.

Document No. 39

Answers dated 13-11-1957, of Dr. Shrimali (on behalf of Maulana Azad), to the questions asked in the Lok Sabha

HINDI LITERATURE IN N.E.S.

Shri Keshava: Will the Minister of **Education and Scientific Research** be pleased to state:

(a) whether it is a fact that in the National Extension Service Blocks in Uttar Pradesh the literature prepared in Hindi for the villagers was not understood by them; and

(b) if so, the steps, if any, taken to remedy the situation?

Dr. K.L. Shrimali: (a) Government have no such information.

(b) Does not arise.

Document No. 40

Answers dated 13-11-1957, of Dr. K.L. Shrimali, on behalf of Maulana Abul Kalam Azad, to the questions asked in the Lok Sabha

MONUMENTS IN ASSAM

Shri Amjad Ali: Will the Minister of **Education and Scientific Research** be pleased to refer to the reply given to Starred Question No. 850 on the 13th August, 1957 and State the sum of money allotted to each of the monuments of National importance in Assam with their names?

Dr. K.L. Shrimali: A statement is laid on the Table of the Lok Sabha. [See Appendix I, Annexure No. 47.]

Document No. 41

Answers dated 13-11-1957, of Dr. K.L. Shrimali, on behalf of Maulana Abul Kalam Azad, to the questions asked in the Lok Sabha

SCHOOLS IN HIMACHAL PRADESH

Shri D.C. Sharma: Will the Minister of **Education and Scientific Research** be pleased to state the number of primary, middle and high schools in the Himachal Pradesh and the number of students studying in them?

Dr. K.L. Shrimali:

	No. of Institutions		*No. of Students*
(i)	High Schools	45	20,927
(ii)	Middle Schools	108	17,446
(iii)	Primary Schools	771	36,054

Document No. 42

Answers on behalf of Maulana Azad, by Dr. Shrimali, to the questions asked in the Lok Sabha on November 18, 1957

ENGINEERING COLLEGE AT WARANGAL

Shri E.M. Rao: Will the Minister of **Education and Scientific Research** be pleased to state:

(a) whether any representation has been received from the Government of Andhra with regard to the establishment of an Engineering College at Warangal;

(b) if so, the steps taken in the matter; and

(c) whether it is also a fact that a building worth Rs. 6 lakhs had been donated by Pingle Brothers of Warangal for utilisation for educational purposes?

Dr. K.L. Shrimali: (a) and (b) Government of the former Hyderabad State had proposed in October, 1956 that a new engineering college be established in Warangal. The State Government was informed that as new technical institutions can only be established in accordance with the Second Five Year Plan the question of an engineering college in Warangal could be considered if the State Government made the necessary financial provision in its five Year Plan. The matter is under the consideration of the State Government of Andhra.

(c) Government of Hyderabad had indicated the possibility of getting some buildings in Warangal as a gift from a local landlord.

Document No. 43

Answers[1], dated 18-11-1957, of Dr. M.M. Das, to the questions asked in the Lok Sabha

NORTH AND SOUTH HIGHER TECHNOLOGICAL INSTITUTES

Shri S.C. Samanta:
Shri Subodh Hasda:
Shri R.C. Majhi:
Shri T.B. Vittal Rao:

Will the Minister of **Education and Scientific Research** be pleased to state:

(a) whether any progress has been made in the establishment of the North and South Higher Technological Institutes;

(b) whether the sites for the location of the Institutions in Kanpur and Madras have finally been selected;

(c) whether any planning committee has been set up for the purpose; and

(d) whether any expert or experts and any equipment have arrived either from West Germany or U.S.A.?

Shri M.M. Das: (a) to (d) A statement giving the required information is laid on table of the Lok Sabha. [See Appendix I, Annexure No. 95.]

Shri S.C. Samanta: May I know the constitution of the Planning Committee? How many meetings have been held so far?

Shri M.M. Das: Each one of these planning committees consist of fifteen members. The southern committee has been set up under the chairmanship of Dr. A.L. Mudaliar and the northern, under the chairmanship of Lala Sri Ram. The members consist of representatives of the Central Education Ministry, Ministry of Commerce and Industry, Vice-Chancellors of universities, industrialists, directors of national laboratories and some Principals of technical institutions.

---

1. On behalf of Maulana Azad.

No meeting have been held so far; they are going to meet in the near future.

Shri S.C. Samanta: May I know whether the topmost priority will be given to these schemes because of the shortage of engineering personnel in the country? If so, how many admissions will be there of under-graduates and post-graduates?

Shri M.M. Das: Originally, the decision of the Government was that these two higher technological institutions will be established during the latter part of the Second Plan. The present decision is to establish them as soon as circumstances permit. The ultimate enrolment figures are: under-graduates – 1500 and post-graduates – 500 in each institution.

Dr. Ram Subhag Singh: The hon. Deputy Minister has said that no meeting has been held so far by these committees though it is a matter of great importance. May I know whether, at the time of setting up such committees, the Government enquire whether the persons who are going to be appointed on them as members or as chairman are having time at their disposal becaue they are on several committees ?

Shri M.M. Das: The committees have been recently set up and we have got every hope and we expect that they are quite fit to take up their work and do the job as efficiently as possible.

Shri V.P. Nayar: I want to know whether one of the terms of reference to these committees is the location of the institute. Have the Government decided in an irrevocable manner about the location of the two proposed institutions?

Shri M.M. Das: The question of allocation has been irrevocably decided by the Government. The decision is that the Southern Institute will be established in Madras and the Northern Institute in Kanpur. So far as particular sites are concerned, the respective State Governments have offered certain plots. With regard to the selection of these plots no final decision has yet been taken.

Shri Narayanankutty Menon: May I know whether before the selection of the sites for these institutions the Central Government consulted the various State Governments and gave them an opportunity to place their claims before the Central Government?

Shri M.M. Das: We have got four Regional Committees in the four different parts of India. So far as the question of location of these technological institutes is concerned, the matter was discussed in the C.T.E. Committees where every State belonging to the particular region is represented.

Shri N.B. Maiti: May I know the date of appointment of this Committee?

Shri M.M. Das: The exact date is not at my disposal, but I know that these planning committees were set up only recently.

Shri Ramakrishnan: May I know whether the standards set up for the courses would conform to university standards of the respective States, or whether the standards would conform to countries which are participating in the establishment of these institutions?

Shri M.M. Das: The standards of these institutions will be fixed according to the standards of the Kharagpur Institute.

Document No. 44

Answers dated 18-11-1957 (on behalf of Maulana Azad), by Dr. Shrimali, to the questions asked in the Lok Sabha

HINDI SHIKSHA SAMITI

Shri V.C. Shukla:
Dr. Ram Subhag Singh:

Will the Minister of **Education and Scientific Research** be pleased to state:

(a) whether Hindi Shiksha Samiti has urged the Central Ministry of Education to give direct grants to All India Hindi Organisations for the purpose of propagation of Hindi in non-Hindi speaking areas;

(b) whether the Government have accepted this recommendation; and

(c) if so, by what time Government propose to implement this recommendation?

Dr. K.L. Shrimali: (a) to (c) A statement is laid on the Table of the Lok Sabha.

STATEMENT

(a) The Hindi Shiksha Samiti suggested that direct grants be given by the Government of India to All-India Hindi Organisations for the propagation of Hindi.

(b) No.

(c) The question does not arise.

Shri V.C. Shukla: What are the specific reasons for not accepting the recommendations of the Hindi Shiksha Samiti?

Dr. K.L. Shrimali: As the hon. Member is aware, prior to 1954 grants were given to private organisations and the main work of propagation was done by private organisations. Later on it was found that there was no harmony, and sometimes there was conflict between States and these organisations. Therefore, in 1954 the Government took a decision that propagation of Hindi would be done by the State

Governments. This question was again discussed at the Conference of Education Ministers, and it was decided that for one year at least the State Governments should be given a trial and the position reviewed after a year.

Shri V.C. Shukla: May I know whether it is a fact that grants to various States for propagation of Hindi have been continuously lapsing for the last few years because of non-implementation of the recommendations?

Dr. K.L. Shrimali: I am sorry it is a fact that every year a certain amount has been lapsing because the grants sanctioned are not utilised by the State Governments.

Shri Dasappa: What has been the total amount spent in non-Hindi-speaking areas during these three or four years?

Dr. K.L. Shrimali: As far as propagation of Hindi is concerned, amount is spent only in non-Hindi-speaking areas. As far as development of Hindi is concerned, that is a work which is sometimes given to organisations in Hindi-speaking areas. There is a difference between development of Hindi and propagation of Hindi. The hon. Member is probably referring to development of Hindi.

Shri Dasappa: My question was simple and specific. I want to know how much has been spent till now on propagation of Hindi in non-Hindi-speaking areas, because propagation is not needed in Hindi-speaking areas.

Dr. K.L. Shrimali: In 1956-57 a sum of Rs. 2,83,905 was sanctioned out of which only Rs. 1,65,502 was utilised in non-Hindi-speaking States.

Document No. 45

Answers by Dr. Shrimali, on behalf of Maulana Azad, to the questions asked in the Lok Sabha on November 21, 1957

RESEARCH ON SECONDARY EDUCATION

Shri Shree Narayan Das: Will the Minister of **Education and Scientific Research** be pleased to refer to the reply given to Starred Question No. 971 on the 15th September, 1954 and state:

(a) whether the results of researches made under the programme drawn up for encouraging training colleges and education departments of Universities to undertake researches on specific problems of Secondary Education have been scrutinised by any expert body;

(b) whether the results achieved so far justify the expenditure incurred on this account; and

(c) whether any new Universities have come forward to do the work?

Dr. K.L. Shrimali: (a) The technical staff of the Ministry is responsible for scrutinizing the results of such researches. The research reports are then placed before the annual conference of Principals of training colleges concerned. Suggestions made by the conference are carefully considered.

(b) and (c) Yes, Sir.

Shri Shrree Narayan Das: May I know what is the strength of the technical committee at the Centre, which scrutinises the result of the researches carried on?

Dr. K.L. Shrimali: There is no regular committee. There is a staff in the division of secondary education which, along with other work, also looks into the reports about these researches.

Shri Shree Narayan Das: May I know whether any period has been fixed, whether any regular reports have been asked for from the various institutions, whether those reports have been compiled by this committee and whether the committee has formulated any results and, if so, whether they have been published?

Dr. K.L. Shrimali: A report is already ready. All these investigations which have been carried on so far has been compiled into a report and the report is under print. I shall also place a copy of it in the Library for the information of the Members. I do not know what other questions the hon. Member asked.

Shri Shree Narayan Das: I wanted to know whether any periodical reports are asked for ?

Dr. K.L. Shrimali: Yes, Sir. We ask the institutions to send us regular reports. There is no fixed time-limit for the researches. It will take two or three years, and sometimes more. It all depends on the nature of the research.

Raja Mahendra Pratap: What is the object of this secondary education?

Mr. Speaker: That has to be debated at the time of the budget session and the budget discussion. If the hon. Member wants that the budget on education should be given up, then he may press the issue then.

Shri C.R. Pattabhi Raman: Will the Government ensure that a uniform policy obtains so far as secondary education is concerned throughout India?

Dr. K.L. Shrimali: This is beside the question.

Shri Thimmaiah: May I know the names of the universities where this research is being conducted?

Dr. K.L. Shrimali: It is a long list. There are 20 institutions. If the hon. Member is interested, I shall place a list on the Table of the House.

Shri Shree Narayan Das: As a result of the results achieved in this direction, may I know whether the Government propose to continue this programme for research, and, if so, what is the period?

Dr. K.L. Shirmali: Yes, Sir. It is going to be continued.

Mr. Speaker: Before I call upon the sponsor of the question, the hon. Members will get up in their seats and catch the eye of the Chair.

Document No. 46

Answers dated 21-11-1957, of Dr. Shrimali, on behalf of Maulana Abul Kalam Azad, to the questions asked in the Lok Sabha

EDUCATION MINISTERS' CONFERENCE

Shri Shree Narayan Das:
Shri Bibhuti Mishra:
Shri Radha Raman:
Dr. Ram Subhag Singh:
Shri Naval Prabhakar:
Shri Kumaran:
Shri Sanganna:
Shri N.R. Muniswamy:
Shri Mahanty:
Shri Tangamani:

Will the Minister of **Education and Scientific Research** be pleased to state:

(a) the subjects discussed at the conference of the State Ministers of Education held at New Delhi on the 19th and 20th September, 1957 under the auspices of the Union Minister of Education;

(b) the nature of decisions arrived at on various subjects, especially in respect of–

(i) introduction of universal free and compulsory education for children up to the age of eleven,

(ii) constitution of a smaller joint body of the representatives of the Union and State Governments in place of the Central Advisory Board of Education,

(iii) nationalisation of text books, and

(iv) sanction of grants directly to Hindi organisations of a national character for propagation of Hindi in non-Hindi-speaking areas, and

(c) the steps taken so far for implementation of these decisions?

Dr. K.L. Shrimali: (a) to (c) A statement is placed on the Table of the Lok Sabha. [See Appendix II, Annexure No. 34.]

Shri Shree Narayan Das: From the statement, it appears that there was a large number of questions with regard to each item and that there are some conclusions reached by the Conference. May I know whether any time-limit has been fixed during which the State Governments and other concerns have been asked to implement those resolutions?

Dr. K.L. Shrimali: No, Sir. No time-limit has been fixed. From the nature of the work, it is difficult to place any time-limit, but we have already sent the minutes of the Conference to the State Governments and have requested them to implement them as early as possible. As far as the Central Government are concerned, they are examining their own proposals and they are taking necessary action.

Shri Tangamani: In the statement, we find that the three-year degree course has also been discussed, and may I know whether this proposal is being opposed by Bombay and Uttar Pradesh?

Dr. K.L. Shrimali: As far as I know, there are two universities which have not yet accepted this scheme–the Bombay University and the University of Agra. As far as other Universities are concerned, most of them have accepted this three-year degree course in principle and are implementing it in due course.

Shri Damani *rose*–

Mr. Speaker: Shri Sanganna.

Some Hon. Members: He is not Shri Sanganna.

Mr. Speaker: I have called this hon. Member. I called Shri Sanganna. He did not get up. He did not hear. He is not here possibly. I have called this hon. Member. I know most of them by name. I am trying to get to know the names of others.

Shri Damani: May I know whether Government have considered the changes that take place in the textbooks and whether any decisions have been taken to see that changes of textbooks are made after a long period?

Dr. K.L. Shrimali: This is beyond this question.

Shri R. Ramanathan Chettiar: May I know whether the Kerala Education Bill was one of the subjects that was discussed in this Conference?

Dr. K.L. Shrimali: No, Sir.

Shri Radha Raman: May I know whether the Education Ministers' Conference had discussion with regard to the inclusion of manual work before any degree or diploma or certificate is awarded to the students of higher secondary schools?

Dr. K.L. Shrimali: The whole statement has been placed on the Table of the House, and it gives full information with regard to all the points that have been discussed at the Conference.

Dr. Ram Subhag Singh: The other day, the hon. Minister said that he was thoroughly dissatisfied with the state of affairs in the Delhi schools. May I know what efforts the Government propose to make the education of children between the ages of 6 and 11 compulsory and for that purpose what improvements are they going to effect throughout the country?

Mr. Speaker: How does this arise out of this question? These are decisions of the Conference.

Dr. Ram Subhag Singh: The hon. Minister mentioned the other day specifically. They say that the education of children of the age-group 6–11 should be made free, compulsory and universal by the end of the third Five Year Plan at the latest. What efforts they are going to make in this direction?

Dr. K.L. Shrimali: As far as the Centrally administered areas are concerned, I might inform the hon. Member that we are only making estimates for introducing free and compulsory education for the age-group 6-11. But there is no provision in the Plan for the expansion of education in Delhi. We are now trying to find out if funds could be available from other sources to implement this Plan for Delhi.

Shri N.R. Muniswamy: May I enquire what is the estimate of additional expenditure that will be incurred in giving effect to the proposals taken at the Conference and the conclusions that have been arrived at? What is the amount to be incurred?

Dr. K.L. Shrimali: It is very difficult for me to give the estimates for all the recommendations–for free and compulsory introduction of education, the reorganisation of universities, etc. I would refer the hon. Member to the Planning Commission's report which gives a fair picture of the amount that will be needed and that is allotted to it.

Mr. Speaker: For some time past, I have been considering as to what I should do with respect to questions to which a number of names have been added. I cannot obviously give opportunity to every hon. Member who put the question–even to all those Members whose names appear here. Others also want to take part. Therefore, in such cases, I would rather more easily grant a half-hour discussion if the hon. Members are not satisfied with the answers given here and some more elucidation is necessary, in which case, those hon. Members will each put a question and in the end the hon. Minister will give a reply.

Now, with respect to matters where a statement is laid on the Table of the House, the hon. Minister, whoever might be incharge, cannot be expected to go into the details of everyone of the items. Then it becomes a discussion. The House wants to know what has happened at the Conference. Here and there, one or two questions may be put, but the details regarding the Conference as to why a particular decision was taken or was not taken would not come within the scope of the questions here. I do not know; I would like to consult the Business Advisory Committee or the General Purposes Committee as to what we shall do with regard to such matters--how far an opportunity is necessary and how an opportunity can be given.

PART II: REMAINING DOCUMENTS

Document No. 47

Letter From Mahatama Gandhi to Azad[1] and Das[2]

Sabarmati,
Ahmedabad,
19th December, 1921.

Your wire composition (and) date (of) conference should be previously determined. Release should include prisoners convicted for fatwas, including Karanchi ones. Subject to these conditions in additon (to) yours, we can, in my opinion, waive Hartal.

Gandhi

1. Maulana Abul Kalam Azad.
2. Mr. C.R. Das.

Document No. 48

Telegram from Maulana Azad and C.R. Das to Mahatma Gandhi

Calcutta
19th December, 1921

Mahatama Gandhi
Sabarmati, Ahmedabad

We recommended calling off hartal on following conditions :

1. Government calling a Conference (which shall) soon consider all questions raised by Congress;
2. Withdrawal of recent Government Communique and Police and Magisterial orders;
3. Releasing all prisoners under this new law unconditionally.

Reply immediately, care Suprintendent, Presidency Jail, Calcutta.

A.K. Azad
C.R. Das

Document No. 49

Letter of Begum Abul Kalam Azad to Mahatama Gandhi, dated 9-2-1922 and Gandhiji's comments on it

'Begum Abul Kalam Azad[1] sends me the following telegraphic message by letter post:

"Judgment has delivered today in the case against my husband Maulana Abul Kalam Azad. He has been sentenced to only one year rigorous imprisonment. This is astoundingly less that what I was waiting for. In conviction and imprisonment, be the reward of national service, you will admit that great injustice has been done to him in the inadequacy of the sentence. It does not even approximate to the minimum of his deserts. I make bold to inform you[2] that I offer my humble services to fill up the gap caused by the absence in the rank of national workers in Bengal. All those activities which he performed will still continue to be carried on normally. This is a heavy burden for my soldiers, but I have fullest faith in God's help undoubtedly the void created by his absence is not merely in work in Bengal but also in all-India activities. It is, however, beyond my fragile frame to endeavour to make up for the bigger void. Before this, during his last four years internment. I have gone through a first test, and I am confident that in this my second trial, I will with God's grace come off triumphant. For the last six years my health has been very broken down and mental exertion has become a positive torture. That was why the Maulana hitherto insisted on my not taking active part in his activities and patriotic strivings. I had, however, all along determined to consecrate my whole being completely and unreservedly to national duties after his conviction from today. I will discharge all the duties connected with the Bengal Provincial Khilafat Committees with the assistance of my brother. My husband has asked me to convey to you his loving and

1. Begum Julaikha Khatoon: Courageous, brave and religious household woman, Begum Julaikha Khatoon was the Great wife of Great Maulana Abul Kalam Azad.
2. Mahatama Gandhi: Supreme leader of National Liberation Movement and the father of the Nation.

reverent greetings and the following message (in a letter's shape): "Dear Mahatma ji, at the present juncture both the sides – the government and the country – are wholly unprepared for any compromise. The only duty before us is to prepare ourselves. Bengal will, in the next stage, also retain the lead which it has established today. Kindly add the name of Bengal to that of Bardoli Taluka. And if any time comes for a settlement, do please not give to our release the importance which is unfortunately being attached to it today. Have the terms of settlement fixed with the single end in view of our national aspirations, concerned with the question of our release."

I have not yet received the telegram although the letter of advice tells me that it was sent both to Ahmedabad and Bardoli. I am able to give the telegram to the public only because the secretary of the Bengal Provincial Khilafat Committee has very kindly sent me a copy by letter post at the instance of the Begum Sahiba. It is matter of no small comfort that ladies, occupying the highest station in life, are coming forward one after another to step into the breach created by the withdrawal of male national workers. I tender my congratulations to Begum Abul Kalam Azad for her having offered to take her share in the public work. The readers will take to heart the message of the Maulana. It is perfectly true that neither the Government nor the country is tody prepared for any compromise. The Government will not – be till we have suffered long and suffered more. Bengal has certainly led in the direction. Bardoli has yet done little. Twice has it been baulked of its privilege by cruel nature, bill is a matter of consequence weather it is Bengal or Bardoli which leads, so long as we get rid of a system which, as it daily becoming more and more clear, is based upon terrorism. In the present mood of the country there is little danger of the vital interests being sacrificed, as the Maulana fears, to the morally pleasure of securing the release of Non-Co-operation prisoners.

Mohan Das Karam Chand Gandhi.

Document No. 50

Maulana Abul Kalam Azad's letter to Mahatma Gandhi after his statement to the court to the Chief Presidency Magistrate of Calcutta

Calcutta
9-2-1922

My dear Mahatma ji,

At the present juncture both the sides – the Governmer and the Country – are wholly unprepared for any compromise. The only duty before us is to prepare ourselves. Bengal will, in the next stage, also retain the lead which it has established today. Kindly add the name of Bengal to that of Bardoli Taluka[1] and if any time comes for a settlement, do please not give to our release the importance which is unfortunately being attached to it today. Have the terms of settlement fixed with the single and in view of our national aspirations, unconcerned with the question of our release.

Yours sincerely
Abul Kalam Azad

Mahatma Gandhi,
Sabarmati Ashram,
Ahmedabad.

---

1. Bardoli Taluka, of Surat District in Gujrat, was chosen for complete Non-Co-operation in 1922 before the suspension of the Non-Co-operation, and Khilafat Movement, by Mahatma Gandhi.

Document No. 51

A Great Statement

"Maulana Abul Kalam Azad's statement to the court has been just received by me. It covers thirtythree closely typed fulscap sheets. But it is worth reading. The original is naturally in the Maulana's polished Urdu. The English translation is not bad, but could wish it was possible to get a better translation. The statement has much literary beauty. It is elaborate and eloquent. It is bold and uncompromising but subdued. A sarcastic vein runs through the whole of it. It is an eloquent thesis given the Maulana's views on the Khilafat and Nationalism. I hope that it will be possible to procure printed copies of the statement. I would advise the Maulana's secretary to have the statemetn carefully revised.

As I laid down the statement I felt more clearly than ever the necessity of boycott of law courts. But for the boycott, we would never have evolved the fearless strength that we have. Instead of the noble declarations of the president, Lalaji[1], Pandit ji[2], we would have had pettifogging lingual quibbs which cannot raise a nation. Without the boycott we could never have had the Maulana's statement which in itself constitutes good political education.

What a change between 1919 and 1922 nervous fear of sentences and all kinds of defences in 1919, utter disregard of sentences and no defence in 1922. In 1919 the nation could have done no otherwise; in 1922 it could have done no less without deserving execration of the world. The effect of the boycott is not to be measured by the number of suspensions of practice. The true measure is to be found in the departure of the halo that only two years ago surrounded the courts of law. They still remain the haunts of money changers and speculators. They are no longer repositories of national or even individual liberty. That is to be found in the stout hearts that the nation is fast developing.

The Maulana's statement is hardly meant for, though addressed to the court. It is meant for the public. It is really an oration deserving

---

1. Lala Lajpat Rai.
2. Pandit Moti Lal Nehru.

penal servitude for life. Well, might the Maulana exclaim after his one year's rigorous imprisonment. This falls far short of what I was waiting for.

The following extracts which I have called from the statement will enable the reader to form his own conclusion.

— Mohan Das Karam Chand Gandhi

Extracts from the statement of Maulana Azad

"I had no intention of submitting here any statement oral or written. This is a place in which there is for us no hope, no demand, and no grievance of any sort. This in turn, without passing through which, we cannot reach our goal. Non-Co-operation is essentially the result of absolute desperation at existing circumstances......I want to make it quite distinct that the term Non-Co-operation applies only to the government, its administrative system and its executive and political principles and not to any persons or individuals.

"Like most occurrences of the present era this movement also is nothing novel. History bears ample testimony to the fact that whenever a ruling authority has taken up arms against liberty and truth, courts of justice have lent themselves admirably to purposes of a most facile and unfailing weapon for the practice of such iniquity. The authority of law courts is a power which can be and equally to do justice and to perpetrate injustice. In the hands of an equitable government they are the best instruments of justice and truth, but in the hands of tryrannical and autocratic governemnts no weapon is deadlier than those for purposes of revenge and iniquity. No pure-minded and truth-loving section of humanity can be found, including even the inventors and savants of science, which has not some time or other stood in the dock before a court of law.

"The iniquities of courts of law constitute an endless list and history has not yet finished singing the elegy of such miscarriages of justice. In that list we observe a holy personage like Jesus who had to stand in his time before a foreign court convicted even as the worst of criminals. We see also in the same list Socrates who was sentenced to be poisoned for no other crime than that of being the most truthful person of his age. We meet also the name of that great Florentine martyr to truth, the inventor Gallileo, who refused to belie his observations and researches merely because their avowal was a crime in the eyes of constituted authority......when I ponder on the great and significant history of the convicts' dock and find that the Honour of standing in that place belongs to me today, my soul becomes steeped in thankfulness and praise of God....

"The bureaucracy in India is nothing more nor less than the domination which powerful individuals will always normally attain over a nation decaying by its own neglect and internal weaknesses. In the natural course of things such dominant authority cannot possibly countenance any nationalistic awakening or agitations for progress, reform or justice. And as such agitation would spell the ineviatable downfall of its dominant power, it seeks to kill all agitation by declaring it a crime against constituted authority. No power would tamely submit to movements likely to bring about its own decline, however much such decline might be in the ultimate interests of justice. This posture of affair is merely a struggle for existence in which both sides fight desperately for their principles. An awakened nation aspires to attain what is considered its birth-right and the dominant authority would fain not budge an inch from its position of unquestioned sway. The contention might almost be advanced that the latter party even like its opponents is not open to any blame in as much as it merely putting up a fight for its own survival and it is quite an incidental matter that its existence happens to be inimical to perpetuation of justice. We cannot deny facts of human nature and its inseparable characteristics. Like good, evil also desires to live in this world and struggle for its own existence. In India also such a struggle for the survival of the fittest has already commenced. Most certainly, therefore, nothing can be a higher crime against the domination of government, as at present established, than the agitation which seeks to terminate its unlimited authority in the name of liberty and justice. I fully admit that I am not only guilty of such agitation but that I belong to that band of pioneers who originally sowed the seed of such agitation in the heart of our nation and dedicated their whole lives to the cherishing and breeding of this holy discontent....

"The history of Politics teachs us that foolishness and recklessness of consequences are always the companions of a decadent power. The government thought that by sheer repression it would annihilate the Khilafat and the Swaraj movements and stop the hartal of the 24th. Accordingly it declared the volunteer corps to be unlawful and many workers were indiscriminately arrested. It fancied that the Khilafat and the Congress committees would become inane and inactive by the mere arrest of the executive and prohibition of the volunteer corps. Thus would the hartal automatically stopped. But very soon the government came to learn that repression when practised against National awakening is no fatal thing for a nation but instead breathes new life into it. Neither was the hartal stopped, nor did the Kilafat and the Congress committees become moribund, nor was the work of the volunteers stopped even for a single day....

"According to my belief it is my duty to speak out at the present movement and I cannot fall short of the full performance of my duty, just because it might be construed into a crime...... Most certainly I have stated that the present governemnt is oppressive. If I do not say this, what else am I to say? I fail to understand why it should be expected of me that I should call things by any but their right names. I refuse absolutely to call black white......I have cartainly been asserting that only two paths are open to us in this matter of our duty. The govenment has to refrain from all this iniquity and deprivation of liberty; or it cannot bring itself to do so, it has to be wiped off.... believe in the evils of the present government most assuredly. I could not at the same time pray that it may not mend its ways and yet be long-lived....

"Now, what is the reason that such is the firm belief of my self and of millions of my countrymen? The reason for this have now become so patent to common knowledge that in the words of Milton, ' Next to the sun itself they are about the clearest and most manifest facts in existence. About such universal facts all that I can say is don't deny them.' I will only add that this faith of mine exists because I am an Indian, because I am Muslim first and last because I am a man....

"It is my belief that liberty is the natural and God given right of man. No man and no bureaucracy consisting of men has got the right to make the servants of God its own slaves. However attractive be the euphimisms invented for 'subjugation' and `slavery', still slavery is slavery and it is opposed to the will and to the canons of God. I therefore do not consider the bureaucracy of India to be a legitimate sovereign and I consider it a bounden duty to liberate my country from its yoke. The notorious fallacies of -Reform' and gradual transference of Powers can produce no illusions and pitfalls in my unequivocal faith. Liberty being the primary right of man, it is nobody's personal privilege to prescribe limits of or apportion shares in the distribution of it. To say that a nation should get its liberty in graduated stages in the same as saying that an owner should by right receive his property only in bits and creditor his dues by instalments..... whatever philanthropic acts might be performed by a man who has usurped our property, his usurpation would still continue to be utterly illegal....

"Evil cannot be classified into good and bad. All that in fairness possible is to fix its gradations with respect to quality. Foir instance we can say very heinous robbery and less heinous robbery, but who can speak of good robbery and bad robbery? I cannot, therefore, at all conceive of any justification for such domination because by its very nature it is an act of iniquity.....

"Such in my duty as a man and as an Indian and religious injunction have also taught me (that) the same lesson. In fact in my view the greatest proof of the truth of my religion is that it is another name for the teaching of the rights of man. I am a Mohamedon and by virtue of being a Mohamedon this has become my religious duty. Islam never accept as valid a sovereignty which is personal or is continued of a bureaucracy of a handful of paid executive. Islam constituted a perfected system of freedom and democracy. It has been sent down to get back for the human race and liberty which has been snatched away from it. Monarchs, foreign dominations, selfish religious pontiffs and powerful sections and alike misappropriated this liberty of man. They had been fondly nurving the belief that power and possession spell the highest right. The moment Islam appeared, it proclaimed that the highest right is not might but right itself. No one except God has got the right to make serfs and slaves of God's creatures. All men are equal and their fundamental rights are on a par. He only is greater than other, whose deeds are the most righteous of all....

"The sovereignty of the prophet of Islam and of the Khalif was a perfected conception of democratic equality and it only could take shape with the whole nation's free will, unity, suffrage and election. This is the reason why the sovereign or President of a Republic is like a designated Khalif; Khilafat literally means nothing more nor less than a representation; so that all the authority a Khalif possesses consists in his representative character and he possesses no domination beyond this representative authority.

"If then Islam defines it as a duty of Mohamedans to refuse to acknowledge the moral justification even of an Islamic Government, if full play is not granted in it to the will and franchise of the nation, it is perfectly superfluous to add what under Islam would be the ruling given about a foreign bureaucracy. If today there was to be established in India an Islamic Government but if the system of that government was based upon personal monarchy or upon bureaucratic oligarchy, then to protest against the existence of such a government would still be my primary duty as a Mohamedan. I would still call the government oppressive and demand its replacement.

"I frankly confess that this original conception of Islamic sovereignty could not be uniformly maintained in its prime parity on account of the selfishness and personal domineering of the later Mahomedan sovereigns. The mighty magnificence of the Emperors of ancient Rome and of the Shahas of Persia had attracted the Mahomedan sovereign powerfully to the dubious glory of great monarchical empires. They began to prefer the majestic figures of a Kaiser or a Khosroe to the simple dignity of the original Khalifs clad oftentimes in old tattored docks. No period of the dynastic soverignties of Islam has however failed to produce some true Muslim martyrs who have made public declarations of the tyrarnnties and transgressions of such monarchies and had joyfully and triumphantly suffered all miseries and hardships which inevitably confronted them in the thorny paths of duty.

"The holy prophet of Islam has preached the following doctrine to the Muslims: `That man is blessed with the best of deaths who proclaim the truth in the face of a tyrannical administration and is slaughtered in punishment of this deed.' The scripture of Islam, the holy Quran defines the greatest attribute of the true Muslim to be `that they fear not any being except God and whatever they consider to be the truth, they reck not any authority in the public proclamation of such truth. The Quran further defines the national charcteristics of the Múlims as follows: `They are the witnesses to the truth on God's earth.' As long therefore they continue to be Muslims they cannot desist from giving this public evidence. In fact it has designated Muslims as withnesses *i.e.* givers of the evidence of truth. When the prophet of Islam extracted a promise of righteousness from any person one of the clauses of such a bond used to be, `I will always proclaim the truth in whatever condition and wherever I may happen to be....'

An outstanding object lesson in speaking the truth which their nattional history presents to the Muslims is to be found in the order of an autocratic monarch by which each organ of a victim's body was cut off. The charge against the victim was that he had proclaimed the iniquity of the tyrant. Firm as a rock he stood and took his punishment in all its heinous stages, but his tongue right on to the moment when it was severed went on proclaiming that that outocrat was a tyrant. This is an incident of reign of the Emperor Abdul Malik whose dome is extended from Syria to Sind can any one then attach any weight to a sentence under section 124 as compared to this terrible penalty? I concede that it is the moral decadence of Muslims and their renouncing the real Islamic life that is responsible for the bringing about of this fallen state.

"While I am penning these lines I know there is still living in India many a Muslim who through his weakness pays homage to this very tyranny. But the failure of man to act up to the spirit of certain tenets cannot belie the intrinsic truth of those principles.

"The tenets of Islam are preserved in its scriptures. These, under no circumstances, make it permissible for Muslims to enjoy life at the expense of liberty. A true Muslim has either to immolate himself or to retain his liberty, no other course is open for him under his religion. Today the Muslims have come to a firm decision that in freeing their country from its slavery they will take their fullest share along with their Hindu, Sikh, Parsi, and Christian brethren..... It is now their belief that to expect any justice from the British government would be nothing but pure self-deception, so that if they really aspire to obtain justice there is only one single avenue leading to it, which is the attainment of Swaraj – meaning the government of India for India and by the Indian themselves. In short, on these points my admission have ever been absolutely clear and unequivocal.

"The present government is a most-illegitimate form of burearucracy. It is openly sparsing the wishes and aspirations of millions of humanity. It has always given the preference over justice to prestige. Does tyranny acquire a right to be given a different cause simply because it happens to be powerful and to possess jails?

"In the words of the good and truthful national here of Italy, Joseph Mazzini, I repeat we cannot possibly deny your evil doing just because temporal power happens to be in your possession for a time....

"Continuously in the last twelve years I have been training my community and my country in demanding their rights and their liberty. I was only 18 years old when I first started struggle and writing on this them. I have consecrated my whole being to it and sacrificed the best part of my life, during the whole of my youth in my situation (of) for this ideal. For four years I have suffered internment but during my internment even, I have never desisted from pushing on my work and inviting people to this national goal. This is the perennial mission of my life and if I live at all I elect to live only for this single purpose. Even as the Quran says, `My prayer and my observances and my life and my death are all for my lord, the God of Univers'. I am the first pioneer in this latest phase of that Islamic movement in India which has created a tremendous revolution in the political world of the Indian Muslims and has gradually elevated them to that pinnacle of national consciousness on which they are seen today. In 1912 I started an Urdu Journal, the Al-Hilal, which was the organ of this movement and the object of the publication of which was mainly what I have declared above. It is an actual fact that within the three years it had created a new atmosphere in the religious and the political life of Mohammedans of India....

"In this war of liberty and justice, I have adopted the path of non-violent non-co-operation. Opposed to us stands an authority armed with the complete equipment for oppression, excess and bloodshed. But we place our reliance and trust, next to God, only upon our own limitless power of sacrifice and unshakeable fortitude.

"Unlike Mahatma Gandhi my belief is not that armed force should never be opposed by armed force. It is my belief that such opposing of violence with violence is fully in harmony with the natural laws of God in those circumstances under which Islam permits the use of such violence. But at the same time for purposes of liberation of India and the present agitation, I entirely agree with all the arguments of Mahatma Gandhi and I have complete confidence in his honesty. It is my definite conviction that India connot attain success by means of arms nor it is advisable for it to adopt that course. India can only triumph through non-violent agitation and India's triumph will be a memorable example of moral force....

"This is the reason why I have always preached to the masses peaceful agitation and have invariably prescribed it as the first postulate of success. This would appear distinctly from these speehes also. I am one of the handful of Muslim leaders who can honestly claim that if it was not for the determined and effective control that they have exercised in keeping the Muslim public within the bounds of non-co-operation, there is no knowing where the excitment of the mobs, under the recent trying provocations, may not have led them and what grave situations may not have taken shape with respect to the Khilafat problem....

"What I have asked in the begining I will repeat in conclusion, that what the government is doing with us today is no extraordinary procedure for which it can be particularly blameable. It is second nature to every usurping authority to put up a determined opposition and repression to suppress national awakening and we know that human nature cannot be altered to suit our own end. This natural failing finds expression equally in individuals and communities. How many people are there in this world who would give back any article which they had already got in their possession for the mere reason that they are not legitimately entitled to it ? How then can we nurse a fond hope of such voluntary-surrender with respect to a whole continent ? Power also is not normally prone to admit facts just because they are logical and proved. As a matter of fact it waits for the emergence of a counter-strength and when this does present itself, it bows its head down before the most improper demand. Patience, therfore, and a tug of war of strength are unavoidable.

"This position is one which should be accepted as a normal and everyday occurrence without surprise and without demur. I will even go the length of admitting that the present repression is certainly not too drastic as compared to the worst instances of inhuman oppressions and terrible presecutions which history presents to us. I am not quite certain whether this is due to immaturity of the national sense of sacrifice or to the imperfect development of the present system of repression. The future alone will decide this. Just as the beginning of such political tug of war has uniformally been on a more or less similar lines, even so its end has been the same in the history of all nations. I know that if our spirit of liberty and justice proves by actual demonstration to be real and unconquerable, this very government which is today putting us into the dock, will be obliged to give us a right royal reception as triumphant patriots....

"Before I conclude my statement, I want to say a few words about those countrymen of mine who are working against me in this prosecution. Previously I have stated somewhere that the work of the C.I.D. is a combination of ignorance and trickery. This I have said from the personal experience that I have gained from countless prosecutions. All the same, however, I admit that all the C.I.D. people who have given evidence against me have not delibertely made any lying statements, barring perhaps the confidence which they have expressed in their own work...... I believe that the confidence which they have expressed on the result of their own work and the motives which have dictated their actions are certainly sinful. But at the same time I also know their weakness. They are only doing this for the sake of the appointments which bring them a few rupees and their only crime is that they do not possess the moral courage to give preference to truth over everything else. In my heart, therefore, lingers no rancour or accusation."

Mohan Das Karam Chand Gandhi

Young India
February 22, 1922

Document No. 52

THE COMPROMISE

Maulana Azad and the Working Committee's Statement

The all India Congress Committee met at Allahabad on February 27th[1], under the Presidency of Deshbandhu Das and Maulana Abul Kalam Azad, and on the motion of Mr. C. Rajagopalacharya, seconded by Pandit Moti Lal Nehru adopted the following resolution:

Resolved that the following terms of Compromise be confirmed and given full effect :

1. suspension of council propaganda on both sides till the 30th April;

2. both parties to be at liberty to work the remaining items of their respective programmes in the internal without interfering with each other;

3. the majority party will be at liberty to carry on their propaganda in accordance with the Gaya programme about money and Volunteers;

4. the minority party will co-operate with the majority party in appealing for and raising such funds and enlisting such workers as may be necessary for the constructive programme and other common matters;

5. each party to adopt such course after the 30th April (1923) as it may be advised; and

6. the above arrangement is subject to the condition that there is no dissolution of the existing councils in any province before the expiry of the full term for which they have been constituted.

The working committee issues the following statement for the information of the public regarding the negotiations which terminated in the above terms of compromise:

At a meeting of the working committee held at Bombay in the last week of January (1923) Maulana Abul Kalam Azad proposed the following scheme of settlement:

1. That both parties should whole-heartedly unite to work the Gaya Congress Programme for the next three months.

---

1. 1923.

2. That there should be no propaganda or talk about any change of the programme relating to the councils during that period or the formulation of a new party.

3. That it at the end of that period civil disobedience was decided upon, both parties should to work for it.

4. That it, on the other hand, no such step was found possible, a special session of the Congress should be held in June to consider the situation.

5. That for one month before the special session of the Congress both parties should be free to educate public opinion according to their views.

6. That the decision of the Congress should be carried out by both sides, without forming separate parties.

After some discussion, the above terms were unanimously agreed to by the working committee, and the Maulana Saheb[1] was requested to place the matter before Mr. Das[2] for the acceptance of himself – and his party. Maulana Saheb placed them before Deshbandhu, but they were not acceptable to him. The members of the working committee also met Mr. Das and had a discussion with him. He expressed his inability to accept Maulana's scheme of settlement but proposed other terms which involved suspension of the boycott of elections at once and without reference to any special Congress. The working committee considered this proposal but found it impossible to accept it. Maulana Abul Kalam Azad however, undertook to press his own scheme again on the leaders of the new party. As a result of his further efforts he was in a position to inform the general secretary by telegram on the 12th of February (1923) that Hakim Ajmal Khan[3] and Pandit Moti Lal Nehru[4] had whole-heartedly accedpted his terms and he proceeded to Calcutta to discuss matters again with Deshbandhu Das. After further consultation and discussion with Maulana Saheb and Pandit Moti Lal Ji, Deshbandhu

1. Maulana Abul Kalam Azad.
2. Deshbandhu Chittaranjan Das was a renowned Swarajist leader and was elected the President of Indian National Congress at Gaya in 1922.
3. Hakim Ajmal Khan: Veteran freedom fighier and prominent Nationalist leader of Delhi, was the President of Indian National Congress in 1921, member, Working Committee of A.I.C.C. in 1920, 1923 & 1925; one of the leading figure of Non-Co-operation and Khilafat Movement in 1920-21.
4. Pandit Moti Lal Nehru: A well known Barrister of Allahabad; Pandit Moti Lal Nehru was a leading Swarajist leader, elected President of Indian National Congress in 1928.

Das re-drafted Maulana's terms with the addition of a clause regarding election machinery for the special session of Congress. The terms of his draft and his letter annexed therto are given below:

1. A meeting of the All India Congress Committee will be called without delay with a view to summon a special Congress about the middle of June (1923).

2. In case special Congress session is summoned by the All India Congress Committee as stated above both the parties while adhering to their respective opinions, agree to suspend their differences and jointly work the programme as laid down at Gaya till the end of April (1923).

3. There should be no propaganda by either party concerning Council Election till the end of April.

4. The All India Congress Committee will meet in the first week of May and if in view of situation at the time it decides to undertake immediate civil disobedience genereally throughout the country, *i.e.* in the majority of the Congress provinces both parties will join in such civil disobedience and there will be no session of the Congress.

5. If however the All India Congress Committee declare against civil disobedience both parties will thereafter be free to educate public opinion according to their views.

6. Further, if the All India Congress Committee in May declares against such civil disobedience arrangements will be made in all the provinces of early as possible in order to enable the election of delegates to take place on fair and impartial lines;

7. The decision of the special session will be binding on both parties.

8. The compromise shall cease to have effect (binding forces in the parties) in case the existing Councils are dissolved by the Government before the expiry of the full term for which they have been constituted.

LETTER OF MR. DAS TO MAULANA ABUL KALAM AZAD

148, Russa Road,
Kalighat
7th February, 1923

Dear Maulana Saheb,

The accompanying draft expresses the terms upon which I am prepared to enter into a compromise with the majority party. This will not prevent my party from raising funds without making any propaganda on the question of the councils from those who are willing to trust to the judgment of the members of our party as to the way in which such funds are to be spent. I undertake not to call any meeting or raise such funds. It is understood that to give effect to the term No. 6 the following or a similar arrangement to my satisfaction must be accepted:

1. For every constituency, district or local, returning delegates to the special Congress an additional secretary will be appointed belonging to the party to which the existing secretary is opposed.

2. In the provincial Congress Committees too the same arrangements will be made.

3. There will be two returning officers for constituency one belonging to each party.

4. There will be an election board in each province consisting of two members, one to be nominated by each party. These two members will decide upon a third person to whom all election disputes will be referred in case of difference. The board will be at liberty to modify the existing election rules to suit the circumstances of the special Congress and for such purpose power of the provincial Congress Committee will vest in them. This board will (be) in all matters be responsible for conducting election of delegates.

I further desire to make it clear that my acceptance of terms mentioned is subject to the approval of our party.

Yours sincerely
C.R.Das

The new party met at Allahabad on February 20 and appointed a special committee with authority to agree on their behalf to such terms of settlement as they might approve after discussion with the working committee which was to meet at Allahabad on February 26th. Four sets of proposals were considered during the conversation at Allahabad between the working committee and the new party's special committee. Two of them implied suspension of the resolution regarding the boycott of the councill elections without references to any fresh Congress sessions of the other two—one was Maulana's[1] proposal as modified and added to by Deshbandhu Das and the other was the following –

1. Suspension of Council propaganda on both sides till the 30th April.
2. Both parties to be at liberty to work the remaining items of their respective programme in the interval without interfering with each other.

1. Maulana Abul Kalam Azad.

3. Each party to adopt such course after the 30th April as it may be advised.

4. No special Congress.

The new party, however, made all the four proposals subject to the following conditions :

"Every proposal subject to the condition that there is no dissolution of the existing councils in any province before the expiry of the full term for which they have constituted."

The Working Committee decided against accepting any of two proposals that involved a reversal of the resolution regarding council boycott without reference to Congress. It decided to accept either of the other two sets of proposals but modified the terms drafted by Deshbandhu Das in same particulars and by substituting for the special election machinery proposed by him a clause that the All India Congress Committee should proivde at its meeting in May satisfactory machinery for disposal of disputes regarding election of delegates to the special Congress in a fair and impartial manner.

To the other alternative proposal the Working Committee added terms to secure co-operation in collection of funds and enlistment of workers.

The two sets of proposals either of which the Working Committee agreed to accept were as follows :

AZAD-DAS DRAFT AS AMENDED BY THE WORKING COMMITTEE

(No. I)

1. Both parties while adhering to their respective opinion agree to suspend their differences and jointly work the programme as laid down at Gaya.

2. There should be no propaganda by either party concerning Council election till the end of April,

3. The All India Congress Committee will meet before the end of May and if in view of the situation at the time it decides to undertake individual civil disobedience on a large scale both parties will join in such civil disobedience and there will be no special session of the Congress.

4. If, however, the All India Congress Committee declares against such civil disobedience both the parties will be thereafter free to educate public opinion according to their views.

5. If the All India Congress Committee to be convened before 31st May declares against such civil disobedience a special session of the Congress should meet about the end of June.

6. The All India Congress Committee Meeting in May will provide satisfactory machinery for the disposal of disputes regarding the election of delegates in a fair and impartial manner.

7. The decision of the special session will be loyally carried out by all parties and there will be no separate organisations for taking action contrary to that decision.

(No. II)

1. Suspension of Council propaganda on both sides till the 30th April.

2. Both parties to be at liberty to work the remaining items of their respective programme in the interval without interfering with each other.

3. Majority party will be at liberty to carry on their propaganda in accordance with the Gaya Programme about money and volunteers.

4. The majority party will co-operate with the minority party in appealing for and raising such funds and enlisting such workers as may be necessary for the constructive programme and also in working the constructive programme and other common matters.

5. Each party to adopt such course after the 30th April as it may be advised.

The Working Committee left these two proposals with the committee of the new party for the latter to decide whichever they might accept after consultation among themselves. The latter intimated their acceptance of the terms of Scheme No. II which were accordingly placed before the All India Congress Committee at its meeting of February 27th and confirmed.

It will be seen from the terms thus finally adopted that unless the Government advances the date of the Council elections, there will be no controversial propaganda, that the collection of money and enlistment of workers by the majority party will be supported by the co-operation of the minority, and that the majority party's efforts at launching a compaign of individual civil disobedience will not be opposed by the minority party. It is hoped that all workers will observe the letter and spirit of the compromise and help to secure an atmosphere of peace and co-operation; and taking full advantage of it, strengthen the Congress organisation throughout the country. The collection, for the Tilak[1] swarajya fund and enrolment of workers and volunteers should be pushed on with vigour, and all Congress Committees should resume their activities by which alone real faith and losting enthusiasm can be restored.

Rajendra Prasad,
Vallabhbhai J. Patel
Muazzam Ali
General Secretaries,
Indian National Congress.

1. Tilak (Bal Gangadar): A great Congress leader of Maharashtra, Bal Gangadhar Tilak, popularly known as Lokmanya, was a prominent leader of the Swadeshi Movement in 1905; editor of 'Kesari' and 'Maratha', imprisoned several times during National Liberation Movement; one of the founders of Theosophical Society.

Document No. 53

Letter from Maulana Azad to Pt. Moti Lal Nehru

Delhi
1-11-1923

Dear Sir,

It is more than five weeks since the conclusion of the Delhi Congress and the swift passage of time will soon bring us to the last week of the year when the Congress reassembles at Cocanada. None can deny the fact that we attained a considerable measure of success in terminating the domestic squabbles of the Congress and paying the way for fruitful efforts in a new direction, but the preliminary steps taken in grappling with a more formidable evil, namely the recent accentuation of communal differences and the embitterment of inter-communal relations, did not go beyond arresting its rapid progess. Singers of a recrudescence of the progressive tendencies of the said evil so far from being wholly wanting lay upon us the imperative duty of immediately resuming our adjourned deliberations and devoting effectual endeavours to the final solution of the questions connected therewith. An informal Conference of prominent leaders of thoughts appears to me to be the need of the hour not merely for this object but also for considering the programme of work we have to place before the country for the ensuing year to ensure the concentration of the country's energy on a vigorous renewal of our struggle for freedom. I take the liberty of supposing that you will endorse the view that the Congress in the present condition of its organization seems almost unequal to the task of taking any definitive steps; the existing Congress Committee being almost without any motive-power behind or a realiy practical programme of work before them. Virtually, the Congress Committees seem to have ceased to function. Such activity as is observable is centred on the electioneering campaign for the Councils, and is, therefore, necessary confined to a section of Congressmen. This is a state of affairs, which in my humble opinion, calls for an informal conference of leading Congressmen for devoting their earnest thought to the question of the hour with a view to evolve a mature and effectual programme of work to be placed at the Cocanada Congress. I have consulted Hakim Ajmal Khan[1], Pandit Madan Mohan Malviya[2], Lala Lajpat Rai[3], Pt. Nehru[4], Smt. Sarojini Naidu[5], Dr. Ansari[6] and some other friends, all of whom have endorsed my view. The informal Conference has accordingly been fixed for the 30th November 1923 at Delhi, and I earnestly hope that recognising the eminently urgent nature of the object for which the Conference being conveyed, you will not fail to allot it the first place in your engagements, will contribute your indispensable quote to its deliberations. Kindly intimate your arrival to Mr. M. Asaf Ali, the Secretary, Provincial Congress Committee, Delhi.

I beg to remain,
Sir,
Yours sincerely
Sd. A.K. Azad
(Abul Kalam Azad)

Pandit Moti Lal Nehru Saheb,
Allahabad.

---

1. Hakim Ajmal Khan:
   Hakim Ajmal Khan Saheb was elected the the President for Indian National Congress in its 36th session in 1921, held at Ahmedabad.
2. Pandit Madan Mohan Malaviya:
   Founder of Banaras Hindu University. Pandit Malviya was a leading Congressman who participated in the Second Round Table Conference held in London in 1931.
3. Lala Lajpat Rai:
   One of the extremist tricumvirate — Bal, Lal, Pal — Lala Lajpat Rai was popularly known as the lion of Punjab and a leading figure of National Liberation Movement for India.
4. Pt. Nehru (Jawahar Lal):
   Pandit Jawahar Lal Nehru, three times elected the President of Indian National Congress in 1929, 1936 and 1946, became Prime Minister of free India in 1947.
5. Sarojini Naidu:
   Sarojini Naidu was the Chairperson of Indian National Congress in 1926, appointed Governor of U.P. in 1947.
6. Dr. M.A. Ansari:
   Great patriot and veteran freedom fighter.

Document No. 54

Statement by Motilal Nehru and Abul Kalam Azad on the Hindu-Muslim dispute at Nagpur, 13 January 1925

In October last leading Hindus and Musalmans of Nagpur agreed to be bound by our decision on the question whether there was any and if so what custom prevalent in the city of Nagpur from of old relating to the playing of processional music in front or in the vicinity of mosques at all or any specified times of the day and night. This reference involved the taking of evidence for which we were then unable to spare the necessary time. We came back to Nagpur on the 11th January and on the following day held a sitting with a view to go into the question. We had a most pleasant surprise in store for us. At the commencement of the proceedings it was stated on behalf of the Musalmans that while they fully believed that there was a custom to stop all music when passing their mosques they had after full consideration of the matter and in the interests of an abiding unity between the two communities determined to surrender their legal right and to leave it to the good sense of the Hindus to play or stop music as they thought fit. They made it clear that although the playing of music in front of mosques while they were at congregational prayers was most annoying to them they have made up their minds to suffer such annoyance rather than proceed with an enquiry on the merits of the question which in any event was bound to leave unpleasantness behind and retard a speedy restoration of amicable relations. We congratulate the Musalmans on their wise and patriotic determination and thank them for having relieved us of the painful duty of deciding a controversy between the sister communities which had caused considerable bitterness. We asked the Musalmans to give us in writing the substance of their generous offer and close the formal proceedings reserving to the Hindus liberty to submit any statement they might be advised to make in response to the Musalman offer. Both parties filed written statements in the course of the day. The Musalman statement repeated the offer we have set out above. The Hindus expressed their full appreciation of the spirit in which the Musalmans had withdrawn their objection to the playing of music in front of mosques and undertook to see that the Musalmans were put to the least inconvenience consistently with the due discharge of what the Hindus considered to be their religious duty. They reserved liberty to play music along public streets and thoroughfares at all times of the day and night only when such music accompanied what they described as the "traditional annual processions of the royal family, of the Bhonslas" and the "traditional Jajoba procession". In regard to all other processions they offered to stop music when passing five specified mosques named below between the hours of one and one thirty p.m. and five and five thirty p.m. in the months of October to February and six and six thirty p.m. in the remaining months of the year. It will appear from the above statements that the Musalmans of Nagpur have fully complied with the resolution passed on the subject, by the Unity Conference at Delhi in withdrawing their objections and leaving it to the good sense of the Hindus to avoid causing them any inconvenience. This resolution was passed after full and matured consideration by representative Hindus and Musalmans and affords a clear guidance to both communities as to the duty each owes to the other. In the last clause of the resolution the Hindu members of the Conference call upon their co-religionists to refrain from playing music in front of mosques in such a way as to cause any disturbance to Muhamedans at the times of their congregational prayers.

The Hindus of Nagpur felt themselves compelled by their religious obligations to limit their offer of stopping music to five mosques only and that at the time of only two out of five daily congregational prayers. Various reasons more or less of a local character were assigned for this limitation but in view of the unconditional offer of the Musalmans we thought it unnecessary to enquire further into the matter. We therefore express no opinion as to the soundness or otherwise of these reasons. It is however obvious that no discrimination can be made between one mosque or another or between one prayer and another in regard to playing of music.

We hope and trust that in the absence of any question of custom the special case of Nagpur will not only be not treated as a precedent for such discrimination in other parts of India but that the Nagpur Hindus themselves will do away with it in course of time. We have reason to believe that the friendly relations which have now been restored will in due course acquire sufficient strength to render all distinction and discrimination unnecessary. We note with pleasure that the Musalmans declared their full adherence to their offer after they came to know of the terms of the Hindu undertaking and that Dr. Moonje as President of the Public meeting addressed by us assured the Musalmans on behalf of the Hindus of Nagpur that the brotherly feelings of the former would be fully reciprocated by the latter.

We congratulate both parties and also the Hindus and Musalmans of India in general at the happy settlement arrived at.

Motilal Nehru
A.K. Azad

Document No. 55

An Appeal for All India Deshbandhu Memorial dated 24-7-1925

We, the undersigned, are of opinion that an All-India Memorial Fund is as much a necessity as an All-Bengal one to perpetuate the memory of Deshbandhu Chittaranjan Das. He was as much an All-India man as he was an All-Bengal man. Just as we know what Deshbandhu would have himself wished us to do as an All-Bengal Memorial, so do we know what he would have wished us to do regarding an All-India Memorial. His idea was clearly expressed over a year ago and repeated in his Faridpur speech that village reconstruction was the thing dearest and nearest to his heart for the regeneration of India and for the attainment of Swaraj, along peaceful and evolutionary lines.

We know too that he believed that the beginning and the centre of such activity lay in the revival and development of hand-spinning in the villages and universalisation of *khaddar*. It is the one activity that can be made common to All-India and yet can be handled with the least cost. It is the one activity that is calculated to yield immediate returns be they even so small. All people, rich and poor, young and old, men and women can personally help and engage in it if they will. It can as nothing else can bind the city people to the villagers and introduce the educated class to them in a most useful manner. It is the one activity that can be common to all the provinces and all the sects of India and produce the largest economic results. Lastly, though it has a political side, it is in the nature so obviously social and economic that it should enlist the support of all, without distinction of party, who believe in the spinning wheel as a great economic factor and as a factor in village reconstruction.

We, therefore, cannot conceive a more fitting memorial than the universal propagation of the spinning wheel and *khaddar*, and, therefore, invite funds for that purpose. we refrain from naming the sum required for this memorial, as it can absorb all it can receive. The subscriptions given by the public will be the measure of their regard for the memory of the deceased patriot, of their belief in the usefulness of the form the memorial is to take, and of their trust in those who are to handle and operate on the funds. They will be M.K. Gandhi, Pandit Motilal Nehru, Maulana Shaukat Ali, Dr. Prafulla Chandra Roy, Shrimati Sarojini Naidu, Syt. Jamnalal Bajaj and Pandit Jawaharlal Nehru, with power to add to their number.

Pandit Jawaharlal has consented to act as Hon. Secretary for the Trustees and Syt. Jamnalal Bajaj as Treasurer. Remittances should be sent to Syt. Jamnalal Bajaj, 395, Kalbadevi Road, Bombay or Pandit Jawaharlal Nehru, 107, Hewett Road, Allahabad.

A full list of donations will be sent to the press for publication from week to week.

M.K. Gandhi
Motilal Nehru
A.K. Azad
P.C. Roy
Jamnalal Bajaj
Rabindra Nath Tagore
Shyam S. Chakravarty
C.F. Andrews
Sarojini Naidu
J.M. Sen Gupta

Document No. 56

Confidential Censored letter from Abul Kalam Azad 42, Ripon Street, Calcutta to Aga Safdar[1]

Dated : 16-8-1925

Date of Censorship : 20-8-1925

Addressee : Aga Muhammad Safdar,
Secretary, C.K.G. Bombay.

Copy, Substance or Extracts etc.

States that he[2] was writing a detailed letter to Shaukat Ali[3] when he received the letter from the addressee. The Writer has to say many things to the addressee but his presence is at once required in a meeting and therefore he cannot pen a letter in details. God willing he will write a letter tomorrow and at present he is giving his opinion about the meeting. The need for the present is for a meeting of the C.K.C.[4] and not of the Working Committee above. The condition at present is such that unless the Khilafatists do not at once take to practical work, the Khilafat Committee are in danger of extinction. Amongst the Muslims except a band of Khilafatists there is no other society. If the Khilafatists whose number is dwindling stop work, the result of this will be that amongst the Muslims political and national work will come to an end.

The Writer has considered the question of "Time". The need for the present is of "Funds", "Programme" and "Workers". There is at present a programme which in its present form is not workable. The Writer has decided to give his final advice to the co-broker now, though he had decided to retire and spend his time in writing and compiling books. He cannot bear to see the condition of the Khilafat Committee. It is impossible for the Writer to leave alone Shaukat Ali[5] after what happend at Amritsar. It is necessary in every way to call a meeting of Central Khilafat Committee on the 24th September a meeting of the All India Congress Committee is to be held at Patna. It is advisable to hold meetings of the Central Khilafat Committee and of the Working Committee on this occasion. The addressee had suggested 6th September for the meeting of the Working Committee of the Central Khilafat Committee. There is not much differences between the 6th and the 24th September. Morever Patna will be a Central place and many members of the Congress are the members of Central Khilafat Committee. The Congress meeting will be on the 24th September and the addressee can fix 25th, 26th or 27th for the Khilafat meeting. The agenda may be fixed after great deliberations. As regard the Hedjaz the policy of the Central Khilafat Committee is settled of course there will be a discussion about this year's Haj, the proposed Islamic Congress and the new programme. Await subsequent letter from the Writer.

No. M/4061

The original letter has been allowed to go on; no photo copy kept on record.

Sd/- P.A. Kelly
Commissioner of Police

---

1. Aga Muhammad Safdar was a prominent leader of Khilafat Movement.
2. Maulana Abul Kalam Azad.
3. Maulana Shaukat Ali.
4. Central Khilafat Committee.
5. Maulana Shaukat Ali, one of the Ali borthers.

Document No. 57

Confidential Censored letter from Abul Kalam Azad 24, Ripon Street Calcutta to Aga Safdar

Dated : 24.8.1925

Date of Censorship : 27.8.1925

Addressee : Aga Muhammad Safdar
Secretary, C.K.C. Bombay.

Substance, Extracts etc.

States that in reply to his[1] telegram he received a letter from the addressee[2]. The idea of holding a meeting of the Central Khilafat Committee came to the Writer as according to him delay in settling the programme and policy of the Central Khilafat Committee is dangerous. If immediate action to organise the Khilafat Committee is not taken then there is no doubt all will collapse soon. After seeing what had happened at Amritsar it is impossible for the Writer to leave Shaukat Ali[3] alone and therefore he had to find out time for the organisation of the Khilafat Committees.

The facts are that at this time amongst Muslims there is no Society of Workers except the Society of Khilafatists. If there was (only) any other Society of Workers then the Writer would have been willing to burn down the signboards of all Khilafat Committees. The situation is quite different and the result will be (by abolishing Khilafat Committees) a death blow to the public life of the Muslims for years together and there will be no society of true workers in the country.

The condition which is prevailing now in the country if allowed to go on, sooner or later, will bring about the dissolution of the Khilafat Committee. It is high time therefore to reorganise them. The "Tansion" programme in its present form is unworkable and should be reconsidered.

---

1. Maulana Abul Kalam Azad.
2. Aga Muhammad Safdar.
3. Maulana Shaukat Ali.

Paucity of workers and funds should be removed with prudence and intelligence and not by promises, patience and individual seal. The Writer is pondering over all these problems and for that very reason he advises the calling of the meeting of the *Central Khilafat Committee* to devise means and new programme for further work.

The addressee's explanation as to the indivisibility of holding another meeting of Central Khilafat Committee soon after the Amritsar meeting is worth considering for the present. These problems may be discussed in the meeting of the Working Committee of the Central Khilafat Committee and if thought necessary a meeting of the Central Khilafat Committee may be called afterwards.

The argument of the addressee[1] against the holding of the meeting at Patna was not convincing to the Writer.[2] In the opinion of the Writer Patna is the best place to hold the meeting of the Working Committee of the Central Khilafat Committee as Shaukat[3], Mohammad Ali[4], Mohammad Shafi[5], Dr. Ansari[6], Murtaza[7], Abul Kader[8] (Qader), Kitchlew[9], Shobani[10] and the Writer who will be there in connection with the Congress Committee meeting; will be able to attend it only Maulana Majid[11] and Syed Sulaiman Nadvi[12] will have specially to come down to Patna for the Khilafat Committee's meeting. With all these facilities if Shaukat Ali[13] still persists in to hold the meeting at Delhi, the Writer has no objection, but the date must be changed so that all may be able to attend the Patna Congress Meeting.

The Hajdis affairs are being criticised in a severely and mixed up manner. It is correct that demolishing of the domes of tombs is a mistake committed by the Hajdis because it was not the time for the

---

1. Aga Muhammad Safder.
2. Maulana Abul Kalam Azad.
3. Maulana Shaukat Ali, one of the Ali brothers.
4. Maulana Muhammad Ali 'Zohar', one of the Ali brothers.
5. Muhammad Sarif, a prominent leader of Khilafat Movement.
6. Dr. Mukhtar Ahmad Ansari.
7. Mohammad Murtaza, a well-known non-cooperater and a leader of Khilafat Movement.
8. Abdul Qader, prominent Khilafatist.
9. Dr. Saifuddin Kitchlew.
10. Maulana Azad Shobani.
11. Maulana Abul Majid, a well-known leader of Khilafat Movement.
12. Maulana Syed Sulaiman Nadvi, member of the Central Committee of the All India Khilafat Conference.
13. Maulana Shaukat Ali.

internal improvement. The Writer himself has repeated by writing to Ibu Saud for the last one year about this matter and personally Ibu Saud agrees with the writer.

At the same time it cannot be tolerated that this act may be dishonouring tombs because whatever is done according to Shariat[1] and with a motive of improvement, it could not be sacriligious act. However the Writer is sending series of articles with a translation of the last letter of Ibu Saud to the press for publication.

No. M/4061
Bombay, 28th August, 1925

The original letter has been allowed to go on, no Photo copy kept on record.

Sd/-x-x-x-x-
For Commissioner of Police

1. Muslim Personal Law.

Document No. 58

Letter from Mahatma Gandhi to Maulana Azad

The Asharam
Sabarmati,
8-5-1926

Dear Maulana Saheb,

I have your telegram[1]. It was received after the All India Congress Committee session was over. But do you think that any purpose can be served by calling a special session of the Congress ? It can be of use only when there is a Policy or Programme that requires confirmation by it. But unfortunately we have neither Policy nor Programme. On the contrary, the tallest among us distrust one another and even where there is no distrust there is no agreement as to facts or opinion.

In the circumstances a Congress session can only accentuate the existing depression. It seems to me that time alone can solve the difficulty which seems to baffle us.

I wish that it was possible for us at least to devise means of ascertaining the causes and of defining the results of each riot. But it seems that we have become incapacitated even for this very simple.

Yours sincerely
M.K. Gandhi

Maulana Abul Kalam Azad
Calcutta

---

1. Telegram of Maulana is not available.

Document No. 59

Letter from Sardar Patel to Maulana Azad

Bardoli
October 15, 1931

Dear,

You will remember the Working Committee fixed the 24th October as the date for the next meeting of the Working Committee to be held at Delhi. I was asked by you,[1] Dr. Ansari and some other Muslim friends to change that date in view of the fact that the Muslim Nationalist Conference was going to meet at Lahore on that date. I have had considerable difficulty in fixing a date which will suit the convenience of all members and have been in telegraphic communication with some of them. Having considered all points of view I have decided that the most convenient date for meeting will be the 27th and it will accordingly be held at Dr. Ansari's House at Delhi on 27th at 12 noon. As several matters of importance will be coming up for discussion, I hope you will make it a point to attend. Even if you are going to attend the Muslim Conference I think there will be sufficient margin for you to reach Delhi in time for the meeting which has been shifted particularly to suit your convenience as suggested by you and Dr. Ansari.

Yours sincerely
Vallabhbhai Patel

Maulana Abul Kalam Azad.

---

1. Maulana Azad had requested Sardar Patel, sending him an express telegram at Bardoli on 8th October 1931, to postpone the Working Committee Meeting to be held at Delhi on 24th October.

Document No. 60

An open letter (as a circular) of Maulana Abul Kalam Azad, Acting President of the Indian National Congress to all Provincial Congress Committees

Calcutta
Feb. 20, 1932

I have learnt to my great astonishment and regret that in some cases even the humiliating parole conditions have been obeyed. I consider compliance with such order as most injurious for our causes. It produced demoralisation in our ranks and undermines the basis of civil disobedience besides running the prestige of the individuals concerned.

I earnestly hope that all Congressmen (workers) in provinces will seriously consider the above suggestions and try their best to work them into practice. I on my part assure you of my full co-operation. I shall always endeavour to hope to the best of my ability.

Abul Kalam Azad
Acting President
All India Congress Committee

Please circulate it.

Document No. 61

Telegram from Maulana Azad to Mahatma Gandhi

Mahatma Gandhi
Yervada Central Prison

Calcutta
Oct. 19, 1932

Muslim leaders Conference unanmiously not to press separate electorate if other demands accepted. In present situation no letter solution possible. Your absence hindering success. Bless us by message. At least trust Government. Won't object.

Abul Kalam Azad

Document No. 62

Letter from Mahatma Gandhi to Maulana Azad

Oct. 20, 1932

Thanks for wire from this place of seclusion I can only say I wish with all my heart that we may achieve the real unity between Hindus, Muslims and Sikhs as symbol of All India Unity for which you and I and other co-workers have been wishing and praying all these long years. On merits I may say nothing in ignorance of full facts and situation. But for me personally any solution that is acceptable to parties concerned will be acceptable. Therefore I wish all success to you and all other friends working for achievement of long deferred peace in this distracted country of ours. Saradar Vallabhbhai joins.

GANDHI

Maulana Abul Kalam Azad,
Calcutta.

Document No. 63

Letter from Dr. Sampurnananda to Maulana Abul Kalam Azad

Ministry of Education,
United Provinces,
Lucknow,
January 31, 1939

Dear Maulana Saheb,

Some time back you sent to Pantji a letter making certain enquiries about two schools in Sikandra Rao. Recently, a letter on the same subject has been sent to Pandit Jawaharlal by the Editor of the *Comrade*.

In this correspondence, some blame has been sought to be thrown on me personally, but I do not care to reply to such criticism. The actual state of affairs as regards this question will be clear from a perusal of the accompanying note by the Director of Public Instruction. You will thus see that the recognition has been granted in spite of the recommendations to the contrary of the Education Department. I have only to point out that the law makes the Board of High School and Intermediate Examinations an autonomous body whose decisions are normally binding on the Department.

I would also point out that in a letter addressed to the Director of Public Instruction on November 14, 1938, the Inspector of Schools, Khan Saheb M. Faiyaz Bahadur, says, "At this stage it would not be advisable to attempt the closure of either of the schools. In my opinion the school results should be watched for at least two or three years. "I find myself helpless, therefore, to do anything, for the present, although I agree with the complainant about the main facts of the case.

Yours sincerely,
Sampurnananda

Maulana Abul Kalam Azad Saheb,
Member All India Congress Parliamentary Sub-Committee,
19A, Ballygunge, Circular Road,
Calcutta.

Document No. 64

Letter from Mr. Nirmalananda Jeshtha to Maulana Azad

17th January, 1940

From,

Bhikshu Nirmalananda,
Jeshtha, The Gandhi Mission Society,
Kripa-Asram, Gandhikuppam,
Triuvennainallur P.O.(South India)

Respected Sir,

Pray permit the undersigned to submit the following grievence for your kind and sympathetic consideration and judgement.

1. Triuvennainalllur is a village in the Tirukoilur Taluq in the South Arcot District (Tamil Nadu). It has a population of over 4500 and is an ancient pilgrimage centre. Here, there are about a dozen temples among whom three are important. The main deity of this village is Sri Kripapuriswarar, a Siva murthy. Legend has it, that in this temple it was that Sri Sundaramurthy Nainar, one of the four of the foremost of the Tamil saints got his divine inspiration on the occasion of his being prevented from marrying by the Lord Himself coming in the form of an old man and claiming him as his bond slave. Thousands of hymns of Sri Sundaramurthy are being sung all over the Tamil Nadu today and this place attracts thousands of pilgrims every year. Two other temples are also important and have associations with sacred memories. But the most important kshetramurthy is Sri Kripapuriswarar. This temple is an ancient one and was renovated and enlarged about 35 years ago by a generous Chettiar of Chettinad. It has some properties and gets a government grant of about Rs. 600 annually. This is the biggest village in this taluq with the largest number of Harijans, about 800. Within a radius of five miles there are over 5000 Harijans in this tract.

2. The undersigned Bhikshu Nirmalananda (Govinda Rao V. Gurjale) belongs to an ancient Maharashtra Brahmin family which migrated to the South and domiciled here a century ago. Though trained for a factory life the call of the village was so strong and insistent

that he has come back to his home and settled among peaceful surrondings. He has been actively in public life since 1917 from during the Home Rule movement days and has played his humble part in every movement therefrom. He has been a whole-time worker since 1929 and had the privilege of being a ward under the government twice afterwards.

3. From a humble beginning in general Congress work this centre evolved itself into an Asram with activities of different kinds. Mahatma Gandhi's memorable fast of 1932 reulting in the famous Yerrowada Pact took us into deeper waters in the field of Harijan service. The Kripa Asram has stood the severest storms and little by little has effectively undermined the opposition of the general masses. (A fair idea of the life of the Asram workers in the beginning stages can be had by a reference to the article titled "EXCELSIOR" in the Harijan ,Vol. II, issue No. 24, page 185). Gandhiji's visit to the Asram on 17- 2-34 was a landmark in the life of the institution in as much as from that occasion the opposition has been gradually on the decline. The visit of Babu Rajendra Prasad to the Asram on 7-11-35 was utilized to reorganize the Asram under the name of the Gandhi Mission Society. All the activities of the Asram are thenceforward carried on under that name.

4. Through the continued work of a band of workers in this centre the outlook of the general masses has undergone a considerable change. From a fierce opposition, passing through several stages they have now come to passive sympathy.

There are many among them who even come to dine with us in the Asram along with the Harijans. We can today look back to those days of sufferring with a real pride and satisfaction.

5. At this stage the opening of the Sri Meenakshi temple at Madura came upon us as an unforeseen help. It enthused some of the local men and induced them to covet the honour here also. Vigourous activity was visible and the people were also in a good mood. The ameliorative measures of the Congress Ministry, the daring lies of the oppositionists during the District Board Elections in 1937 all contributed to enhance the prestige of the Congress. It was a time when anything in the name of the Congress could be carried on.

6. With this knowledge of the attitude of the masses the undersigned wrote a letter to the Trustee of Sri Kripapuriswarar temple at Tiruvennainallur on 19-7-39 (Appendix. I.1) requesting him to open the temple for the worship of the Harijans. The effect of this letter was a report to the police by the trustees of the Siva and Vishnu temples complaining that the undersigned proposed to enter the temple along

with the Harijans by force and appealing for protection. The local Sub-Inspector wrote to the undersigned asking for definite information about the proposed entry into the temples (Appendix III.1). A reply was sent to the S.I. that he did not propose to force entry into the temple and that all that he did was, he requested the trustee of the Sri Kripapuriswarar temple to open the temple to the Harijans and on hearing favourably from him he would lead a batch of Harijans (Appendix III. 2). Having waited for ten days the undersigned wrote a second letter to the trustee on the morning of the 29th July in which he wished to impress upon him that the opening of the temple was inevitable and that if he did not choose to do this thing at the right time gracefully, the Harijans would themselves wrest it from our hands (Appendix I.2). The above-mentioned letter from the police was received in the evening of the 29th. That day the father of the undersigned was obstructed from going in the temple which incident reaching the ears of the Panchayat Court President, the trustee was advised by the latter not to indulge in such methods. The next day the undersigned was sent for by the trustee. During the meeting the undersigned explained how the Harijans were impatient and how the Savarnas who promised the Harijans during the fast of Mahatma Gandhi in 1932 absolute equality were bound to honour their word. He also brought to his notice that Harijans were already entering the temples stealthily and that it would be adharma to obstruct worship of the devotees who were yearning for the holy communion. Besides he also pointed out that Harijans were allowed into the temple compound for all menial services but were refused admittance even in the Sannadhi Street (street opposite to the temple) if for worship. He also made him know the law which was passed only a year ago which conferred upon the Harijans unrestricted freedom in the use of all public places, wells, tanks etc. and that the Temple Entry Ordinance was an emergency measure to protect the trustees from the persecution of the oppositionists. But the trustee was adament. He said that he would not allow the Harijans at any cost and if the fight was inevitable he would face it. Just the previous evening news was brought to the undersigned by co-workers that they were subjected to foul abuse by a drunkard from the varandha of the house of the trustee.

This incident was also brought to his notice by the undersigned at the time of the personal talk. The trustee also told the undersigned that the people of the village were not in favour of the reform. But would not accept any method by which the will of the public could be known. From that day onwards hooliganism was let loose. Finding that the workers and sympathisers of the reform were insulted by the drunkards the undersigned wrote a letter to the local Police officer giving him a clear idea about the course of the movement and bringing his notice the appearence of the drunkard on the stage (Appendix III. 3).

7. According to the program of the Society the temple entry propaganda was begun in right earnest on the 5th August. It was decided–

(1) that meetings were to be conducted every Sunday in different parts of the village;
(2) that the people should be approached individually and the reform explained;
(3) that signatures were to be secured for a memorial and sent to the Honourable Minister of Religious Endowments.

This program was fairly kept up and several meetings were addressed by the local workers. A memorial was prepared and houses were visited. Signatures from every literate were obtained. It took about two months to secure the signatures of about 120 people. While this work was going on the goondas were doing their work with added vigour. It was always noticed that one of the rich men was guarding these rowdies from a distance. The police who promised to bring them under control took no notice of the daily happenings. Even when they were shown they began saying that they were unable to take any action unless something untoward had happened. This encouraged the goondas and they would go to the houses of the local workers and sympathisers at 11 p.m. in the night and abuse the workers and their women-folk in the most obscene language. Some nights they would stand opposite to the *Khadi* shop and abuse one and all. In spite of all these humiliations some of the local people encourged the workers.

8. The month of August was one of trial and test for this firka as a whole. The South Arcot District Conference was conducted in this Firka in a village two miles from the Asram on 6-8-39. It was almost a temple entry conference in as much as the opening of the Sri Meenakshi temple at Madura was the predominant subject. Almost all the prominent leaders spoke on it. The movement at Tiruvennainallur was also referred to and supported. When the support for this subject was sought all of the 2000 except one solitary figure raised their hands. As the audience contained the local people in a major proportion the voice of the conference was almost the voice of the people of this Firka. The

second test came during the elections to the seat of the District Board on the 12th of August. None of the anti-Congressites or the Sanatanists showed their head. The third test was the most important and covered the whole of the district. The vacancy in the Madras Legislative Council created by the death of Sri R. Sreenivasa Iyangar was contested by Sri P. Ramaswamy Reddiar of Omandur, the President of the Tamil Nadu Congress Committee. He was opposed by a Justice Party and a Sanatanist canditate. The issue of the contest was the temple entry question. The opposing parties combined their forces against the Congress and spread all kinds of falsehoods. Enormous money was also spent. But the Congress candidate won the contest with credit. He got half the votes polled while the other half was equally divided between the two. This was a clear demontration of the attitude of the conservative elements in the district. This election took place on 20-8-39.

9. With these proofs about the attitude of the masses so clearly expressed the undersigned again wrote to the trustee to reconsider the appeal and accede to the wish of the public. Here, he had suggested that the opening could be done on the occasion of the birthday of Mahatma Gandhi (Appendix I. 3). There was no reply. Meanwhile the hooliganism extended to the day time also. This was brought to the notice of the police and was spoken of in public meetings. The unfortunate situation in the village is that most of the peasants are indebted to the rich men and are under their grip. They dare not say anything against the action of the rich men. This grave state of affairs was brought to the notice of the trustee in the letter of the 20th September (Appendix I. 4). The temple Entry Ordinance was promulgated to protect the reformer trustees from the persecution of the antireformers. The trustee of Sri Kripapuriswarar temple was availing the benefit of the Ordinance against the very purpose for which it was passed. It was a gross misuse of the Act which if tolerated without challenge would do more harm than the existing disadvantages. The hooliganism had also advanced to such an extent that it had become impossible to express their views on the reforms for which there was so much of support. That the trustee should refuse to the will of the public in their very name was an insult. The undersigned aware of the fact that the law required the trustee to apply for permission and obtain it before actually opening the temple gave him sufficient time. He was also aware that the trustee could only apply for the permission. So he was satisfied if he applied for the necessary sanction. Since the trustee would not do this the undersigned wrote to him that if he did not accede to the public verdict he would enter into a fast from the 5th October.

10. After this letter was recieved by the trustee there were signs of brisk work going on the other side. Gates which had not held a shutter since their construction got new ones. Any one wearing Khadi were refused admission in the temple. All the inlets to the temple were closed at all the hours of the day and guards posted at the main entrances. Only people who were in their good looks were allowed in. Strangers had to appear before the trustee and make a request to be allowed for worship. People in the surroundings were inconvenienced by the barring of all the entrances, thus preventing them from taking drinking water from the temple well. The condition was day by day growing worse and none of the public had the courage to raise a finger against these acts of the rich men. Under the circumstances the undersigned wrote the last letter to the trustee about the fast (Appendix I.5). At the same time he wrote two other letters one to the local Police Officer (Appendix III. 4) and another to the District Magistrate (Appendix III.5) and requested them to maintain peace at all costs, and make it possible for the people to take sides in a fight that was purely religious.

11. During the period between the 30th September and the 5th October news was brought by the public that the trustee was collecting signatures in a document in the weekly market telling that it was a protest against the tobacco and sales taxes. The village Munsiff went house to house telling that if they sided the reformers the reduction of 2 as in the rupee which the Government was giving in the land tax would be discontinued. The Harijans brought news that the Police Sub-Inspector, to whom they had to go in connection with a theft case, reprimanded them with dire consequences if they should dare to heed to the advice of the undersigned in connection with the temple entry work. Signatures were also taken by the trustees from the Harijans in a document which expressed unwillingness to enter the temples. From the 3rd October the hooligans were not very much in the scene.

12. At the appointed time the fast began. There were 200 people at the place. The Police had made good arrangements. The public was addressed by the undersigned and the object of the fast explained. Being rainy season the public were anxious about the undersigned being in the open. When there was a slight drizzle in the night, people from the neighbourhood came with blankets and shawls. The next morning the public put shed in the spot where the undersigned was fasting. These minor incidents are mentioned here to give an idea of the attitude of the public. Hundreds of people visited the spot and they felt sorry for the attitude of the trustee. On the 6th October the trustee complained to the Police twice against the friends of the undersigned

and charged them as inciting the Harijans to force entry into the temple. He objected to the erection of the shed on the ground of the materials being combustible. The Congress flag which was hoisted above the shed on the unfinished construction of the Gopuram was objected to in the complaint. The man who was attending upon the undersigned was summoned to the police station and warned.

13. Meanwhile Sri K.S. Jambunathan one of the workers of the Gandhi Mission Society sent an invitation to all the workers of the district to assemble in the Asram on the 4th to consider the situation (Appendix II. 1). Some wrote that they were unable to come as they were engaged in election work elsewhere. The local workers and sympathisers met on the 4th and formed a Temple Entry Satyagraha Committee with seven members. They also passed some resolutions (Appendix II. 3). They were very anxious for the discontinunce of the fast. They tried to meet the trustee and his group, but they would not see them. Sri Chinnasamy Reddiar however was kind to promise to arrange for a meeting between the two parties. But this did not take place.

14. On the fourth day (8-10-39) the Revenue Sub-Divisional Officer and the Tahsildar visited the place. They had long talks with the trustee. They also visited the undersigned and discussed with him for over half an hour. They found that both claimed to represent the public opinion. They tried to feel the pulse that had gathered then. There were about 50. But those who raised their hands for and against were barely half a dozen. All the rich men also were there. They were convinced that the public felt timid to express their opinion. The S.D.O. suggested a referendum. The undersigned accepted the proposal on condition the S.D.O. would undertake to conduct it and see the verdict was honoured. But the S.D.O. would do no such thing without the permission of the Government. When he left the place he requested both the parties to keep him informed about the developements.

15. The same night a meeting of the trustee's party was held in the house of Sri Chinnasamy Reddiar. All the rich men and their tenents were assembled. It was a crowd of about 50. The Secretary of the Satyagraha Committee was also present by invitation. There was no discussion. A document was taken round and signatures were obtained by Sri Reddiar and the trustee. When a few young men asked what it was about Sri Reddiar was heard to say that those who did not know the purpose of the meeting can go away. Some people proptested against this procedure and left the meeting. Next morning a complaint was lodged with the Police stating that the undersigned sent some men to

their meeting to create confusion. Since it was spoken of that the document of the previous night was to be sent to the S.D.O. the next morning a letter was written by the President of the Satyagraha Committee to the S.D.O. as to what happened the previous night (Appendix II. 7).

16. Having failed to approach the temple trustee and his group the President of the Temple Entry Satyagraha Committee wrote to several friends in and outside the district to help them in bringing this to an amicable settlement. Sri P. Ramaswamy Reddiar, President of the Tamil Nadu Congress Committee being a resident of this district, was being put in touch with every detail. In response to this invitation the President of the Tirukoilur Taluq Congress Committee G. Ramaswamy Naicker; Sri T. Vadivelu Mudaliar, retired Tamil Pandit and Superintendent of the Harijan Hostel at Tirukoilur; Sri C. Krishnaswamy Pillay, an old Congress worker; Sri A.V. Sreenivasan, an ex-reporter of the *Bombay Chronicle* and a Congress worker, all from Tirukoilur, came on the 12th October. While they were meeting people one by one they were joined by Sri R. Subba Iyer, Public Prosecutor of Chenglepet, and a member of the Tamil Nadu Congress Committee and Sri A. Krishna Rao also a pleader of Chenglepet. This group met the trustee, Sri Chinnaswamy Reddiar and the undersigned alternately. On the morning of the 14th they brought the news that the friends of the trustee were acceptable for the arbitration by Sri P. Ramaswamy Reddiar, President of the Tamil Nadu Congress Committee. This arbitration proposal was not acceptable to the undersigned for delicate reasons.

17. Sri P. Ramaswamy Reddiar, President of the Tamil Nadu Congress Committee is a native of this district. He has influential relatives in the surrounding villages here. Some of them are anti-Congressites and most of them are against the Harijan movement. Sri Chinnaswamy Reddiar, the local anti-Congressite is a close relative of his. Though Sri Ramaswamy Reddiar contested the elections for the seat of the Upper Council on the Temple Entry issue, his conduct in this village was harmful to the Harijan cause. It is this small incident which gave them the courage to suggest his name for arbitration. The undersigned explained the whole thing to the friends and pointed to them the risk in accepting the proposal for arbitration. At this juncture the proposal of the Sub-Divisional Officer for a referendum was considered. The undersigned had no objection for it provided the verdict of the referendum was binding upon the trustee also. The undersigned accepted to suspend the fast if the referendum could be undertaken by competent authority and its verdict made binding on

both the parties. The friends again met the trustee's group. They seemed to consider it favourably and had even given hopes. But when they came to know about the acceptance of the proposal by the undersigned they sent word about their inability to accept the proposal. They withdrew at the last moment. The friends again met them. All their persuasions were useless. They came to the undersigned and pressed to accept the proposal of referendum and said that if its result was favourable for the reform they would give the undersigned all the strength of the Congress organization in his efforts to have the temples opened. They also said that through this open verdict of the masses they would help the undersigned in moving the Government to respect this popular will. Finally on the insistence of the undersigned it was agreed that the referendum should be conducted by a committee over which Sri P. Ramaswamy Reddiar, President of the Tamil Nadu Congress Committee should preside, and the personnel of the Committee should be appointed by the President. The Committee was to include Sri R. Subba Iyer also. Messrs G. Ramaswamy Naicker President of the Tirukoilur Congress Committee and Sri R. Subba Iryer agreed to make the necessary arrangements for the appointment of the Committee. It was also agreed that the referendum was to take place within two months from that date *i.e.* 14-10-39. A letter was accordingly drafted by the President of the Taluk Congress Committee to the President of the Tamil Nadu Congress Committee in which the terms of the suspension of the fast were mentioned. Three copies were taken. One was handed over to Sri R. Subba Iyer to be delivered to the President of the Tamil Nadu Congress Committee. Since this letter was considered to be as good as an agreement another copy was given to the undersigned. The third was taken by the President of the TirukoilurTaluq Congress Committee for his office file. When this was done the fast was suspended at 5 P.M. on 14-10-39 (Appendix V.1). On the way to the Asram the throng who gathered in the place where usually public meetings are held, was addressed by the undersigned for a couple of minutes explaining the circumstances leading the suspension of the fast. Messrs Ramaswamy Naicker and Subba Iyer also addressed the audience for a longer time and explained the course of the movement and the future work ahead. They exhorted them to give support to the reform at the time of the referendum. The Satyagraha Committee was also requested by them to prepare a voters' list of all the adults of the village above the age of 18.

18. Next day when the President of the Taluq Congress Committee reached his headquarters wrote a letter to the undersigned requesting him to take care of his health and instructing to prepare a voters' list with the help of local helpers (Appendix V. 2) Though the stipulated period of two months elapsed none of the above-mentioned gentlemen who were concerned in the suspension of the fast wrote any letter to the undersigned. The agreement was not given effect to either by those who were responsible for the creation of the document or by the President of the Tamil Nadu Congress Committee. Several letters were written to the Taluq and the Provincial committees as also to Sri Subba Iyer (Appendix VI. 1 to 4). They did not even care to reply.

19. On a casual talk with the Secretary of the Taluq Congress Committee he expressed that the Congress organization was not bound to honour any understanding that the President might have entered into in his personal capacity. The undersigned showed him the documents concerned and convinced him that there was nothing of personal concern in it and whatever was done was done in his official capacity. Dr. Sakuntala Bai Gurjale met Sri Ramaswamy Naicker in the last week of November and enquired him about the progress of thier efforts in the formation of the Committee. The President of the Taluq Committee said to her that he was in correspondance with the President of the Tamil Nadu Congress Committee and that he would meet the undersigned in the course of the first week of December as he would be meeting Sri Ramaswamy Reddiar meanwhile. He again sent word through the Secretary of the Taluq Congress Committee that he would go over to the Asram after the 15th December.But he did nothing. Pained at their callousness the undersigned wrote an appeal to the other members of the group who had taken part in the negaotiations to exert their influence with them in bringing into being the committee and fixing the date of the referendum (Appendix.VII). No information has been received from them upto the time of submitting this appeal.

20. Finally, since all the people had neglected and no action was taken to fulfil the agreement it had become necessary to the undersigned to intimate to the President of the Taluq Congress Committee that he would be forced to submit the case before the President of the A.I.C.C. and Mahatma Gandhi if no favourable reply was received before the 3rd of January 1940 (Appendix VI.5). In reply to this the President of the Taluq Congress Committee wrote to the undersigned on the 28th December requesting him to be patient and explaining the difficulties in the path of committees subject to discipline (Appendix V.3). The

undersigned has waited all along hoping that there may be some favourable turn even though much belated. But there seems to be no hope of any such event.

21. The days in the future are full of uncertainty. Fresh elections are taking place all over the province for all the Congress Committees. In a few days many of the members of the old committees may be unseated and new ones found in their places. Authority may passes into the hands of new sets of people. Even those who were directly responsible for the document have shown scant respect for it. The possibility of others showing due regard for it is doubtful. The undersigned is deeply pained that those friends should have entered in his life at a time when he was fighting against an injustice, insult and misrepresentation with his life staked, given him hopes of redress and then left him in the lurch making him the mocking stock of the place. Secondly, this interference of these people and the subsequent inaction will harm the cause more than affecting the undersigned in as much as it will once for all betray the Harijans who had shown no little enthusiasm in the advent of the reform. Lastly, this letting down of an institution and a band of workers working under its auspices will make any good work impossssible here as the anti-Congressites will not let the chance pass without trying to ruin the institution and its workers. The undersigned has no other object in his life but the service of humanity and has chosen this spot as his Kurukshetra. He has stood the severest storms of the opponents. But nothing hurts him more than the feeling that his own co-workers should cripple him and render his life a burden for all time to come.

Though conscious of the unlimited call upon your good-self's time and physical strength the undersigned is painfully driven to add to them with this case and hopes that he may be pardoned. He has waited for a reasonable period and has tried to appeal to the good sense of the party concerned. Having failed in his efforts to make them realize their responsibility he approaches your good-self for justice and redress. He has presented in this document every available evidence. A few letters in the appendices may not be necessary here, but they are not irrelevant. To give a thorough idea of the case they have also been included. Under the circumstances the undersigned prays that this case may be given due consideration and favourably disposed.

Awaiting Sir, for your esteemed self's orders.

He begs to remain,
Your obedient servant,
(Nirmalananda)
Jeshtha

Document No. 65

Statement of Maulana Azad dated 19-2-1940

Maulana Sahib said the he regarded his election as vote of confidence in the leadership of Mahatma Gandhi and the country's approval of his programme.

Asked if the solution of the Hindu-Muslim problem would form the chief plank in his programme during year, Maulana Azad said that the real issue before the country was political but they could not ignore the Hindu-Muslim problem.

He had, however, no hesitation in saying that the struggle for the achievement of Independence could not await the settlement of internal problems.

He wanted to make it clear that the settlement of the political issue was not dependent on the solution of the communal problem which was, after all, a domestic affair.

The Congress had taken a definite step and could not wait any longer. "The present state of suspense," added Maulana Azad, "cannot continue longer and I can say that after the Ramgarh session the Congress must take a step forward. That step would surely take the form of a new struggle."

Replying to a question whether it would mean the launching of civil disobedience once again, Maulana Sahib said: "Yes naturally."

Maulana Sahib also indicated the possibility of examining the question of forming coalition ministries in the provinces provided a satisfactory solution of the political question could be arrived at with the British Government.

Maulana Sahib said it was to a certain extent essential for launching a civil disobedience campaign that a favourable atmosphere should prevail in the country but he did not think that there was much danger of communal disturbances.

Commenting to Mr. Jinnah's[1] recent statement to the "Time and Tide" Maulana Azad said that Mr. Jinnah's two-nation theory was entirely based on misunderstanding and he did not agree with him.

1. Mr. M.A. Jinnah.

Maulana Azad said that the possibility of forming coalition ministries in the provinces was not precluded if the British Government acceded to their political demand but hastened to add that there could be no question of the Congress taking up office under the Government of India Act of 1935.

Referring to social relations of Congressmen with non-Congress Ministers, Maulana Sahib said that the Congress had never banned social relations.

"The Muslims have every right to struggle for their safeguards. They should not look to the British Government for these safeguards but they should look to their countrymen," declared Maulana Azad, addressing the first public meeting since his election as President of the Indian National Congress.

It was one of the biggest meetings held in Lahore in recent times and was attended by a very large number of Muslims. The Maulana received a great ovation on arrival. He was presented with a guard of honour by Ahrar and Congress volunteers.

Dealing with the communal question, Maulana Azad said that nobody could deny its existence. Everybody was anxious to solve this question as early as possible. It was rather the bounden duty of every Indian to help in solving the thorny issue. But so far as the question of independence was concerned he would appeal to his countrymen to join hands in achieving the freedom of their country.

The Muslims had every right to press for their safeguards. They should not look to the British for their safeguards but they should look to their own countrymen. The foremost problem at this juncture was to achieve independence other questions could be solved later on.

Proceeding Maulana Azad said that if they asked the British for their safeguards they would be strengthening the roots of British Imperialism in India. He would advise his nine crore Muslim brethren that they should not look upon their countrymen with suspicion. Their rights were not at all in danger in the hands of the Congress. There was no other alternative for the Muslims than to join in the stuggle for the freedom of the country. The doors of the Congress were open to all and it represented all communities. They should dispel all suspicions and muster strong under the banner of the Congress.

Document No. 66

Message of Azad for "News Chronicle" dated 10-3-40

"India had put a clear and simple question to the British Government to clarify their war aims with particular reference to India. If these were meant for maintaining and extending democracy and freedom of nations then inevitably they must be applied to India also and Indian people enquired if the British Government were prepared to acknowledge their right of self-determination. Britain's answer was a definite 'no'. Our question was answered though not to our liking and the real object of the war became clear. Whatever pronouncement might have been made about the war the fact stood out that the British Imperialism still persisted with all the traditional characteristics as previously.

India has condemned Fascism and Nazism, but she condemns Imperialism equally. She had no option left and only line of action remained to her to refuse to be a party to any Imperialist war and to think in terms of her own final struggle for freedom.

Mr. Chamberlain[1] has frankly stated the British and French war aims in his Birmingham speech of 24th February, "We are fighting to secure that small nations of Europe shall henceforth live in security, free from constant threat of aggression against their independence". This statement implies that the object of the war is limlited by geographical boundaries to Europe. It is a clear negation of freedom not only to India, but to all peoples of Asia and Africa who must continue in subjection.

The independence of three hundred and seventy millions of people of India is not even worthy of thought. Whatever the British Empire exists it must remain untouched and be perpetuated. Small European nations under British influence should in the name of freedom be kept under that influence. That seems to be Mr. Chamberlain's conception of freedom. That is not ours. Certainly small European nations should retain independence, but no real freedom unless other nations, great and small, are also freed and imperialist system ended.

Countless human souls all over the world agitated for the dawn of a new world order based on reason, justice and peace. Can such order be

---

1. British Premier during the World War Second.

dreamt of when the people of India forming one-fifth of the human race are deprived of their birth-right?

We believe that the world will appreciate our position and not blame us for our decision. We have vigilantly kept control on our heads and hearts lest we might take a hasty step at a critical juncture. We wanted and waited patiently but certainly we cannot wait indefinitely.

India was prepared to throw her weight on the side of freedom, if freedom were really in issue and her free choice and will acknowledged, but the British Government has banged the door in her face.

Much importance is being attached to the communal problem, especially the Hindu-Muslim problem of India. But the world should not remain in the dark about the real situation. Such problems are the result of foreign domination for a century and a half. Its origin lies in the traditional policy of balance and counterpoise pursued by British imperialism in India. India like other countries has her internal problems and it is her bounden duty to solve them to the satisfaction of all concerned. The achievement of this is obviously impossible when she is deprived of the atmosphere in which nations have solved such problems. If this is a real impediment and the British Government does not wish to exploit our differences the solution is simple. Let Britain declare clearly her intentions about Indian independence and allow us to remove all differences by common consent.

The offer of the Indian National Congress ends all disputes pertaining to this problem. The Congress has accepted that Muslims can send representatives to the Constituent Assembly purely by their own votes. A majority of votes in the Assembly are not the deciding factor so far as the communal problems are concerned, but a decision can only be arrived at by mutual consent. In case of difference, reference of the issue to an impartial tribunal is the only advisable course.

If any people outside India entertain the opinion that Indian Muslims are opposed to independence I would tell them with the fullest sense of responsibility that this is absolutely a false impression. Not a single responsible Muslim group is opposed to it. The general trend of Muslim thought in India has compelled even the Mulim Leage to change its creed of "full responsible government" to that of "democratic independence".

Document No. 67

Remark of the League Scheme for Partition dated 22-4-1940

The Muslim League has presented at its Lahore session[1] the idea of dividing India into Hindu and Muslim India. This conception is so unreal, crude, fallacious and impracticable that on reconsideration the League[2] itself would probably not insist on its realisation. But so far as the Congress[3] is concerned, it has no hesitation in saying that this matter may also be entrusted to the Muslim representatives of the proposed Assembly. The right to take such a step can rest only in the Mussalmans who are elected by Mussalmans themselves for such a purpose. The League can present any scheme, but it cannot claim that the scheme is acceptable by the totality or even the majority of the Mussalmans, I have no misgivings about the attitude of the Muslim members of such an Assembly. They would never favour a vivisection of India.

---

1. Of 1940.
2. The All India Muslim League.
3. Indian National Congress.

Document No. 68

Maulana Azad on Hidnu-Muslim Unity

9-6-1940

In connection with the Press report that the former Premiers of Congress provinces would meet in Delhi on June 13, under the presidency of Maulana Abul Kalam Azad with a view to examine the possibility of the Minister's return to office. Maulana Azad expressed surprise on the above statement and said that it was absolutely baseless. The Maulana has no knowledge of any such conference and so far as the Congress was concerned, he added, the resumption of office under the present circumstances was quite out of question. The Congress, he continued, firmly adhered to the decision taken on October 17, 1939.

Continuing, the Maulana said "The Hon'ble Mr. Fazlul Haq[1] met me in Calcutta and we had some talk about the solution of the Hindu-Muslim problem. He proposed a Premiers' conference to discuss the matter. I told him that such a conference might not be of much use under the prevailing circumstances and suggested that if he along with Premiers of the Punjab, Sind and the N.W.F.P. could meet me on some future occasion we may then discuss the problem informally and see if we could reach some tangible solution. Then we may pursue it still further. I have promised him to try and find out an occasion for such a meeting. After coming to Nainital, I had correspondence with Sir Sikandar Hyat Khan[2] also about the matter. It is quite possible that someone might have got scent of this matter and gave it the shape of a Premiers' conference for the purpose of resuming office."

---

1. Premier of West Bengal.
2. Premier of Punjab.

Document No. 69

Public Address dated 10-7-1940 in New Delhi

An address of welcome on behalf of the citizens of Delhi was presented to Maulana Abul Kalam Azad, Congress President, at a mammoth meeting held at the Gandhi Grounds in New Delhi on July 8, evening. Mr. Asaf Ali, M.L.A. (Central) presided and among those present were Mr. Jawaharlal Nehru and Mrs. Sarojini Naidu.

Maulana Azad said that at the very outset he wished to make it clear that it was incorrect to say that the deliberations of the Congress Working Committee during the last four days were confined only to the Gandhi-Viceroy talks at Simla. It was true that this subject was one of the several items that came up for discussion but there were several other matters left over from the last Wardha meeting. He pointed out that the resolution passed by the Congress Working Committee at its last meeting in Wardha put the Congress position in clear and unequivocal terms, and there was little that he could add to it by way of explanation.

Exphasising that the Congress still adhered to the creed of non-violence in the country's fight for freedom Maulana Azad said that during the last twenty years they had achieved noteworthy results. It was an indisputable fact that it was through strict adherence to this creed that they had been able to develop political consciousness among the masses not only in towns but also in remote villages. The Congress was still committed to the principal that India should reach her goal of independence by non-violence methods.

Ever since the outbreak of war in Europe in September last year Mahatma Gandhi wanted the Congress to go a step further and accept the proposition that a free India should have no need for armed forces, for defence purposes. This was the issue with which the Congress Working Committee was confronted, and the members with full sense of responsibility took the decision after prolonged deliberation. The Wardha resolution was self-explanatory and he did not think that any further elucidation was necessary.

Maulana Azad alluded to the Working Committee's resolution passed last evening demanding that Great Britain should make an unequivocal declaration according complete independence to India as the only solution of problems facing India and Britain. He pointed out that there was nothing new in the resolution nor was their going back on the Congress policy or principles. Pointing out the difficulties in the way of a composite national government, Maulana Azad said that there were no political parties in India except the Congress. There were communal parties whose programme were not confined to political issues. He thought that this was a serious obstacle to the formation of composite governments.

Maulana Azad further mentioned that during the period of nearly three years when the Codngress was running the administration in the provinces there were occasions when the Congress Parliamentary Sub-Committee had sought the cooperation of other parties for a solution of the problems that confronted them but he regretted to say that such cooperation had been refused.

Document No. 70

Maulana's Statement on China-Burma Road

Poona
July 27, 1940

Maulana Abul Kalam Azad, the Congress President, has issued the following statement in regard to the closing of the Burma-China Road:

The decision of the British Government to close the Burma-China Road is a matter of the most serious significance for China, India, Burma and Britain. This road had been built at enormous sacrifice by China and already it had become one of the main arteries of traffic between China and the outer world. It had brought China and Burma and India nearer to one another and their contacts grew from day to day. The people of India welcomed this new relationship and their goodwill flowed out to the people of China struggling for their freedom against an aggressor nation. The closing of the Burma Road means a severe restriction on these growing contacts and a flouting of Indian opinion. It is in complete conflict with the foreign policy which the people of India desire to pursue. It is a violation of international usage as well as of Sino-British treaties, and is evidently meant to hamper China in her struggle for freedom. It is clearly an encouragement of the aggressor nation who for over three years has been carrying on an undeclared war on Chinese territory. It is support of a policy against which Great Britian claims to be fighting in Europe. Its greatest significance lies in this light it throws on British policy which claims to do one thing in Europe and follows an entirely different course in India and China. We must therefore wholly disapprove of the action of the British Government in closing the Burma-China Road.

Document No. 71

Opinion expressed on Wardha Meeting dated 27-7-1940

The Congress President was of the emphatic opinion that there was no departure whatever in the present position of the Congress from what it was before the Wardha meeting. He explained that neither the Wardha statement of the Working Committee regarding non-violence nor the Delhi resolution offering co-operation in the matter of organizing the country's defences on the condition that Indian independence was recognized and a national Government enjoying the confidence of the elected members of the Central Assembly formed, marked a departure from the fundamental position taken up by the Congress in its resolution adopted at Wardha immediately after the declaration of war in September 1939.

The resolution, continued Maulana Azad, made it clear that the Congress was prepared to cooperate with the British Government if the latter satisfied the Congress with regard to its war aims in their application to India and also recognized India's independence.

On the question of non-violence the Maulana was clear that at no stage had the Congress declared that it would pursue the stage had the Congress declared that it would pursue the policy of non-violence in the matter of meeting external aggression and internal disorder for the simple reason that the issue had never arisen before. He emphasized that in regard to every other aspect of the Congress programme the Congress still adhered to the policy of non-violence. Even today no external situation had actually arisen necessitating such clarification of the Congress attitude. But Mahatma Gandhi felt that the Congress owed it to the country to clarify its position in the matter, and the Working Committee had accordingly defined its attitude. In doing so the majority of the members of the Committee felt that while they fully endorsed Mahatma Gandhi's views on non-violence, they did not feel that the country was ready to adopt non-violence in respect of meeting external aggression and internal disorder.

Document No. 72

Statement dated 5-9-1940 on the Sikh Support

Maulana Abul Kalam Azad, Congress President, has issued the following statement to the Press:

"When I was at Wardha, on the occasion of the last Working Committee meeting, I received a telegram from Sardar Sampuran Singh, Leader of the Congress Party in the Punjab Assembly, saying that he has been invited to a dinner to the Maharaja of Patiala, in which after-dinner speeches may also be delivered on the present, political situation. He asked my advice whether he should participate in it or not? I replied that his participation would not be advisable. He, therefore, informed me on August 20, that he has declined to deliver any speech at the function."

But while returning from Wardha, I was astonished to find the following Press report (in the *Bombay Chronicle*):

"According to talks here (Simla) the Sikh dinner at Patiala last night was intended to serve three main objects: firstly, the importance of the Sikh community during war; secondly, unity of Sikh parties behind Patiala's leadership and demand for Patiàla Maharaja's membership on the War Advisory Council and thirdly inclusion of a Sikh in the enlarged Executive Council, Master Tara Singh, Akali Leader, Gyani Kartar Singh and Sampuran Singh leader of the Congress Party in the Punjab Assembly, participated and showed their support to the three demands. The Sikh leaders are prepared for a panel for election or an Executive Councillor from among them to be forwarded to the Viceroy. This includes Sir Jogendra Singh, Sant Singh M.L.A. (Central), and Sampuran Singh. Two others, Sardar Bahadur Ujjal Singh (of Round Table Conference) and Sir Datar Singh of Indo-British trade negotiations are also trying their luck."

No sooner had I reached Calcutta, then I asked him (Sardar Sampuran Singh) telegraphically the truth or otherwise of the report, as I could not believe that he, being a responsible member of the Congress Party, could associate himself with any demand based on the declaration rejected by the Congress.

In reply to the above telegram, Sardar Sampuran Singh wired to me saying that the Press report was wrong and that he had no association with these demands. Now I am writing to him to fully clarify the situation by a detailed statement to the Press.

The above-mentioned Press report also mentions Master Tara Singh in this connection. Master Sahib is a member of the Punjab Provincial Congress Committee, and a member of the All India Congress Committee as well, I have written to the Punjab Provincial Congress Committee to inquire into the matter and apprise me of the situation.

Document No. 73

Maulana Abul Kalam Azad's reaction on the action taken against Mr. Sarat Bose by the Congress Working Committee

October 11, 1940

In communication to the decision of the Committee to Mr. Bose, the Congress President says that the Committee is definitely of opinion that Mr. Bose[1] has knowingly adopted an attitude which is not only against Congress discipline but creates in the party a general state of confusion, which effects the whole work of the Congress organisation in the province.

The Committee has, therfore, removed him from the Bengal Assembly Party and demands his resignation from the membership of the Assembly as he has broken the pledge he had signed by going against Congress discipline, adherence to which was the condition precedent to his getting the Congress ticket.

In informing him of the decision of the Parliamentary Sub-Committee, the Congress President, Maulana Azad, wrote the following letter to Mr. Bose yesterday (October):

"It is my painful duty to let you know of the decision of the Parliamentary Sub-Committee, which it has reached after fully considering the events since March last to the present day. The committee gave you several chances, one after the other, to make an explantory statement in this respect, but it did not receive any satisfactory explanation. The Committee is definitely of opinion that you have knowingly adopted an attitude which is not only against the Congress discipline, but creates in the Party a general state of confusion which affects the whole work of the Congress organisation in the province. Now there is no other alternative for the Committee but to discharge its duty–the duty for which it is responsible to the great national organisation.

"The Committee, therefore, removes you from the Bengal Assembly

1. Mr. Sarat Chandra Bose, a front ranking Congress leader of Bengal and elder brother of Netaji Subhas Chandra Bose.

Party, and demands your resignation from the membership of the Assembly, as you have broken the pledge you had signed by going against Congress discipline, adherence to which was the condition precedent to your getting the Congress ticket. "

"It is useless to recapitulate all the facts which have come before the Committee during the past months, as we had already a long correspondence about them. However, it is necessary to refer to some of them briefly."

"During the Bengal Council bye-elections of March last you had recommended the name of Babu Namini Kumar Dutt to the Parliamentary Sub-Committee on behalf of the Provincial Congress Committee. He was working as the party leader in the Bengal Council Party at that time. The Parliamentary Sub-Committee had accepted your recommendation. But later on, owing to some unknown reasons, you changed your opinion all of a sudden, and began to work for Mr. Birendra Kishore Roy. This gentleman was a member of the Assembly and wanted to resign his seat for that of the Council. The Parliamentary Sub-Committee could not understand why he wished to resign from the Assembly and to become a candidate for the membership of the Council. Moreover, this application which you had presented, could in no way be granted. He wanted to sign the Congress pledge with the reservation that he should be exempted from all the Party mandates which affected the Zamindar interests. Obviously the Parliamentary Sub-Committee could not accept the pledge with such reservation, and it rejected it.

"When the Parliamentary Committee did not approve your recommendation, you wired to me at Patna on the 30th February, 1940, that you would get the decision of the Parliamentary Sub-Committee faithfully acted upon, but in that case you could not remain the Party leader, and would resign. But despite this assertion you issued your own whip against that of the Parliamentary Sub-Committee on the Ist March and flatly denounced its decision. You gave directions to the party to give its votes to Mr. Birendra Kishore Roy as against the accepted nominee of the Parliamentary Sub-Committee. Thus, on the one hand you went against the decision of the Committee, while on the other hand you voted, and asked the party also to vote for a candidate whose name had already been rejected by the Committee and whose pledge could not be accepted being against the acknowledged principles of the Party.

"After this another occasion arose regarding the Mymensingh bye-election of the Assembly. Again on this occasion some members of the Bengal Congress Assembly Party were made to work against the Congress nominee. And this was not the end. You did not even hesitate to send a congratulatory telegram, and get it published in the papers, on the success of a candidate who stood against the Congress nominee. Moreover, you instructed the party Secretary to find a place in the Party benches for this gentleman, but this could not be carried out owing to my interference."

Document No. 74

Statement[1] dated 25-11-1940

"On the eve of my departure from Sind, I am in a position to announce with the fullest satisfaction that I have succeeded in efforts and I am leaving with the belief that a Stable Ministry has been established here which has the backing of all parties in the Sind Legislature," observes Maulana Abul Kalam Azad, Congress President, in the course of his statement at Karachi on November 23. The Maulana adds, "I am satisfied that nothing better is possible under the existing circumstances in Sind. I received all round co-operation. Both the Moslem groups in the Assembly unanimously responded of my appeal for unity and all the four Muslim Ministers were at one with the decision of the Muslim members of the Assembly to respond to my appeal for unity. My success would have become doubtful had not the Hindu party in the Assembly helped with the fullest confidence. This party was prepared to support any Ministry which would establish law and order in the province with a firm hand. It went still further and was prepared to leave the administration of the province to the goodwill of Muslim Ministers only without there being a Hindu Minister in the Cabinet. I admit this spirit is nothing but praiseworthy but no single group of Muslim members of the Assembly was prepared to work without Hindu colleagues. I too did not consider it to be in any way conducive to the best interests of the province that Hindu members should not participate in the Cabinet. I am glad that the Hindu party has accepted my advice and let its representatives remain on the Cabinet and the party sincerely helped me in the achievement of the common object."

Turning to the Congress members of the Assembly the Congress President says:

Just at a time when I was expecting all Congress legislators to find themselves behind prison have as soon as possible, the situation in Sind engaged me in an activity of the opposite nature. I shouldered this responsibility with my own choice and it was my duty not to shrink it under its special circumstances. I have to admit that it is impossible to tread two contradictory paths one and the same time. Therefore if we

1. To the Press

were forced by the prevailing circumstances in Sind to participate in the formation of a provincial Government it is necessary that we remain in the Assembly and not grudge support to the Cabinet as far as possible. I have directed both Sind Assembly members and members of the A.I.C.C. from Sind to abstain from civil disobedience. Congress members of the Assembly will confine themselves only to constructive criticism and at the same time strain every nerve to consolidate the present Ministry. Outside the Assembly the work of the provincial Congress Committee will be mainly devoted to constructive programme, specially, Hindu-Muslim unity."

Maulana Azad prefaced his lengthy statement with the following observations:

"It is a matter of common knowledge that the root cause of the Ministerial tangle here was the outcome of mutual differences and rivalry between the Allah Baksh group of Muslim Assembly members and the other Muslim group in the Assembly." Maulana Azad said: "On arrival at Karachi, I found there were three lines of action open to me: first, the ministry might be formed on an all party basis, secondly the present ministry might be dissolved and a new single party ministry formed and third, so far as the Congress party was concerned it might resign from the Assembly and all its responsibilities come to end under the present circumstances."

Continuing he said "I studied all aspects of the problem and every link in the chain of reasoning led me to conclude that the first and fundamental need for the welfare of Sind lay in establishment of a stable Government. I also concluded such Government could not be established unless two conditions were fulfilled first, the group led by Khan Bahadur Allahbux joined ministry; secondly the Congress party was prepared to help it. No other menthod could solve the existing tangle in Sind. Such a structure could only be on an all-party basis. I therefore, decided to exert all my energies to achieve the above-mentioned object, which I did achieve."

The Advisory Committee includes Sir Ghulam Hussein Hidayatullah, Mr. R.K. Sidhwa, Doctor Choitram and two members from the Hindu Independent Party, the ex-Minister Pir Ellahi Baksh, Mr. M.H. Gazdar, Mr. Naraindas Anandji Bechar and the one European member of the Assembly. Mr. G.M. Syed, ex-Education Minister, will act as Secretary.

Document No. 75

Extracts for the address dated 2-1-1941 at a public meeting in New Delhi

"Future historians will have to write that there can be no better example of political blunder than one shown by British statesmen in rejecting the old Poona offer and other offers made by the Congress from time to time to give their whole-hearted support for a successful prosecution of the war. The Congress wanted India to be a self-respecting and equal partner with the British Government." Thus observed Maulana Abul Kalam Azad addressing a public meeting held in the morning at New Delhi on Jan. 1.

The Congress President also explained the significance of the individual satyagraha movement, and said that the Congress wanted to show that the war was declared without the consent of the people of India and even members of the Central Legislature which, was "Government's own creation." The British Government, he said, should change their attitude towards Indians.

Maulana Azad replied to the critics who condemned the Congress of having accepted office for capturing power, and crushing political opponents. Had then been so, the Maulana said, the Congress Working Committee would not have and half-an-hour's time decided to withdraw Ministries from the 8 provinces out of 11 after the outbreak of the war.

Document No. 76

Statement regarding the Entry of Subhas Bose in the Congress fold dated 3-1-1941

"The Congress will always welcome Mr. Subhas Chandra Bose to come to the Congress fold, provided he regrets his past activities in respect of the breach of the Congress discipline," observed Maulana Abul Kalam Azad, Congress President prior to his leaving for Allahabad at New Delhi on January 3, in the evening."

Maulana Azad added: All members of the Forward Block and other parties who wnated to offer satyagraha would be required to comply with the Congress discipline and the conditions laid down by Gandhiji.

Regarding the Frontier Province and Calcutta where Government did dnot arrest satyagrahis Maulana Azad stated that from January 6 arrangements would be made throughout the Frontier Provinces and different parts of Calcutta to hold meetings where the Congress stand would be explained to the public.

Document No. 77

Clarification of the Congress Attitude on War, dated 3-1-1942

"Before proceeding to Bardoli to attend the meeting of the Congress Working Committee I had said in a speech in Bombay that nothing had happened during the last fourteen months to warrant a change in the attitude of the Congress *vis-a-vis* the present war; after the conclusion of the deliberations of the Working Committee I must repeat the same thing," said Maulana Abul Kalam Azad, the President of the Indian National Congress at a Press Conference at Bombay on Jan. 2, 1942.

The Congress President was explaining the decisions arrived at the Bardoli meeting of the Congress Working Committee.

The Congress President averred, that the main resolution passed by the Working Committee left the position exactly where it was in September 1940 except for the fact that it relieved Mahatma Gandhi of responsibility of leading the Satyagraha movement on behalf of the Congress. The Bombay resolution had given him full powers for the conduct of the Satyagraha movement but at Bardoli he expressed his wish to be relieved of responsibility and this was done.

No Prediction As to Next Step.

The Congress President added:

"The fact that two resolutions, namely, one relating to non-violence and, the other about the attitude of the Congress in regard to the political situation came simultaneously before the public had given rise to some misunderstanding. I want to clear this.

"Before proceeding to Bardoli, I had not the least idea that once against the question of violence and non-violence would come before us. This question was raised by some friends but I did not like it as in my opinion there was no scope for raising this question at all. But I was very much surprised to find that when Gandhiji first addressed the meeting of the Working Committee he raised the question and said, that the speech I made in Bombay and the short statement that I issued on my release from jail went against the spirit of the resolution passed by the A.I.C.C. at Bombay in September 1940. You might remember that I had emphasised the fact that it was the attitude of the British Government which was responsible for our decision about the war and unless she changed no question of change came before us. Gandhiji thought that this was not in line with the Bombay resolution."

He also felt that the statement given by Pandit Nehru to the "News Chronicle" was also against the spirit of the Bombay resolution. It was quite clear to me that in the Bombay resolution the Congress had taken up the position that it would not participate in this war, because of political considerations. It was not because of non-violence. However, the interpretation now put by Gandhiji took us back to the same controversy which was raised on June 3, 1940 at Wardha. I told Gandhiji that I felt it was the first time that the Bombay resolution was being interpreted in that manner to us."

"Then I invited every member of the Working Committee to express his opinion. Last time when this question was discussed at Wardha there was a section in the Working Committee who were ready to go whole hog with Gandhiji. I invited these friends to express their opinions first. They all said apart from the question of violence or non-violence the Bombay resolution was based on political grounds only. There was only one member out of the 14 who were present, who held a different view. The Bombay resolution was studied again and Gandhiji admitted that it could bear the interpretation that was being put on it. On the next day, Gandhiji wrote a letter to me in which he said that he had committed a mistake in interpreting the Bombay resolution differently and that the proper thing for him and for the Congress would be that he should be relieved of the responsibility of leading the movement.

The Committee was faced with a very difficult situation. None of us was prepared to hear this from Gandhiji. Efforts to persuade Gandhiji not to give up the stewardship of the Congress proved of no avail. The discussions were suspended for three days. I was asked in company with Jawaharlal to see Gandhiji and try to find a way out. Both of us tried our best, but we found that Gandhiji would not budge and he stood like a rock on his decision. Gandhiji said that for him it was no more a question of meeting them half way or finding a formula on which they could agree. The question before him was whether we were prepared to take up the position that the Congress would not participate in the present war on the ground of non-violence alone.

We found ourselves unable to go so far despite our utmost desire to do so. It is quite possible that Congress may not find a way, when it would be possible for the Congress to participate in the war or to come to a settlement with the British Government, but in political life it is never possible to arrive at decisions beforehand or to close all doors for all time. In these circumstances, there is no other way before us but to bow before Gandhiji's decision. Consequently, he addressed the letter to me which was placed before the Committee and the Committee arrived at the decision which is not before the country."

"There were two parts of the Bombay resolution. In one of them, we had declared that it was not possible for the Congress to participate in the war. In the other we had requested Gandhiji and had authorised him to launch Civil Disobedience on behalf of the Congress. Now after Gandhiji's decision, the Satyagraha movement is naturally suspended. What he now wishes is to continue it, not on behalf of the Congress, but in pursuance of his own mission. The Working Committee had made it clear that those Congressmen who wished to participate in that movement their individual capacity may do so and naturally nothing would please the Congress more than to see his mission succeed.

I must however make it clear that even if Gandhiji had not raised this question of non-violence at this juncture, the main resolution would have been the same. Nothing would be more incorrect than to think that the Committee's main resolution was influenced by Gandhiji's present decision. As a matter of fact, it was at Gandhiji's suggestion that a Sub-Committee consisting of four members, besides me, drafted the main resolution. These members were Babu Rajendra Prasad, Pandit Jawaharlal Nehru, Mr. C. Rajgopalachari and Pandit Govind Vallabh Pant. It is common knowledge that the five members of the Committee hold different views on several issues. But the fact that ultimately they could come to the decision which is now before the country shows unanimity of opinion in the Working Committee on the particular issue."

Questioned what would be the next step of the Congress the Maulana said that it was difficult to predict what the Congress would do. One thing was very clear and that was that the position of the Congress regarding the present war remained unchanged.

Asked whether the Congress Members of the Central Assembly would be permitted to attend the Assembly session, the Maulana said that Mr. Bhulabhai had placed before Gandhiji the views of the

Congress Assembly Party before his release. He had not personally seen the report. He, however, thought that compared to big issues now before the country, the question of attending the Assembly was a minor one and to him it was meaningless too. However, there was no hard and fast rule and if ever it was considered necessary to allow members to attend the Assembly, they might be allowed.

With regard to the participation of Congressmen in A.R.P. work, the Maulana said that so far as accepting the membership on the Committees was concerned, Congress members were not allowed to accept it. But it was the duty of Congressmen to do all to save life and property in any eventuality. But he made it clear that Congressmen were not to come into conflict with the authorities in the A.R.P. work.

Document No. 78

Remark on the Bardoli Resolution dated 9-1-42

The Congress President, Maulana Abul Kalam Azad has issued the following statement on the Bardoli Resolution of the Working Committee *vis-a-vis* Mahatma Gandhi's attitude:

"If there is any man in this country, or outside, who has interpreted the Bardoli Resolution in the sense that Mahatma Gandhi has withdrawn from the Congress leadership, I would say that he knows nothing about Gandhiji, or about the Congress. Neither Gandhiji can withdraw from the leaderhsip of the Congress nor it is possible for the Congress to remain without his guidance. The simple meaning of the Bardoli Resolution is that Gandhiji now does not want to carry on Satyagraha on behalf of the Congress. He wants to carry on Satyagraha against all wars on the ground of non-violence only, and only with those of Congressmen whom he finds to be well up to his standard."

"And after all, what is the Indian National Congress of to-day? What is the national life of India, which has developed with such an amazing speed during the last 22 years? It is nothing but an outcome of the creative genius of Gandhiji. He alone is the author of all the chapters which the national life of India is preparing for the future historian of the world. Every tune that rises from the strings of our national life is the creation of his finger touch. How can it be possible for him to leave the Congress: how can the Congress even think of it?"

"The world requires some illustrations in order to understand our relation, but the difficulty is that no illustration can be given in this respect. Like all his other characteristics, Gandhiji is matchless in this respect also. If he finds out you can follow him with full conviction according to his standards, he would lead you as no other leader of the world can. If he finds that you cannot, then he would stop; but even in such a situation he would treat you in a manner which you cannot expect from any other leader of the world.

You will not see even the faintest shadow of complaint or bitterness. He will simply admit the differences, and in spite of them he will treat you in the same manner as he used to do before. Even in the matter in which you differ from him, he will give you every kind of guidance which you expect from him. What happened at Bardoli? He differed from us in a particular matter. But we are so much accustomed to take his guidance and he too is so much accustomed to give it to us, that in spite of difference there was nothing that would reflect the slightest change in our attitude. The Working Committee remained looking towards him for guidance in every matter, and he continued advising it in every manner, as usual. We relied on him even in the matter in which we had differed. I requested him to draft that very resolution which the Committee had to adopt about his decision. He readily acceded to it, and the draft was ready the next morning. We only added a few lines to it, in which we have assured him that our position regarding non-violence remains the same as we had accepted in the Bombay Resolution."

Document No. 79

Statement dated 5-3-1942 about the resignation of Frontier Gandhi

Maulana Abul Kalam Azad, Congress President, has issued a statement announcing the acceptance of the resignation of Khan Abdul Gaffar Khan of his membership of the Congress Working Committee and nominating Dr. Khan Sahib in the vacancy.

The statement runs as follows:

At the occasion of the last A.I.C.C. session at Wardha, Khan Abdul Ghaffar Khan had a long talk with me, as how to promote the constructive programme of the Congres in the N.W.F.P. I found that the Khan Sahib keenly believed that he would be able to serve this purpose better if he be relieved of the membership of the Congress Working Committee. He also emphasised the fact that he was an out and out believer in non-violence in all walks of life; and he found himself quite at one with Mahatma Gandhi in that matter. Considering this aspect as well, he thinks that he will be more useful in the great work which he wishes to undertake in his province, if he is relieved from the membership of the Committee. It is needless to say that I and my colleagues were at first not prepared to agree to this proposal. But on further consideration I preferred to leave it to his judgement. I said I would not prevent him from adopting this method, provided that his decision remained unchanged even after consultation with Provincial Congress Committee. Now I have received his resignation in which he writes:

"As per our conversation I have talked to my friends and co-workers here. We have all come to the conclusion that the Congress will be better served by my being relieved of official connection with the Congress and devoting myself solely to the Congress constructive programme. As I have told you I am a believer out and out in the non-violent method in all walks of life, I will be better able to carry the message of non-violence to the Pathan mind if I am detached officially from the Congress, whose policy can vary according to the exigencies as they may arise from time to time. My bond with the Congress will thus be richer than hitherto."

"I therefore accept his resignation, and nominate in the vacancy thus created Dr. Khan Sahib.

Whether Khan Abdul Ghaffar Khan is in the Working Committee or not, he will always hold a high place in the heart of every Congressman."

Document No. 80

M. Azad's Call To Congressmen

TESTING TUNE

To Defend Motherland By Fighting

A.B.P. – March 17, 1942

Wardhaganj, March 16. "I will not shirk my responsibility weather in peace or war time even when India is ablaze with war but would defend my motherland by fighting foreign aggression, even by shedding my blood", observed Maulana Azad, Congress President, while addressing the Nagpur Provincial Congress workers here this afternoon. Pandit Jawaharlal Nehru was present.

"We do not know what will happen tomorrow as war is knocking at India's doors, so without losing heart we must organise ourselves better for helping the needy in any emergency such as panic, internal troubles like looting, arson, goondaism, riots, air raids etc." He exhorted them to produce more grains and foodstuffs, also Khadi and revive cottage industries which would greatly relieve economic tension and supply our daily demands.

Continuing Maulana Azad Said, "The testing time has come, so I hope you will stand it and not be found wanting. Realize the gravity of the occasion and play your part well as this is a time not for speeches but solid work which alone will create confidence in the public."

"I will be the first to face the enemy's bullet rather than submit", replied Maulana Azad to a question. The Congress never bowed before Imperialism nor would she do so even before any aggressor enemy, he added.

"It is foolish and useless to resort to Satyagraha where the enemy is threatening", was Maulana Azad's and Pandit Nehru's prompt reply when questioned about Satyagraha.

This evening Mahatma Gandhi received Maulana Azad and Pandit Nehru after breaking his weekly silence.

"As everything is nebulous about Sir Stafford Cripps' proposals nothing can be said but the Working Committee will give its thought to them if they are worth considering otherwise the whole business will be finished soon if nothing substantial is immediately granted,'' said Maulana Azad when approached by Pressmen about Staffords' mission to India. Maulana Azad and Pandit Nehru are seeing Mahatma Gandhi this evening after his weekly silence. -- (A.P.)

Document No. 81

Clarification on the news published in the "News Chronicle" dated 20-3-1942

"It is entirely unfounded," said Maulana Abul Kalam Azad, the Congress President, on his attention being drawn to a report from India published in the London newspaper "News Chronicle" that Sardar Vallabhbhai Patel was leading the opposition in the Congress Working Committee to Sir Stafford Cripps' mission and that Pandit Jawaharlal Nehru and Mr. C. Rajgopalachariar know Sir Stafford Cripps' proposals beforehand and that they are in favour of their acceptance and that in the event of Sir Stafford Cripps proposals being accepted by the Congress, Sardar Vallabhbhai Patel along with his supporters might resign from the Congress Working Committee and lead an opposition to the programme in the country. The Congress President averred that there was no basis whatever for such a report.

Document No. 82

Maulana Azad's advice dated 23-3-42 to Indian Muslims

Indians should take a lesson from the experience of various European countries. India was no longer a spectator. The time for her trial had arrived. The question of the future of Muslims in India was a vital question and it had been worrying him for the last thirtyeight years. During this period there had been no change in his attitude towards this question. He had been trying to find out the root cause and had come to the conclusion that until they were free from foreign domination no other question should be raised.

The Maulana Sahib said that the Muslims should not ask for any safeguards but should try to attain the country's freedom first. He was confident that no earthly power could efface nine crores of Muslims in this country. Not any constitution or safeguards could save them if they had no confidence in themselves and did not attempt to stand on their own legs.

Concluding Maulana Azad advised the Muslims not to stand in the way of freedom by presenting different schemes.

Document No. 83

Maulana Azad's condolence on the Death of Subhas Bose

A.B.P. – 30-3-1942

New Delhi
March 29, 1942

Maulana Abul Kalam Azad, Congress President, issued the following statement to the Associated Press:

"I was shocked to read this morning the news of an aerial crash in which Mr. Subhas Chandra Bose and some other Indians were involved. The tragic end of Mr. Subhas Bose, while he was still in the prime of life, will cause deep sorrow to all those who knew him. In spite of differences with him as regards the means of attaining India's freedom, it must be recognised that he lived and died for the cause to which he had dedicated his life.

Document No. 84

Congratulations of Gandhi and Azad to the Mother of Subhas Bose

A.B.P. – 31-3-1942

New Delhi
March 30, 1942

Mahatma Gandhi and Maulana Abul Kalam Azad have sent the following teleagram to Mr. Subhas Chandra Bose's mother:

"Thank God, what purported to *i.e.* authentic has proved to be wrong. We congratulate you and the Nation" – (A.P.)

Document No. 85

Statement on Cripps' views dated 11-4-1942

Maulana Abul Kalam Azad, Congress President revealed at a Press Conference on April 11, 1942 at Delhi that he had given indications to Sir Stafford Cripps during his very first interview with him on March 25 that the Government's proposals might not be acceptable to the Congress. The Maulana Sahib gave his impressions of his interviews with Sir Stafford and General Wavell.

The Maulana Sahib admitted that at times he had heated arguments with Sir Stafford but added that did not mar the general spirit of friendliness or cordiality.

Referring to the failure of the talks, the Congress President said: It is deeply to be regretted that the end all of us had passionately desired was not reached but all the discussions were carried in a friendly atmosphere and, in spite of profound differences, which at times led to heated discussions, the cordiality of our talks with Sir Stafford was maintained throughout. We met as old friends and I am glad to say that we parted as friends.

Continuing the Congress President said: "I met Sir Stafford on March 25, for the first time when he read out the draft proposals and gave a copy of the draft to me. This was followed by discussion. I must make it clear that the entire approach of the Indian problem as evidenced by his proposals was fundamentally wrong and likely to create fresh complications. I also made it clear that if the British government were sincere in their desire to transfer real power to the people of India even at this eleventh hour, and thus create a new atmosphere, then the proper course for them was to send him to India armed with a definite decision to that effect. I assured Sir Stafford that if the problem had been approached in that spirit, his mission would have been surely crowned with success, and if it had failed he would not have been responsible for the failure".

The second point which I emphasized was that the draft proposals were largely concerned with the future rather than the immediate present, which was more important. The draft contained just a few lines about the present arrangement and those lines do not give any positive picture. On the contrary, they are negative in their charaacter. I plainly told Sir Stafford that so far as the Congress was concerned there was no likelihood of their accepting such a scheme.

The third point I emphasized was that in tackling the political problem of India, the communal and other problems are bound to arise at some stage or the other and would have to be solved. I assured him that as soon as the main political problem was settled the responsibility for finding a satisfactory solution of communal and other problems would be ours and I could confidently assert that we would find a satisfactory solution.

With reference to clause (e) of the draft, Sir Stafford assured me that it provided for complete freedom and transfer of power with only the reservation for defence. I then pointed out that the defence was the demand of the moment so far as the country was concerned and during the war the civil administration of the country disappeared and the problems of defence, permeated every civil department. If he reserved defence, he pracaticallly reserved all the powers, which he said, we are being transferred to India. Sir Stafford then said by way of re-assurance that reservation related only to the functions of the Commander-in-Chief.

Reverting to this point, I said,"This is that the first impression of the present created by my earlier interview with Sir Stafford began gradually to fade away as the discussion proceeded on material points from stage to stage and when I last met Sir Stafford on April 9, the whole picture had completely disappeared."

I next referred to my interview with General Wavell and said, "In the course of our talks Sir stafford had over and again emphasized the technical difficulties in the way of transfer of defence to the Indian Member. In this connection he suggested, that we should meet General Wavell, because he could explain the technical side of the question much better. Curiously enough not a word was mentioned by General Wavell about the technical difficulty throughout our discussions, which were entirely on political lines. It did not strike me for a single moment that we were interviewing a military expert. It appeared as if we were talking to a politician. In fact when I told this to Sir Stafford Cripps, he gave me no reply but merely smiled.

Referring to reports in certain sections of the Press suggesting that the working committee's decisions on the proposals had been influenced by Mahatmaji's views, the Congress President said,"Mahatma Gandhi's view as regards participation in any war are well known and it would be entirely untrue to suggest that the working committee's decision have in any way been influenced by that view. In fact, Mahatma Gandhi made it perfectly clear that they were free to come to any decision on the merits of the proposals. Mahatmaji did not want to participate in the earlier sittings of the working committee but he was persuaded by me to stay on from day to day."

Document No. 86

Statement dated 13-4-1942 in connection with the mediation of Johnson

"Sir Stafford Cripps is reported to have said in the course of an interview at Karachi before leaving India that Congress leaders first went to see colonel Johnson who acted as a mediator in his personal capacity," says Maulana Abul Kalam Azad, Congress President.

The Maulana adds: "This is likely to create an impression that this mediation was sought by us. Facts, however, are otherwise. On or about April 1, a common friend informed Pt. Nehru that Col. L. Johnson was anxious to meet him and would be glad if a meeting could be arranged at his residence. Accordingly, Pt. Nehru met him. Again it was by pure accident that on April 3, while I was on my way to a meeting of the working committee, I went to Pt. Nehru's residence, which was on my way, to pick him up, and there I found Col. Johnson. Naturally we met and had a brief talk. At the end of this talk Col. Johnson expressed desire that in the event of the Working Committee coming to an adverse decision, he should be allowed a chance to see if he could be helpful, before the committee's final verdict was formally communicated to Sir Stafford Cripps."

"His wish was so obviously in the interest of the common object, namely, the successful conclusion of Sir Cripps mission, that I saw no objection in complying with it. It is hardly necessary to narrate the rest of the story. But I must make it perfectly clear that nobody on behalf of the Congress sought either Col. Johnson or President Roosevelt's intervention although in the very nature of things Col. Johnson's friendly interest was appreciated."

Document No. 87

Remark on the British proposals dated 15-4-1942

"The picture that was given to me of the British was Cabinet's proposals in my first talk with Sir Stafford Cripps on March 25, deteriorated so completely and took such a shape by April 9, that it was clear to me that the proposals were no better than a rehashed and polished version of the August declaration. We could not accept them."

We went far in our desire for a settlement–perhaps too far. But our irreducible and essential minimum was that only a free India could defend herself, and the people at large must be made to feel that they were free in their own country and had to defend their own freedom."

The use of word like 'National Government' and Cabinet by Sir Stafford Cripps in his first interview, I added, had given a certain impression and but for it he would not have called a meeting of the Congress Working Committee. The change in the attitude of Sir Stafford Cripps may had been done to an honest doubt about these terms or the influence of White Hall. I reiterated that when I talked of the National Government, I did not for a moment speak from the point of view of party gain for the Congress or dictatorship of the majority."

Document No. 88

Statement on Cripps proposals dated 30-4-1942

In one sentence Maulana Azad summed up the reasons which let to the failure of the Cripps Mission. (At the A.I.C.C. session held at Allahabad–April 29, May 1.)

"The British Government's distrust of the Indian people."

He emphasized that the Congress position that only a free India could have the strength to defend hereself. Referring to the future, he said, there were only two alternatives before the country – either take up the Government for organising national defence or resist the enemy invasion by adopting non-cooperation which the Congress had been practising for the last 22 years. As the British Govt. had refused the former, they had to prepare for the latter if the contingency arose. In emphatic terms he said that if he believed that entry of Japanese or Germans into India would be helpful to the country he would have said so no matter what the consequences, but he felt honestly that their coming was against the interest of the country and should be resisted by the Indian people. They should not get excited or lose themselves in emotion but they must prepare to meet aggression with courage and strength. "People who know how to die for their country and never be helpless" said Maulana.

Document No. 89

Address dated 17-5-1942 to the C.P.C.

The seriousness of the danger which confronted India today was referred to and the duties of the people in the present circumstances were explained by the Congress President addressing a rally of Civil Protection Corps volunteers organised by the North Calcutta Congress Committee at Calcutta on May 17, 1942.

After dealing with the present situation, the Congress President said that Indians were ready to make sacrifices and even to take up arms to defend their motherland against the aggressor. But they were denied that privilege. So their duty now would be to serve their fellowmen in these critical times and relieve their distress and sufferings resulting from the exigencies of the present circumstances.

The Maulana Sahib exhorted the volunteers to remain true to their pledge of serving their fellowmen and expressed the hope that they would spare no pains to redeem the pledge in a worthy manner.

He exhorted every one connected with the corps to see that they were never found wanting in courage when called upon to serve their countrymen. In particular, he stressed, that in the organisation to which they belonged, numbers did not count. What did count was the spirit of service and sacrifice for each individual volunteer.

Document No. 90

Remark on Rajaji's talks dated 2-6-1942

The Cripps negotiations broke down on defence alone and Mr. Rajagopalachari's statement to the country is entirely baseless, said Maulana Abul Kalam Azad, the Congress President in an interview to the Associated Press at Calcutta on June 2, 1942.

The Maulana was referring to Mr. Rajagopalachari's speech at Coimbatore in which he was reported to have said, "The statement that control over defence was denied in any circumstances represented the position as it stood when the Cripps negotiations started, but at subsequent stages it became clear that as a result of cable exchanges, the British Govt. were prepared to modify the position and gave us a part in defence also. The negotiations brooks over other points and not defence."

The Maulana adds, "When my friend has discovered a new creed all of a sudden that freedom or no freedom, control over defence or no control, National Government at the Centre or no National Government at all we should resume Provincial Ministries which we have given up, no statement from him surprised me. I would only say that all the documents in connection with the Cripps Mission have been published. These are easily available. Every one who has read the correspondence between Sir Stafford and myself can say unhesitatingly that the Statement of Rajaji is absolutely baseless.

In the very first interview with Sir Stafford Cripps, I had said with due emphasis that the trend of events have carried the Indian problem to such a stage that we are not much concerned about the future; the real question is that of the present. The plan offered by the draft declaration does not say anything positive about the present. But the negative side of the matter is quite clear. It shows that defence will remain wholly in British control. The Congress will never agree to it.

As our negotiations proceeded further on, naturally many other problems came under discussion but the main point of our discussion remained the question of defence.

When I handed over the resolution of the Congress Working

Committee to Sir Stafford on April 2, 1942, he said that he was cabling to London from where he expected a specific reply. He therefore, requested the Committee not to publish the resolutions. On April 7, he sent me the new proposal of the British Government about Defence. It was rejected by the Working Committee because although it contained in appearance a seat for an Indian representative as a Defence Member, in reality he was given no share in the control of Defence. As I had promised Col. Louis Johnson to give him a chance of intervention, if our talks did not succeed, he was, therefore apprised of the situation. Col. Johnson handed over to us another formula on April 8. It was admitted in his formula that the Defence Department be placed incharge of a representative Indian Member with the exception of the function to be exercised by the Commander-in-Chief as War Member and a War Department would be constituted which would take over such functions of the Defence Department as are not retained by the Defence Member. A list of all the retained functions has been agreed. Col. Johnson had said about the list mentioned above that if the formula was accepted it would be drawn up by common consent. When Sir Stafford was asked to give the list he informed us that nothing could be added to the list sent to us along with the letter of April 7. The only difference between the first and second formula is that the latter tries to present the same thing in a better form.

As the Working Committee was not after appearances in place of reality, it was forced to reject it also. This put a stop of further negotiations.

It will thus be seen how erroneous and misleading is the statement of Rajaji that as a result of cable exchanges the British Govt. was prepared to modify the position or give us a part in defence also. In fact the part in defence which the British Govt. was prepared to give us was no part in Defence at all. The Congress Working Committee therefore rejected it and the negotiations broke down on this very point."

Document No. 91

Maulana Azad's Editorial Entitled 'The Ancient Gate of Western Asia' for the *Amrita Bazar Patrika* dated 7-6-1942

The latest news show that the long awaited spring drive of Germany has now begun: and as it was surmised by informed circles, it seems to be heading towards Caucasia. If the German forces succeed in crossing the wall of the Caucasus, they will find the countries of Turkey and Iraq on their right, the route of India on their left and Iran in the front. If they succeed in removing all the obstacles in their way, their presence in Northern Iran would be a grave menace to the whole of Western Asia.

It is quite obvious that some kind of agreed plan has been reached between Germany and Japan: and the Japanese navy might try to implement her part of the plan by dominating the Arabian and Red Seas.

When I read the news of German attack on the Kerch Peninsula, I remembered how history was once again going to repeat an oft-repeated story. In nearly 700 B.C. the Scythian hordes had descended these very heights of the Caucasus and attacking the Assyrian Empire, had laid it waste. Herodotus had told this story and we find numerous references to this event in the book of Ezelhiel of the Old Testament. This place comes again into prominence after 200 years, in the days of Cyrus the Great, and Stesias and Xenophon tell us that the northern wild tribes were making constant incursions through this passage. History, is now silent for several centuries. But again in the first century A.D. the famous Hebrew historian, Josephus, mentions this : "Northern gate of Western Asia" and tells us about its military importance. A few centuries later in the days of Sassanian Kings of Persia the Romans began to attack through it. Bellisarius the Roman General led an expedition to this country in 528 A.D. the story of which is told by Procopius, who himself was with the attacking army.

This mountain is a kind of wall which Nature has raised to separate the South from the North. We find in all the stories of ancient history that no invader, intending to march towards the plains of Western Asia, could but pass through the gates of this wall. That seems to be the reason why an attempt was made in the 4th century B.C. to close this natural gate by means of human ingenuity, in order that no invader may march towards Western Asia.

This characteristic of the mountain becomes quite clear by a glance over the map. The Caspian Sea is on the East, the Black Sea is on the West. This mountain stretches from the shore of one sea to that of other as if Nature wanted to close the space between the two seas by drawing a sky-high wall.

There were only two routes to cross this mountain in ancient times. One route passes through nearly the middle of the mountain, which was known later on as the Darial Pass. This Pass is shown between Vladikaukaz and Tiflis in modern maps. The attacks of Scythians mentioned by Herodotus were probably made through this very pass. The second route passes through the Eastern slope of the mountain. It leads to that area of the western shore of the Caspian Sea which was later on known as Azerbaijan. The wild of the North used to descend the border districts through this very route in the days of Cyrus.

History does not tell exactly when, but it is definite that long before the birth of Christ, a superhuman attempt was made to close these passes by erecting impregnable walls. This wall which was built several centuries before the Chinese Wall has no other rival than that of China in the history of the world. The wall, which was erected to close the Darial Passs was made of iron slabs, and molten copper was used to cement them together. That is why this place is known as the "Iron Gate" in Georgia upto this day and the Turks have translated it as "Damar Kapu".

A longer wall had to be built to close the Eastern slope. The slope stretches to several miles, and it was necessary to builld a wall from the shore of the Caspian to that part of the mountain which was absolutely impassable. Accordingly two walls were built from the sea shore. One was only two miles long, but the other was carried up to the place where the mountain is very steep, nearly 50 miles from the Sea. The distance between the walls was about 500 yards near the sea-shore, but as they progressed further their distance decreased, till it became about a hundred yards at the place where the fort is built.

Darband, the famous city of Azarbaijan, grew up between these two walls and is still there. There was an iron gate in the first wall, which gave an entrance to the city. On the other end of the city there was also a gate in the second wall. As this city closed the Northern Pass, it became known as Darband (*i.e.* Closer of the gate) probably in the period of the Sassanians. The Iranians call this double wall, as "Dobaarah" *i.e.*, a double range.

This place has achieved great importance, in the days of Sassanian Kings, owing to its being a strong-hold against the Northern incursions. All the Arab historians, geographers, such as Al-Maqdasi, Al-Hamadani, Al-Istakhari, Al-Mas-oodi, Al-Beruni and Al-Yaqut tell us that the Sassanian emperors considered it to be the key position of the Empire. Whoever could get this key, he could open the lock of the Empire.

When the Arabs conquered this country in the 7th century A.D. they too realised its importance. They began to call it by the names of "Bab-ul-Abwab", or "Al-Bab", *i.e.*, the gate of the gates or the gate of the empire. Al-Mas-oodi and Al-Yaqut have also mentioned it by the names of "Bab-ut-Turk" and "Bab-ul-Khizr", *i.e.*, the gate of the Caspian tribes–because these tribes used to come by this very route.

Who had constructed these walls? All the historic data which are found in this connection are confused and uncertain. Some Arab historians have mentioned Khusru Anushirwan in this connection. This, however, cannot be true. Josephus has mentioned it five hundred years before Anushirwan, and Procopius mentions to have personally visited the place and seen this wall in 528 A.D. The period of Anushirwan is accepted to be between 531 and 579 A.D. by all authorities. Consequently, it is clear that he could not have been the founder of these fortifications.

Josephus and Procopius think that these walls were built by Alexander the Great. But all historical evidence goes against this. The famous American historian, A.V. Williams Jackson, has admitted that it is difficult to ascribe them to Alexander.

I have discussed this question in some of my works and have reached different conclusions. Historical evidence leads us to believe that both these walls were built by Cyrus the Great, between 541 and 521 B.C. Sassanian kings might have repaired them, and it is probable that Khusru Anushirwan might have built them anew.

The double wall of Darband was extant up to the end of the 18th century. Eichwald has given a picture drawn by a Russian tourist in his book Caucasus, who had visited the place in 1796. But when Mr. Williams Jackson examined the place in 1904, the wall had fallen down although its marks were still there. The single wall, however, was still standing. He has given full details in his book "From Constantinople to the Home of Omar Khayyam".

I visited this place five years after the visit of Mr. Jackson. Nothing had visibly changed upto that time, however, a part of the remnants and arches of the double-wall mentioned by him, had disappeared.

The world famous Oil-field of Azerbaijan is adjacent to Darband. Baku is situated to the South. Its original name was Bad Kooba, *i.e.* a wind-beaten city. The ancient Iranians called this country by the name of "Azarpaigan" as the oily dust of this country caught fire as speedily as the sticks of dry wood. "Azarpaigan" means the sacred country of fire. It was pronounced as Azerbaijan by the Arabs.

The revolutionary changes of the world dealt with the difficult routes of the Caucasus in the same manner as they have with all such places. The routes which were stopped by high walls and iron-slabs are now being used by railway lines day and night: which carry hundreds of passengers from one side of the mountain to the other. The inner portion of the Caucasus is now full of places or recreation, sanatoriums and mineral baths. The neligence of this country during the regime of Czars is amply compensated for by the tremendous progress made during recent five years' programmes of the U.S.S.R. It is difficult to predict which route would be chosen by the German armies if they could advance towards this area to cross the Caucasus. The easiest route is that of Darband.

Document No. 92

Message to the U.N.O. dated 17-7-1942

Maulana Abul Kalam Azad, Congress President, in an interview to the United Press on Thursday evening (July 17, 1942) at New Delhi emphasized that the Congress had been wedded to three Fundamental principles, sympathy for the Democracies, policy of non-embarrassment to the War effort and the will to resist any aggression and in the resolution passed at Wardha the Congress had firmly adhered to these principles. The whole spirit of the resolution was one of presenting the case for India's demand, which was dictated by the political situation in the country.

Whether any movement is to be started immediately, Maulana Azad said, would depend on certain developments. He said that the main anxiety of the Congress at this hour, was due to the fact that the defence of the country could never be organised to an effective and efficient degree unless the people could be made to think that their state was involved in the War, which was to be fought in their own interest.

The Congress President added that the Congress would not be satisfied with anything but the immediate declaration of independence and handing over of power to Indians when the British Government made it perfectly clear that they were prepared to part with power and make India free, it would be easier for political parties in India to make adjustments and form a provisional Government pending such times when a Constituent Assembly could agree upon the final settlement. The British might turn to the Congress or the League to accept the responsibility and the Congress and the League, Maulana Azad was sure, would consult each other to form a Government. Maulana Azad went to the length of saying that he would not be sorry if the Congress were left out and Muslim League were given the power to form the Government but the only condition precedent would be the declaration of independence of India.

In reply to the question what he thought would be the attitude of the Muslim masses in the event of civil disobedience movement by the

Congress, Maulana Azad said that the Congressite Muslim would stand by the movement and there was no reason to believe that Muslim League would stand against that. In any case they would not interfere in any movement started by the Congress.

The Congress President said that for the first time in the history of the Congress, a resolution was in actuality addressed not only to the British Government but to the United Nations. The U.S.A., the Congress President continued, had become the main hope of the Democracies today and he expected the right gesture would come from America."

Document No. 93

Emphasis on the resolution of Working Committee dated 17-7-1942

Emphasizing that the resolution of the Congress Working Committee was a unanimous one, Maulana Abul Kalam Azad, the Congress President in an interview to the Associated Press at Wardha on July 14, 1942 stated that the committee had two main problems to tackle, one relating to the achievement of Political independence and the other to meet the present situation.

He said that events had reached such a stage that it had become impossible for the Congress to wait and watch passively. For nine days the committee discussed the resolution in all its aspects to see what should be done and in what form to meet the present situation. He considered the Defence of India as of paramount importance and only Indian independence would enable her to play her part effectively in the defence of the country. It may be possible to wait for the final achievement of India's independence, but India's obligations to her defence could not wait. This point had been made clear in the resolution.

He said that there should be no room for any misunderstanding and hoped that the British Govt. and the Allied Nations would appreciate the position of the Congress. He denied that the resolution was an ultimatum and said that it was only a reiteration of the national demand though there was a warning to the British Government.

The Maulana added "Whatever shape the proposed movement takes it will be a mass movement". He reiterated that there was no longer any occasion for restatement of the Congress position *vis-a-vis* non-violence. The Congress position was that India's defence could not only be with the aid of armed forces. He had explained this position to Mahatma Gandhi who had appreciated the position of the Congress as such.

As for himself, said the Maulana, he would not hesitate to introduce conscription in India, but the presence of the British in the country had made things impossible.

Document No. 94

India and her Independence: remark by Maulana Azad dated 20-7-1942

Maulana Abul Kalam in an interview to the Associated Press said in New Delhi on July 21, replied to the question whether there was any basis for the impression prevailing in certain quarters after the statements made by Mahatma Gandhi and Pt. Jawaharlal Nehru that there was hardly any room left or any negotiation with the Congress. If "said of the Maulana" this refers to India's right of independence, it is certainly not a matter for negotiation. It is a fundamental principle which must be recognised by the United Nations. But if the question refers to arrangements or the duration of war, there is a clear procedure envisaged in the resolution of the Working Committee itself and there is no reason to suggest that there is no room for negotiation. It is quite obvious to my mind that matters of this nature can only be settled by negotiation.

Question: Suppose there is a declaration on behalf of the United Nations guaranteeing India's independence, will it satisfy what you regard as fundamental principle?

Answer: It will depend entirely on the form and contents of the declaration and in any case I can assure you that there is no reason why the Congress should not give the fullest consideration to any declaration of the kind you have mentioned.

Document No. 95

Reaction dated 28-7-1942 on the British Misrepresentation of Working Committee's Resolution of 27 July, 1942

Maulana Abul Kalam Azad, the Congress President made the following statement at a Press Conference this evening (Monday, 27th July, 1942) at New Delhi: "I have carefully watched the reactions of the Working Committee's resolution and have come to the conclusion that in their anxiety to find fault with the Congress adverse circles have completely ignored the frank analysis of the political situation and constructive proposals and only concentrated on the last paragraph which hints at the consequences of the failure to take himself steps. In doing so they have overeached themselves by drawing a lucid picture of anarchy and chaos; particularly pleasing to those who would invade India. It is the height of unwisdom to use to sharp, a double edged weapon for while it is intended to affect public opinion in America and China, it supplies the Axis propagandists with the very material they would wish for.

Sir Stafford Cripps' broadcast to America marks the climax of this propaganda. He has studiously avoided the Working Committee's resolution because it contains a complete answer to his entire agreement. He has selected for his basis a phrase or two from Mahatma Gandhi's writings torn out of their context. Mahatma Gandhi will take care of their misrepresentations. But Sir Stafford Cripps has either misunderstood or deliberately misinterpreted the Congress point of view. Commenting on the failure of the Cripps negotiations, the Working Committee has said that it has resulted in a sense of frustration and a rapid and widespread increase of ill-will against Britain. The Committee has expressed its anxiety to avoid the experience of Malaya, Singapore and Burma, and it has desired to build up resistance to any aggression for invasion of India by the Japanese or any foreign power.

The Committee's much criticized resolution says:

"The Congress would change the present ill-will against Britain into goodwill and make India a willing partner in a joint enterprise of securing freedom for the nations and peoples of the world and in the trials and tribulations which accompany it. This is only possible if India feels the glow of freedom". On the withdrawal of British rule from India, the resolution visualizes a "Provisional Government representative of all important section sof the people of India". It further says, "Representatives of free India and representatives of Great Britain will confer together for the adjustment of future relations and for the co-operation of the two countries as allies in the common task of meeting aggression. It is the earnest desire of the Congress to enable India to resist aggression effectively with the people's united will and strength behind it."

"In making the proposal for the withdrawal of British rule from India, the Congress has no desire whatsoever to embarrass Great Britain or allied powers in their prosecution of the war or in any way to encourage aggression on India or increase pressure on China by the Japanese or any other power associated with the Axis Group. Nor does the Congress intend to jeopardise the defensive capacity of the Allied powers. The Congress is, therefore, aggreeable to the stationing of the armed forces of the Allied powers in India, should they so desire, in order to resist Japanese or other aggression and to protect and help China.

How all this can be interpreted by Sir Stafford Cripps as a demand for "walking out of India leaving the country without any constitutional form of Government and with no organised administration" frames one's comprehension. In fact what is visualized in this resolution is a stable provisional Government as the immediate result.

Another glory on statement which he has admitted himself to broadcast to America as extremely discourageous. Describing the form of Government which he offered to representative India political leaders he calls the Viceroy's Executive Council" a body of Ministers like those who advise your President". This analogy is as totally misleading as that other of the National Cabinet with which Sir Stafford Cripps tried to mislead India. If India's *de facto* independence were recognised and if a President elected by the people of the country were at the helm of the State, the analogy of American Minister of State would be appropriate.

Those who are trying to make out that the demand of India's independence is unreasonable in the midst of War may pause to consider that Free India offers to throw its entire weight on the side of the Allies surely the negotiation and guarantee of Egypt's independence did not present any difficulty in the way of the Allies even though Egypt has remained neutral. But Free India is committed to full participation in the United Nations fight for freedom and peace of the world.

The Congress has no illusion along the extent of the support which India's demand for independence may receive from those who have so far been lugh in their professions of sympathy. Ultimately India will have to depend entirely on such strength as she possesses for achieving her goal."

Independence First

I repeat what I had told Sir Stafford Cripps that "once the British Govt. make up their mind to part with power and hand over the Government of this country to the people we shall produce an agreed solution for setting up a provisional composite Government within 24 hours. I am quite confident about it, let them summon the Muslim League to form a Government. The Congress will not be sorry if the Government summons the Muslim League and give them power. But it must be real independence. The Congress is only concerned about that". This announcement was made by Maulana Abul Kalam Azad at a Press Conference today in reply to a question from an American correspondent.

Elucidating his point, the Congress President said that he had particularly referred to the Muslim League because the League's name is being exploited in the present controversy. The Congress would have no objection if the power was transferred to the No-party leaders. Maulana Sahib emphasized that once the Government would make up their mind the whole outlook of the parties would change and they would be in a more reasonable frame of mind.

At the outset, Maulana Sahib made it clear that for the first time the Congress had passed a resolution which was addressed to the United Nations.

Negotiation

Replying to a question from an American correspondence as to whether the Congress would be willing to open negotiation with the British Govt. if the United Nations particularly Russia, China and America, recognised India's independence, the Congress President said, the very procedure suggested in the Working Committee's resolution pre-supposed negotiation. There was, however, no room for negotiation for the question of recognition of India's right to freedom. Any negotiation must start with that basis.

In reply to a question whether he wanted a guarantee of freedom now or after the war, Maulana Sahib said: "I want a recognition of India's freedom today."

Replying to other questions, the Congress President said that while they were not prepared to go back to the Cripps proposals any suggestion coming from the United Nations, once the fundamental question of the recognition of India's independence was settled, would receive the careful consideration.

Interregnum

Several American correspondents, whose papers had criticised the Congress resolution on the ground that it did not provide for the interregnum between the abdication of the British Government and the setting up of an Indian Government, asked whether civil administration and the authority of the present Government would disappear during this period.

"That was not the position which the Congress had taken up," explained Maulana Azad. He was definitely of the opinion that once the British Govt. had decided to part with power there would be no interregnum and no chaos and anarchy. He made it clear that "when they framed their resolution they had taken the most scrupulous care to see that the change asked for did not weaken the position of the United Nations, and the organised civil administration to be set up would fully co-operate in the efforts of the United Nations to resist aggression. Fundamentally the whole stand was based on a desire to fight for the longer cause of the United Nations and India's defence."

Document No. 96

Maulana's letter dated 13-2-1943 to the Viceroy

CONGRESS PRESIDENT DENIES GOVT. CHARGES

LETTER TO VICEROY

Maulana Abul Kalam Azad, President of the Indian National Congress in a letter to the Viceroy dated February 13, 1943, written from Ahmednagar Fort on behalf of himself and his colleagues, has denied "with all vehemence the false charges that have been repeatedly advanced against the Congress."

He says no sabotage movement was ever contemplated by the Congress and no instructions, secret or otherwise, were issued for a violent movement.

Wardha, Oct.31. – Dr. Syed Mahmud has issued the following statement to the Press:

On reading the correspondnece between Lord Linlithgow and Gandhiji, members of the Working Committee, including myself, conferred among ourselves with the result that a letter was sent by Maulana Abul Kalam Azad, President of the Congress, to Lord Linlithgow on February 13, 1943. A copy of the letter was kept by most of the members if not all. I happened to make a copy for myself. As the letter is of importance, I release it for publication. It speaks for itself and must assist the Congressmen and others to know the mind on non-violence of members of the Working Committee who are interned in Ahmednagar Fort. Messrs Dobble and Sorensen, M.Ps, have asked me to give some indication of my colleagues's mind. This letter gives sufficient indication of their mind. Plenty of other such indications can be given but I ask them if there is any use.

Ahmednagar Fort,
February 13, 1943

H.E. the Marquis of Linlithgow,
Viceroy's House,
New Delhi

Dear Lord Linlithgow,

My colleagues and I have read in yesterday's and day before yesterday's newspapers the recent correspondence that had passed between you and Mahatma Gandhi. In the course of your letter to Mahatma Gandhi numerous references have been made to the Congress and repeated and far-reaching charges have been made against the Congress organization. In your letter of January 13 you express your regret that no word of condemnation for the violence and crime should have come from the Working Committee.

Ordinarily we would refrain from saying anything while we are kept in detention cut off completely from our people and the outside world. Even our place of detention is supposed to be a secret which may not be mentioned or whispered to any one. Our sources of information here are strictly limited and consist only of some newspapers which under existing rules and ordinances, publish only censored news and are prohibited from giving publicity to many kinds of news which are of vital importance to us and to the Indian people. In these circumstances, it is obviously improper for us to give expression to any views in relation to events with which we are so ill-acquainted, especially when the only method of doing so open to us is to address the Government of India.

FANTASTIC CHARGES

We have, therefore, avoided any such expression of views and have refrained from addressing you or any member of the Government of India even though at times the most fantastic charges have been made against us and the organization we have the honour to represent. These charges have now been made even more explicitly in an aggravated form in the course of your recent letters to Mahatma Gandhi. The tone and contents of these letters more especially of your letter of February 5 are such that it will perhaps serve us no useful purpose to address you on the subject. Yet we cannot ignore the fact that the head of the present Government of India has made these charges. I am venturing, therefore, to write to you.

Your correspondence with Mahatma Gandhi raises a large number of issues many of which have great importance. Normally we would have out say in regard to them but at the present moment it is not my desire to discuss all these.

I wish to confine myself more especially to one issue and to make it clear that so far as we are concerned both as individuals and in our corporate capacity speaking on behalf of our organization your charge that the Congress had organized a secret movement of violence is wholly false and without foundation.

There is a vital difference of opinion between you and us in regard to many matters and unfortunately this difference brings us into conflict. But even so as an English patriot and a lover of British freedom it should not be impossible for you to appreciate how Indian patriots and lovers of India's freedom might feel and it should be possible for some element of fair play and square dealing to be kept up in our relation to each other:

To make serious charges against those who are prevented from replying to them, to make those charges without producing evidence to support them by the vast propaganda machine of a powerful Government and at the same time to supply news and views which are contrary to them are not evidence either of fair play or a strong case.

In your letter of February 5 you refer to the Home Member's speech in the Central Legislative Assembly for the charges made by him against the Congress. Further you say that all the mass of evidence that has since come to light has confirmed the conclusions then reached. This procedure of reaching conclusions and later to seek evidence to justify them is not usually considered judicial or proper.

In this letter of February 5 you further say you have ample information that the campaign of sabotage has been conducted under secret instructions circulated in the name of the All-India Congress Committee. What your information is we do not know.

But we do know and can state with authority that the A.I.C.C. at no time contemplated such a campaign and never issued such instructions secret or other.

The A.I.C.C. was declared an unlawful association at the time of our arrest and practically all prominent and responsible Congressmen including the members of the A.I.C.C. were arrested. At the same time the A.I.C.C. office and other Congress offices were seized by the police. Since then the A.I.C.C. cannot obviously function.

NO UNDERGROUND BODY

You mention that an underground Congress organization exists now and that the wife of a member of the Congress Working Committee is a member of it. We know nothing of such an organization and are not in a position to find out, but we are convinced that no Congress organization and no responsible Congressman or Congresswoman can be actually engaged in planning the bomb outrages and other acts of terrorism. Congressmen, no doubt, consider it their duty to carry on civil resistance under certain circumstances to the best of their ability. But this has nothing in common with the charges you have made. It is possible that in the mind of the average official or policeman there is no particular difference between civil disobedience and bomb outrages etc., but we have no doubt in our mind knowing our people as we do, that responsible Congressmen cannot possibly encourage in any way bomb outrages and terroristic acts.

A great deal is said about secret organization, evidence of which the Government claims to possess, but which it does not produce. May I draw your attention to the public speeches delivered by Mahatma Gandhi at the last meeting of the A.I.C.C. on August 8 a few hours before his arrest, wherein he emphasized with all solemnity his appeal for non-violence. The Congress adopted this policy of non-violence 23 years ago and despite popuar lapses occasionally has met with a great measure of success in regard to it. This will be evident from a comparison of the Indian national movement with national movements in other countries which have often openly based themselves upon violence. You have no doubt yourself approved of violence in many forms when you have considered that it was used for a right cause. The Congress, however, has adhered to its creed and practice of non-violence and has for these 23 years preached this method to the people. If the Congress decides to change its policy and method and function in this matter like other national organizations it would do so openly and deliberately by changing its creed to that effect. There would be no secrecy for apart from other valid reasons a conflict between public and secret advice stultifles an organization which is based essentially on open action and constructive endeavour. The Congress may have many faults but it has not been accused of lack of courage in the pursuit of its objectives and ideals.

I would suggest to you to consider what the result in India might have been if the Congress had deliberately instigated and encouraged violence and sabotages since the Congress is widespread and influential enough to have produced a situation a hundred times worse than anything that has so far happened.

In the summer of 1940 when France fell and England was facing dire peril, Congress which had been previously thinking in terms of direct action deliberately avoided this in spite of strong demand for it. It did so entirely because it did not want to take advantage of a critical international situation or to encourage Nazi aggression in any way. Nothing would have been easier than for the Congress during those critical days to produce a situation of the utmost embarrassment to the Government.

DESPERATION

For many weeks prior to our arrest we had been pointing out in Working Committee meetings resolutions and otherwise that public feeling in the country had grown exceedingly bitter against the British Government in India. Not only we, but many moderate leaders stated publicly that they had never previously known such bitterness. Responsible Congressmen tried to divert this feeling into peaceful channels and largely succeeded in doing so. They would have succeeded in doing so. They would have succeeded even more if events had not taken place which suddenly exasperated the public and at the same time removed all prominent and well-known leaders who might have been able to control the situation. These events are better known to you than to us situated as we are, but we have learnt enough to realize what the shock to the public must have been. Wholesale arrests were followed immediately by the prohibition and prevention of all public activity, all public expression of opinion, by lathi charges, tear gas, bombs and shooting. Well-known leaders were spirited away and their destinations were kept secret.

Rumours of death and illness spread and added to the public excitement and resentment. This apparently was the background of the happenings during the second week of August last. I do not wish to deal here with subsequent events for their adequate consideration requires fuller knowledge than we possess here, but I would like you to consider what the effect on the Indian people must have been of all that has been done to them on behalf of the Government since our arrest and how large numbers of people must have been driven to desperation.

MADE UP EVIDENCE

Reference has been made in the Government 'communique'

accompanying the recent published correspondence to a certain circular which is said to have been issued by the Andhra Provincial Congress Committee. We know nothing of this and cannot believe that improper instructions against the fundamental principles of the Congress could have been issued by any responsible Congress authority. It is worthy of note, however, that even official references to this circular contradict themselves. The first mention of it was made in a Press Note issued by the Government of Madras on August 29. In this it was stated that the circular continued instructions 'inter alia' for the removal of rails. Two weeks later Mr. Amery speaking in the House of Commons stated that the circular expressly said that rails should not be removed and that there should be no danger to life.

This is an instructive and significant instance of how evidence is made up and used to influence people.

In your letter of February 5 in refering to the A.I.C.C. resolution you draw attention to the concluding part in it which authorizes Congressmen to act for themselves in the event of interference with the leadership of the movement. This has appeared significant to you and you have drawn certain conclusions from it. You are evidently unaware that similar instructions were given when previous civil disobedience movement of 1940-41 these instructions were repeated by me on many occasions. It is of the essence of civil disobedience or Satyagraha that individuals should become self-sufficient units, should need arise as leaders are always likely to be removed and isolated at an early stage. In the present instance, the phase of civil disobedience was not reached. It is curious that in a fairly lengthy correspondence and in various official statements nothing is said about the merits of the resolution passed by the A.I.C.C. which dealt with the national and international situation and made it clear that a Free India would not only resist invasion to the utmost but would throw all her resources into the world struggle for freedom and align herself with the United Nations. This was made perfectly clear in the resolution itself. It was further emphasized by the speaking as President and by many other speakers. It must be known to you that ever since the early beginnings of Fascist, Japanese and Nazi aggression in Africa, Asia and Europe, the Congress has consistently condemned them. No organization in India or elsewhere has been so clear and emphatic on this subject.

The Congress was anti-Fascist and anti-Nazi when the British Government, under Mr. Chamberlain's leadership, was openly friendly to these regimes. The A.I.C.C. resolution of August last was especially based upon this anti-Axis policy and in particular on the urgent necessity of strengthening India's defence against invasion.

It was made clear and I emphasized it on that occasion that an acid test of the change was this defence of India and the strengthening of the United Nations. It may also be known to you that several members of the present British Government have in the past repeatedly supported or welcomed Fascism and Japanese aggression.

You conclude your letter to Mahatma Gandhi by saying that the charges against the Congress will have to be met sooner or later. We shall welcome that day when we can face the peoples of the world and leave the verdict as to them. On that day others also including the British Government will have to meet and answer charges. I trust they will also welcome that day.

I apologize for the length of this letter. I felt that I owed it to you as well as to myself and my colleagues to be perfectly frank and to deny with all vehemence the false charges that have been repeatedly advanced against the Congress.

This letter has been written on Saturday afternoon February 13. I am told that like all other communications sent from here it will have to be depatched under registered cover to the Government of Bombay. As registration will not be possible on Sunday it will thus have to be sent on Monday and it may not reach you for some days. I regret the delay.

Yours sincerely,
Abul Kalam Azad

Document No. 97

Questions dated 5-3-1944 in the Legislative Assembly about Maulana Azad

THE QUESTION, IS DOWN FOR MEETING ON 15-3-1944

Maulana Zafar Ali Khan: Will the Honourable the Home Member please state:

(a) whether it is a fact that the Taj Company Limited, a Muslim publishing firm of Lahore, recently addressed a letter to Maulana Abul Kalam Azad at present under detention and requested the Honourable Member to transmit the letter to the Maulana;

(b) whether it is also a fact that the letter was of a purely business nature and only asked permission from Maulana Abul Kalam Azad to print and publish a popular edition of his Exegesis of the Holy Quran which has become so rare that its price, Rs. 7, has shot up to Rs. 30;

(c) whether it is further a fact that the Home Department refused to forward the letter, in question, to Maulana Abul Kalam Azad; and

(d) if the answer to (c) of the question is in the affirmative, the reasons for refusing to forward a purely business letter to the Maulana?

LEGISLATIVE ASSEMBLY

Question No. 443

(To be answered on the 15th March, 1944)

Reply to Maulana Zafar Ali Khan's starred question No. 443 regarding the refusal of permission to forward a letter addressed to Maulana Abdul Kalam Azad by the Taj Company Limited.

The Honourable Sir Reginald Maxwell

(a) to (c) Yes.

(d) The letter was withheld in accordance with the rule under which correspondence with members of the Congress Working Committee is restricted to private and domestic matters with members of their families.

Document No. 98

Supplementaries to question in the Legislative Assembly No. 443, dated the 15th March 1944

Mr. Govind V. Deshmukh: With reference to part (b) was permission refused to the publication of the Holy Quran as was sought in the letter?

The Honourable Sir Reginald Maxwell: It is not a case of giving or refusing sanction to the publication of the Holy Quran but of passing a certain communication of a business nature.

Mr. Govind V. Deshmukh: Could not an inquiry be made from Maulana Azad about this request as to whether he would allow the publication of the Holy Quran as was asked for in the letter?

The Honourable Sir Reginald Maxwell: I have explained that members of the Working Committee who are under detention are not allowed to have correspondence or dealings with members of the general public. Their dealings are restricted to private and domestic correspondence.

Sardar Mangal Singh: Cannot the members of the Working Committee even look after their private property? The translation was done by Maulana Azad and if the Holy Quran is published we stand to gain?

The Honourable Sir Reginald Maxwell: Members of the Working Committee and other persons under detention are like Government servants; they are not allowed to carry on business.

Document No. 99

Questions dated 20-3-1944 in the Legislative Assembly about Maulana Azad

(THE QUESTION IS DOWN FOR MEETING ON THE 20-3-1944)

Sardar Mangal Singh: Will the Honourable the Home Member please state:

(a) whether Messrs. The Taj Company, Limited, Lahore, sent a letter through the Government of India to Maulana Abul Kalam Azad requesting him to give permission to them to publish his translation of the Holy Quran;

(b) whether it is a fact that the same was not forwarded to the Maulana Sahib, but that it was returned to the sender without assigning any reason;

(c) whether there was anything objectionable in the letter itself, or the refusal was due to the fact that no letter could be sent to him from other than a relation;

(d) whether Government are aware that it will cause great disappointment to numerous readers of the Holy Quran if his translation is exhausted in the market; and

(e) whether Government propose to reconsider their decision and allow the letter in question?

LEGISLATIVE ASSEMBLY

Question No. 518

(TO BE ANSWERED ON THE 20TH MARCH 1944)

Reply to Sardar Mangal Singh's question regarding the refusal of permission to forward a letter addressed to Maulana Abul Kalam Azad by the Taj Company Limited.

The Honourable Sir Reginald Maxwell: (a) to (e) I would invite the Honourable Member's attention to my reply to question No. 443 put on the 15th March by Maulana Zafar Ali Khan.

Document No. 100

Supplementaries to question in the Legislative Assembly No. 518, dated the 20th March, 1944

Sardar Mangal Singh: What is the answer to part (e). That was not covered by this question.

The Honourable Sir Reginald Maxwell: Yes, it was. I said in answer to the original question that the letter was withheld in accordance with the rule under which correspondence with the Working Committee members is restricted to private and domestic matters with members of their family.

Document No. 101

Questions dated 20-3-1944 in the Legislative Assembly about Maulana Abul Kalam Azad

(THE QUESTION IS DOWN FOR MEETING ON 20-3-1944)

Qazi Muhammad Ahmad Kazmi: Will the Honourable the Home Member please state:

(a) if it is not a fact that purely personal and domestic correspondence is allowed to the President and the Members of the Congress Working Committee;

(b) if it is a fact that Maulana Abdul Kalam Azad has written a commentary on the Holy Quran, which has been published long ago;

(c) if it is a fact that about the end of February, Taj Company Limited of Lahore, who are publishers of oriental literature, addressed a letter to Maulana Abul Kalam Azad in respect of his commentary on the Holy Quran which they wanted to reprint;

(d) if it is a fact that that letter of the Taj Company Limited, was withheld by Government and that it was not allowed to reach Maulana Abul Kalam Azad; and

(e) whether Government have considered the advisability of allowing such personal letters to the President of the Congress?

LEGISLATIVE ASSEMBLY

Question No. 527

(TO BE ANSWERED ON THE 20TH MARCH 1944)

The Honourable Sir Reginald Maxwell : (a) Yes; but with members of their families only.

(b) to (e) I would invite the Honourable Member's attention to my reply to question No. 443 put on the 15th March by Maulana Zafar Ali Khan.

Document No. 102

Question for the Legislative Assembly dated 10-11-1944 regarding a copy of letter of Maulana Azad to the Viceroy

Starred/ D. No. 78.
Notice was received on the 10-11-44.
Notice of admission to be sent out on the 15-11-44.
Department to which the day has been allotted–None.
The question will, if admitted, be put down for the meeting on 21-11-44.

Shrimati K. Radha Bai Subbarayan : Will the Honourable the home Member please state:

(a) if he has seen the public statement of Mahatma Gandhi to the effect that mass civil disobedience is now out of the question;

(b) if he has also seen copies of the letters written by Maulana Abul Kalam Azad, President of the Indian National Congress, to the former Viceroy, Lord Linlithgow and now published in the Press by Doctor Sayed Mahmud, denying the various charges on behalf of the Member of the Working Committee and himself, made by the Government in their pamphlet on Congress responsibility for the 1942 incidents; and

(c) if the Government has considered that in view of these facts, they have no justification for continuing to keep the Member of the Working Committee and other Congressmen in confinement; and, if so, when they intend to release them?

Document No. 103

Answer to the question raised on 10-11-1944 about Maulana's letter to the Viceroy

LEGISLATIVE ASSEMBLY

Question No. 705

(TO BE ANSWERED ON THE 21ST NOVEMBER 1944)

Answer to Shrimati K. Radha Bai Subbarayan's starred question No. 705 regarding Maulana Abul Kalam Azad's letter to Lord Linlithgow and the question of the release of members of the Congress Working Committee.

The Hon'ble Sir Francis Mudie: (a) The reference is presumably to Mr. Gandhi's "Hints for Workers on the constructive programme." In it he wrote "just as military training is necessary for armed revolt training in the constructive effort is equally necessary for civil resistence" and later "It would be different if there was mass civil disobedience. But that is out of the question for the time being at any rate."

(b) Yes.

Document No. 104

Interview to the Press dated 19-6-1945

The Congress President, Maulana Abul Kalam Azad in an interview on June 19 at Calcutta said that in the Wavell proposals nothing had been said about the method of selecting members of the Executive Council. If they were selected by those attending the Simla Conference jointly there should be no objection to the procedure. If, however, any organisation listed on selecting a group of members of the new Council, there might be reason for pessimism about the success of the Plan.

In an interview to "Amrita Bazar Patrika" Maulana Azad said that the first and sacred duty of the Working Committee was to try to secure the release of patriots still in prison. "Without them as freemen, it is difficult for us to take decisions on many political issues (Maulana Azad said that if the Working Committee so felt, a meeting of the All India Congress Committee would have to be convened for approval of the decision taken by the Working Committee on the Wavell Plan. He was aware that the ban on the A.I.C.C. had not yet been lifted.

Referring to future possibility in the event of the failure of the Wavell Plan, the Congress President said:

> *"In my opinion the Congress should not start any movement in furtherance of its cause before the Japanese war ends. After about half-a-century's struggle the Congress has brought the country to a point not far from its goal and the next step, if necessary, will be taken after the war."*

Maulana Azad said that one of the reasons for the exclusion of Hindu Mahasabha from the Simla conference might be that the invitees had been selected more or less on the basis of parties in the Central Legislature, when there is no Hindu Mahasabha Party as such. The Congress President was not inclined to comment on the Wavell Plan until the decision of the Working Committee was taken. What the Congress would do in the case the Wavell Plan was rejected by the Working Committee was a matter to be taken up later on. At present this question was not an immediate issue.

Maulana Azad added that the Wavell Plan would be considered threadbare by the Working Committee. In his personal opinion, clarification of main points would be required before a final decision could be taken.

Document No. 105

Suggestion for the Interim Government dated 28-6-1945

Maulana Azad said in an interview at Simla on June 27, that it was at least as important to get broad minded men on the proposed Interim Council as it was to be sure that each community was represented.

This was made clear by Maulana Azad this morning in a talk with Preston Grover of the Associated Press of America at the cottage which has been placed at the disposal of the President by the Viceroy. "The Congress cannot accept any suggestion that it is a communal body" he said, "and can, therefore never agree to select only the Hindu representatives. It must have a voice in the selection of Indians of all communities, for to do otherwise would be to contradict the whole character of the Congress."

At the same time the President outlined the general background against which the discussions are being carried on. The President who understood English comprehensively occasionally answered the question in English but for the major part he gave the answers in Hindustani which was interpreted by Mr. Humayun Kabir who is acting as his Secretary. As to the meeting between Pt. Govind Ballabh Pant, and Mr. Jinnah last night Maulana Azad said that it was part of a network of discussions which would necessarily be carried on outside the general conference and there would probably be further informal conferences between the Congress and League representatives.

The rumours in conference quarters that Pt. Pant and Mr. Jinnah had carried the talk forward even to the point of bringing up names of the future members were declared by the Congress President as untrue. He said that Mr. Jinnah at the conclusion of yesterday's talk with the Viceroy had asked Pt. Pant to come and see him. "Each question must be considered in relationship to the others" said Maulana Azad, "no final decision can be reached on any point until all the major questions are settled."

He made gestures by the hand to indicate that the whole pattern had to be worked out together. There were questions of appointment of membership among the various groups and of whom those members would be composed of. There was the question of restoration of representative at the Governments in the provinces and how the various parties would reach. There was the question of minority groups whose representation on the Council had to be settled.

His comment emphasized against the vast difficulty of conducting negotiations on such a basis. It is impossible for representatives to agree on one point and dispose it off before going on to the next. No one can be disposed off finally but it must remain in a pending state while the other issues are discussed and brought near agreement. In a sense it is like solving a jigsaw puzzle where most of the parts will stay in their places but where each part is likely to name a little under the influence of another part and even change the shape. But despite all this the Congress President seemed confident of success in reaching an agreement.

One thing on which he insisted was that the Muslim League must yield in its traditional insistence that it is the one and the only representative organization of the Muslims in India. Acceptance of that position would make the Congress a sectarian body.

The President said that a meeting of the Working Committee would be called before any agreement was reached on who would sit in the National Council but he accepted that the negotiations would reach that stage soon.

"The whole thing has been done with speed", he said smilingly, "and we are approaching an agreement rapidly."

While, therefore, it will remain for the Viceroy technically to name the members of his Council, President Azad said that it was now expected that the list agreed on by the representatives at the Conference would be accepted by Lord Wavell. He suggested that after some degree of agreement had been reached on the question of appointment of members the question of names would begin to creep into the discussions. Their broadly national character would become an important factor.

Asked what had induced the seeming change of attitude on the part of the Muslim League, Maulana Azad smilingly commented that it was something for political correspondents to deduce. He, however, remarked that some of the political difficulties which the League had encountered in the Punjab, the N.W.F.P., Bengal and Sind might be the reason.

Finally he said that "when agreement on all phases was accepted by the conference and by the Working Committee the whole plan would be submitted to the general assembly of the All India Congress Committee".

Document No. 106

Congress and its National approach: Statement of Maulana Azad dated 30-6-1945

The Congress President, Maulana Azad, declared on June 30 at Simla that the Congress approach to the Wavell Plan was not dictated by party consideration. It was a national approach. "The Congress approach is independent without reference to what other parties would or would not do", the Maulana Sahib said. It was for the Viceroy to decide.

In answer to a question as to the extent to which the Congress would be prepared to contribute to the success of the proposals, the Congress President said that by the very fact of agreeing to participate in the Conference the Congress had shown its readiness to be constructive in its attitude rather than destructive. The Congress could very well have demanded the release of all political prisoners still under detention in order to create a favourable atmosphere and also the removal of the ban on the All India Congress and other allied organizations before agreeing to participate in the Simla Conference. And nobody could have blamed the Congress had it insisted on the fulfilment of those conditions as a pre-requisite for Congress participation. This Congress did not do and at the risk of being is misunderstood.

That the Congress waived these demands at the risk of being misunderstood by its own followers proved its readiness to contribute its share to the success of the constructive move that had been made by Lord Wavell. "The Congress could not have gone further," the Maulana Sahib said. "All reasonable men should agree that the Congress could not have gone further than this."

The Congress President emphasised again and again that the Congress was not making a party approach to the Plain. "The Congress will always have before it the national point of view and any step which the Congress takes will be in accordance with its traditions and policy pursued all along. For instance, when the Congress prepares the panel it will see to it that it nominates Hindus, Muslims, Harijans and other communities. The personnel for the panel will not be confined to

Congressmen alone. Our object is to have the best men in the country irrespective of the fact whether they are Congressmen or not.

In reply to a suggestion made in certain quarters that the Congress was big enough to afford to yield to the Muslim League without suffering in stature or prestige, the Maulana Sahib said: "I do not share that view. I feel that if the Congress fails to show sufficient strength and determination at a critical juncture like the present to adhere steadfastly to its national outlook and the principles for which it has always stood, the future of the Congress organization will be jeopardized."

Document No. 107

Remark dated 1-7-1945 regarding Jinnah's Statement

"I do not think there is anything new in Mr. Jinnah's statement to the press on the position of the Muslim League," declared Maulana Azad in an interview on July 1, 1945 at Simla.

Regarding further negotiations between the Congress and the League on the question of obtaining a panel of names for the proposed Executive Council, Maulana Azad said that it was up to Mr. Jinnah to make the next approach.

"I made it quite clear during the yesterday's session of the Conference that the Congress door was always open," he said. "The League President thought that there was no common ground."

"As to whether the Congress would be prepared to form a Government even if the Muslim League did not submit a panel, Maulana Azad said, "That is a matter for the Viceroy to decide. So far as the Congress is concerned, it had gone to the limit in showing that its attitude was constructive."

Questioned regarding his own health, Azad said that while he felt none too well yet, he was somehow carrying on because of the urgency of the present work that was to be done.

Document No. 108

Advice to the people about Wavell Plan, dated 4-7-1945

Maulana Abul Kalam Azad, Congress President, has given the following two messages, one to the people of India and the other to Indian Muslims. To the Indian people: "This is a critical moment in our political life, and therefore, it is essential that we should keep before us the real significance of the temporary situation that has arisen in the country. We should neither attach exaggerated or undue importance to the Wavell offer nor should we ignore the real demands and exigencies of the situation. Consistent with the defence of our principles, if the way is opened to a temporary solution leading to our ultimate goal of freedom, then we should unhasitatingly avail of it. If such a way is not opened then we should watch our step and not budge an inch from our position."

To Indian Muslims: "The Muslims of India should not think for a moment that the Muslims in the Congress are blind to the genuine doubts and grievances of the Muslims. Indeed, perhaps they realize the situation better than anyone else. The point, however, is what should be the correct approach to remove these doubts and grievances? The difference between the Nationalist Muslims and the Muslims League is not one of ultimate aim which after all is the well-being and honourable existence of Indian Muslims in a free India, but of methods to be used to achieve the desired end. And if we so desire we can easily remove even this difference over our respective methods. What is needed is a broad visit, large heartedness and a sincerity of purpose."

Document No. 109

Letter dated 6-8-1942 from S.A. Latif

Hyderabad
6-8-1945

Dear Maulana Sahib,

We may be aware that I have been endeavouring to seek, in my own way, a constitutional solution to the Hindu-Muslim problem. Lately some confusion appears to have arisen as regards the validity of a provision contained in the Congress Working Committee's resolution passed at Delhi at the time of the Cripps Negotiation which runs as follows:

"Nevertheless the Committee cannot think in terms of compelling any territorial unit against its declared and established will to remain within the Indian union."

The confusion has been caused by Mr. Jagat Narayan's resolution adopted by the A.I.C.C. at its meeting held at Allahabad because that resolution has been taken generally to have nullified the above-mentioned provision in the Delhi resolution.

May I therefore ask for your authoritative ruling whether this interpretation is correct and whether this Mr. Jagat Narayan's resolution has in any way modified or affected the said provision?

Further, you are reported in the press to have made an offer that if the League were prepared to come to a settlement with the Congress, the Congress Working Committee would appoint a few representatives to meet the League representatives for the purpose. May I know whether representatives of the League would in any way be debarred from discussing any proposals they might put forward for a permanent settlement of the communal problem?

Yours sincerely
S.A. Latif.

Document No. 110

Letter to S.A. Latif dated 6-8-1945

Dear Doctor Abdul Latif,

I appreciate your interest in raising the questions contained in your letter dated the 6th.

Had the speeches of responsible members of the Working Committee been duly noted the confusion to which you refer in your first question would not have arisen. It was made fully clear by Dr. Rajendra Prasad, Pandit Nehru and myself at a time and I repeat it now that no part of the Delhi Resolution to which you refer has in any way been affected or modified by any subsequent resolution of the A.I.C.C. In fact, the Delhi Resolution was confirmed by the A.I.C.C.

With reference to your second question, it was never contemplated that the examination and discussion of the viewpoints of the representatives of the two organisations should not be free, frank and full, in fact, it was fully understood that these representatives would, in no way, be under any restriction in their deliberations and discussions subject only to the usual condition that their agreed decision would be submitted to their respective bodies for ratification.

Yours sincerely
A.K. Azad

Document No. 111

Explanation of Maulana Azad dated 8-1-1950 regarding the Government difficulties implementing education

Maulana Abul Kalam Azad, Education Minister, said here today that the problem before the Government was not what schemes should be prepared for national education but to consider whether they could take any forward step at all in the immediate future.

The Education Minister felt that in spite of the urgency, the Government could not go ahead because of shortage of funds.

Maulana Azad who was addressing the Central Advisory Board of Education added: "In spite of our best efforts we were unable to provide sufficient funds even for the very modest programme of expansion of education which we had framed. Our intention was to provide for an amount of Rs. 11 crores for 1949-50 as this would enable us to start the basic education programme and undertake preliminary work for social education. Our financial position however, allowed us to provide only about Rs. 6 crores. Within six months of the adoption of this year's budget, we have had to face a financial crisis of such magnitude as to force a reduction of 10 to 20 per cent in the already approved budgets. Instead of going ahead as we had originally planned, we suddenly realized that we had to retreat. For 1949-50 we had to surrender about Rs. 153 lakhs out of a total budget of about Rs. 588 lakhs. The result is that a country with a population of almost 350 millions and with hardly 14 per cent. literates cannot provide more than Rs. 4 $\frac{1}{2}$ crores from its Central revenue for education."

EXPANSION NEEDED

"It is true," continued the Education Minister "that education is a provincial subject, but in the existing circumstances, the problem of education cannot be solved unless the Centre assumes appropriate responsibility for expansion and growth." The schemes he said, were ready "but in spite of the urgency, we cannot go ahead because of shortage of funds."

There is no immediate prospect of a large increase in our

revenue," remarked the Minister, "and funds can therefore be found only by diverting a large proportion of our available resources to education and other nation-building activities. The main burden on our finances today is due to the expenditure on import of food, rehabilitation of refugees and defence."

There was every hope the expenses on the food account would be diminished and would ultimately disappear but the expenditure for rehabilitation could not be curtailed till then.

The Education Minister referred to the four-point programme namely the provision of universal, free and compulsory basic education, provision of adult education for liquidation of illiteracy of the masses, improvement and expansion of technical education and reorganization and improvement of university education from the national point of view.

The post-war development plan laid down that would take 40 years to implement a scheme of basic education and it would involve expenditure of Rs. 200 crores a year. But the Education Ministry prepared a plan of junior basic education to be implemented in ten years and at a greatly reduce cost.

In the field of adult education too the programme was revised so that it became one of social education for training in citizenship and aimed at making at least 50 per cent. of illiterate adults literate in the next ten years.

The programme as suggested by the Board might be prepared on the basis of co-operation between the State and the people.

TECHNICAL INSTITUTE

As regards technical education, the programme envisaged the establishment of four higher technological institutes in addition to the strengthening of existing institutions. The Eastern Higher Technological Institute near Calcutta was taken in hand and the schemes was in progress. He hoped the next academly year would see the first batch of teachers and students working in this institute. It had been the aim of the Ministry to strengthen existing institutions by improving their quality and increasing their capacity.

So far as university education was concerned, the report of the Universities Commissioner had been presented and the Board would be considering the recommendations of the Commission.

The Ministry was therefore, ready with its programme in all the four fields, so far as planning was concerned, but finances were the main obstacle in the way of implementation.

Maulana Azad said: "It is necessary to wipe out the illiteracy of 50 years and make our people efficient, productive and responsible citizens of a democratic State. The new Constitution gives powers to the people, but if this power is to be exercised with wisdom and foresight, it is necessary that the people must have the requisite knowledge.

"Even from the point of view of economic and industrial efficiency of the people, it is essential that our educational facilities must be expanded. As a famous economist has said, there are no poor or rich countries but only countries in which the people use their resources and countries in which they do not. Some parts of Africa are among the richest in the world in natural resources and yet because the people are illiterate and ignorant, they are poor and suppressed. There are other parts of the world poor in natural resources which have been developed and enriched through the knowledge and industry of their people. India will have to decide to which category her people should belong."

The Governor of Orissa, Mr. Asaf Ali, who inaugurated the session, said that on the delineation and implementation of long-range and immediate policies of education would depend not mrely on the future of India, but also in due proportion according to India's reaction to international relationships that of the rest of the world.

He said that the future of the human race as a whole was subject to the evolution of a healthier and happier outlook and co-operation between the various peoples and Powers of this globe. Although India was directly and primarily concerned with destiny of one-sixth of the entire human race, its geographical position and economic, potential and cultural heritage made it a pivotal region of the eastern hemisphere.

In his humble judgement the role which the people were to play in the human drama which was being rehearsed on this earth very largely would depend on the ideals, no less than the realism of their educational experts.

ADMINISTRATOR'S VIEW

Placing before the conference an administrator's point of view, His Excellency said none felt the urgency of universal and purposive education more keenly than an administrator who had to answer a multiplicity of social, cultural, economic and political problems of great complexity every moment of his life not in theory but in actual and concrete action.

"He (an administrator) feels," said Mr. Asaf Ali, "that but for insufficient appreciation of the practical problems of life among both the toiling masses and quite a large number of the educated and semi-educated classes of society within his charge, most of the processes of social and material development could be made infinitely easier. He feels like an engineer with great vision of the fabric he wants to raise for providing material comforts to every member of society, but for want of skilled technicians he has to allow the work of months to take years and decades. He (an administrator), therefore, passionately desires the training of the personnel required for the task which he, in co-operation with the people, has to face."

APPENDIX

Document No. 112

Rajya Sabha August 24, 1957

Maulana Azad and the ancient and Historical Monuments and Archaeological Sites and Remains (Declaration of National Importance) Second Amendment Bill, 1954[1]

The Deputy Minister for Education (Dr. Mono Mohan Das): Sir, the legal position with regard to the maintenance and protection of ancient monuments and archaeological sites in this country has undergone a rapid change during the last few years after Independence.

[Mr. Deputy Chairman *in the Chair*]

During the time of the British regime, there was only one Act, the Ancient Monuments Preservation Act, 1904, which provided for the maintenance and protection of the monuments and archaeological sites. Archaeology was a Central subject and the State Governments in British India had nothing to do with the maintenance and protection of ancient sites or monuments. The Indian States, wherever possible, made their own arrangements for the maintenance and protection of archaeological monuments and sites situated in their own areas. Now, after Independence, when the Indian States integrated, the Government of India made the Ancient Monuments Preservation Act applicable to those integrated States. Then came the Constitution of India. Our Constitution envisaged that archaeology should be managed both by the Central Government as well as by the State Governments. So, the ancient monuments and archaeological sites and remains were divided into two groups – one was the group of great national importance to be maintained, managed and protected by the Central Government and

1. Continued from Previous Volumes.

the other group was of lesser importance, to be maintained by the State Governments. Sir, for the effective implementation of our Constitution, so far as these provisions are concerned, a Bill was brought before Parliament by the Central Ministry of Education and it was passed in 1951. It is the Ancient and Historical Monuments and Archaeological Sites and Remains (Declaration of National Importance) Act. As we gained experience in working out the maintenance and protection of monuments, as we visited more and more temples and monuments in this country, we were convinced of the great necessity of bringing another amending Bill for inclusion of some other important monuments which were not up till that time included in the Act. In order to do that, another amending Bill was passed by Parliament on 2nd January 1954 in which additions and alterations were made to the schedule containing the monuments and archaeological sites. Now, in December 1954 my hon. friend, Dr. Raghubir Sinh, brought this amending Bill to the original Act, in which they had declared some of the monuments as monuments of national importance. So our friend, Dr. Raghubir Sinh, the mover of this Bill was requested by the Government of India to postpone the further consideration of this Bill, since the Government themselves were bringing forward such a measure. It is true that twenty months have passed since this undertaking was given by Government. If during the last twenty months the Government of India have not been able to bring forward such a Bill before this House, it is not due to any frivolous cause. There have been potent reasons and powerful reasons which had prevented the Government of India from bringing in such a measure. These are due to the question of the reorganisation of the States. Up till now we have not been able to get a broad picture of the reorganised States. The Government of India could not bring in their amending Bill in this respect for that reason. The States Reorganisation Commission was established. They gave their report and the events after that are all well known to this House and up till now we have not been able to come out of that storm. That very Bill, as we all know, is pending before this House.

So far as the present Bill, that of my hon. friend, Dr. Raghubir Sinh, is concerned, I would like to place before this House certain important points. Taking the Bill with the amendments that he has given notice of, we find that so far as Rajasthan is concerned, only two monuments are sought to be included by him, namely, Parsvanath Jain Temple (Panchayathan) with the inscriptions of the 12th century and the Badoli Temples. The others are Menal (Mahanal) temple, the Math and the ancient well and then the Suhaveshwar temple and the palace of Rani Suhavadevi. These are the monuments that my hon. friend, Dr. Raghubir Sinh, wants to be included in the list. But my submission to him is that this only touches the fringe of the porblem. These do not cover even the whole of Rajasthan. not to speak of the other parts of India. In the comprehensive amending Bill that we propose to bring before this House shortly after the reorgnisation of the States is complete, there will be a large number of monuments, archaeological sites and ruins. They will be included in that Bill. So far as this Bill of my hon. friend is concerned, we find that he wants to add only these two monuments which have not yet been included. The other monuments have already been declared as monuments of national importance. What he now wants is only to add two more to them but that, as I said, does not cover even the whole of Rajasthan. Our officers have visited the different places in Rajasthan and they have found very important monuments which have not yet been declared as of national importance and which are not covered by this amending Bill. For instance, I may point out to Dr. Raghubir Sinh that there are the temples of Osia in Jodhpur district and several other temples, the temples of Harihara, then the temple of Surya, the temple of Mahavira, the temple of Pipla Devi, the temple of Sachiyamata and others. They are very important. They have very important inscriptions engraved on the temples. For instance in the inscription engraved on the temple of Mahavira there is mention of the name of Pratihara dynasty who flourished in about A.D. 770 to A.D. 800. Some of the temples were built in the eighth and ninth centuries A.D. These are all very important temples and they are situatied in Rajasthan. But my hon. friend Dr. Raghubir Sinh, in his amending Bill has forgotten to include them. Then there is the Surya Temple in Ranakpur in Pali district and this temple is dedicated to the Sun and it contains fine sculptures. It is a fine specimen of mediaeval Hindu architecture. There is also the Ambikaji temple of Jagat in Udaipur district which has excellent plastic decorations and is in a good state of preservation. Then there is the main Jain temple in the old city of Jawar famous for its silver mines. The notice of the Archaeological Department was directed to this place and to this temple by Dr. Katju when he visited the place. It is one of the finest monuments in our country. But my hon. friend in his amending Bill has not included it. Then there is the Ghat with inscriptions at Nauchauki. It is in Udaipur. The whole ghat gives us an idea of the secular architecture of ancient times. The inscriptions not only furnish historical data, but are themselves important as a poetical composition. They were built during the great famine of 1660. But my hon. friend here wants to include only two of these monuments. So far as Rajasthan is concerned our officers have found lots of other monuments which ought to be included. This amending Bill of course, does not cover the rest of India, where there are hundreds of monuments to be included in the list and declared as of national importance. But even the whole of Rajasthan is not being covered. In Rajasthan itself there are many more monuments which have all been left off from this Bill. Therefore, my request to my hon. friend is this. The Government has given the undertaking to bring in a comprehensive amending Bill before Parliament which will include all the monuments all over India, which, as I have pointed out, have not yet been included. What is the hurry about this measure? It may be alleged that during the last twenty months since Government gave this undertaking, it has not been possible for the Government to bring in this measure. But I have pointed out the reason why it was not possible for the Government of India to bring in such a measure. The reason was the impending reorganisation of the States. These monuments are strewn all over the country and when we bring forward such a piece of legislation, we have to give all the details in it, mentioning the States in which these monuments are situated. So until we get a full picture of the reorganised States in India, it is not possible for the Government to bring forward such a comprehensive measure.

If my hon. friend is impatient and wants to include these two monumens, then my submission is that even with regard to Rajasthan there are important temples which have not been included in this Bill. So as far as this Bill is concerned, it only touches the fringe of the problem. Therefore, my request to him is either to drop this Bill or to postpone further consideration of this bill, since it does not cover even a fraction of the monuments that have to be covered.

So far as the Government is concerned, if my hon. friend wants to include in the list the two monuments that he has referred to, to be declared as of national importance, we have not got any objection. We are going to include these two temples in the Bill that we are going to bring forward. So far as the Government is concerned, we do not oppose his Bill. But considering the necessity of a comprehensive measure, my request to him would be either to postpone the consideration of this Bill or to drop it. If my hon. friend insists that he must have what he wants, then considering the uphill labour and the great interest that he has taken and has been taking in matters of archaeology and in archives, we fell that it would be unkind on our part if Government were to deprive him of the satisfaction of having his Bill passed.

Shri S. Mahanty (Orissa): I would like to speak.

Mr. Deputy Chairman: All right.

Shri S. Mahanty: Mr. Deputy Chairman, I had no intention of participating in this debate at this stage; but the speech of the hon. Deputy Minister giving expression to the colossal inefficiency that prevails in his Ministry ....

Dr. Mono Mohan Das: I am sorry to say, Sir, ...

Shri S. Mahanty: Yes, I am coming to that. With regard to colossal inefficiency that prevails ......

Dr. Mono Mohan Das: Sir, I rise on a point of order. Sir, when the Chairman was there he was going to ask the mover of the Bill to give a reply, then I stood up under the impression that I was the last speaker before the reply would come from the hon. the mover. Now, Sir, after I spoke some hon. Member got up and the hon. Member said something against the Government. In such a case, Sir, I as representative of the Government am deprived of the opportunity of contradicting him. That is my point.

Shri S. Mahanty: Does it take away my right of speech?

Mr. Deputy Chairman: All right, you carry on.

Shri S. Mahanty: Why does he anticipate me?

Mr. Deputy Chairman: When the Chair called, nobody stood up ....

Shri S. Mahanty: He did not also stand up.

Mr. Deputy Chairman: Then Chairman asked the Government to reply.

Shri S. Mahanty: I was trying to catch his eye.

Mr. Deputy Chairman : He called Dr. Raghubir Sinh to reply and nobody else stood up and then Mr....

Shri S. Mahanty: It is unfortunate that I could not catch his eye.

Mr. Deputy Chairman: I say you did not stand up apart from catching the eye.

Shri S. Mahanty: I was trying to speak.

Mr. Deputy Chairman: Neither Mr. Kapoor nor you stood up.

Shri Jaspat Roy Kapoor (Uttar Pradesh): I submit that this kind of a situation has arisen becuase of the special circumstances of this measure. It was introduced and discussed about two years back and we have practically forgotten as to at what stage....

Mr. Deputy Chairman: There were no speical circumstances. He has made it clear that there is no special circumstance, and they are going in for an all-comprehensive Bill including various other items also.

Shri Jaspat Roy Kapoor: What I was submitting was that some of us who wanted to participate in the discussion thought that perhaps Dr. Raghubir Sinh would himself say something. We had forgotten that he had completed his speech and that we had arrived at the concluding stage of the measure. That was the misunderstanding, Sir.

Mr. Deputy Chairman: Hon. Members are expected to come prepared for all eventualities.

Shri S. Mahanty: What I was saying before I was most unfortunately interrupted by the Deputy Minister is this that the expression of callous inefficiency that pervades the entire Ministry in regard to the maintenance and upkeep of the national monuments and our cultural heritage has provoked me to participate in this debate.

Sir, the hon. the Deputy Minister has already said that twenty months have elapsed and in the meantime the Government could not come to the Parliament with the consolidated measure that they contemplated. The circumstance which has been adduced by the hon. the Deputy Minister is that the States Reorganisation Bill was in the offing; therefore they could not come to this Parliament with the consolidated measure as they had promised but, Sir, I cannot understand, nobody can understand with any stretch of imagination how the States reorganisation could stand in the way of the Ministry in bringing forth that measure. For aught we know, the States reorganisation can stand in the way of delimitation of constituencies or matters relating thereto. Here is a matter which does not involve any question of administrative change. Here is a matter which does not also involve any legalistic matter. Wherever the monuments may be, they will continue to remain in India and what the Bill seeks is merely to declare them of national importance. So, if the hon. the Deputy Minister argues that the States reorganisation can make a monument either of national importance or can make it of local importance, then that is a different matter, but I do not think an intelligent man like him will continue to say that the States reorganisation or the picture of the future reorganised Indian can make a monument of national importance or can make it of local importance.

Then, Sir, another matter which is more serious and deserves consideration is that when the last amending Bill came up before this House the Government was kind enough to accept some of the amendments related to the Chusath Jogni Temple of Ranipur Jharial. I would like to know of the hon. the Deputy Minister if anything has been done in regard to the maintenance of that monument during all these years. Therefore I have been constrained to observe that the Education Ministry takes all along a very formalistic, a very technical view of the matter without trying to appreciate the spirit of it. We all know the great work which had been done by this Department when it was under the direction of foreigners like Sir Mortimer Wheeler. Even the 'Ancient India', a bulletin which was being published, now I understand its publication has become very irregular and very erratic like the moods of the Ministry itself, and the 'Ancient India' which was doing a good deal of work in this field has now suspended its publication. And now the Deputy Minister takes to task the mover of this Bill for bringing forth a measure whose scope is not very much enlarged, and that he would have liked to include many more monuments in this Bill. But may I ask what stops him from doing that even at this stage; he can move amendments to this Bill, but we are not going to rely on the assurances that he gives here that at some future date the Government will come with consolidated measure and that therefore this Bill should be withdrawn. Sir, this is a very strange attitude. I do not wish to make any broadside against the Ministry. I have got every respect for the persons who are in control and incharge of it, but that does not extenuate the many acts of omission with which the Ministry can be charged. I therefore would urge this hon. House not to accede to the request for the withdrawal of this Bill; if the Government feels that there are certain omissions, the hon. Minister can make amendments even at this stage with your permission and the Bill can be passed.

Shri Jaspat Roy Kapoor: Mr. Deputy Chairman, I would like to take this opportunity to offer congratulations to my hon. friend, Dr. Raghubir Sinh, for having brought before us this measure and for rousing the Education Ministry from its slumber. Sir, Dr. Raghubir Sinh, has been regularly showing very keen interest in matters relating to archaeology, ancient history, old documents and so on. There are not many who can persuade themselves to take interest in such cases and...

Dr. W.S. Barlingay (Madhya Pradesh): He is the hope of the old causes.

Shri Jaspat Roy Kapoor: ... we find it very much refreshing when such subjects are brought before us for consideration.

Sir, I am rather a little unhappy to find that with all the grace of my hon. friend, Dr. Mono Mohan Das, he has been a little ungraceful on this occasion in making the speech which he has made. I would have expected him to join me in congratulating Dr. Raghubir Sinh for having introduced this measure the necessity for which Dr. Mono Mohan Das himself has felt so keenly and his own Ministry has been feeling so keenly. He has tried – I do not know consciously or unconsciously; I am inclined to think, perhaps unconsciously – to ridicule Dr. Raghubir Sinh for having not included many more items in this Bill. He has told us that there are innumerable, very many at least, monuments in the country even in the present State of Rajasthan which monuments should have been brought within the scope of this measure so that they could be declared monuments of national importance. What was the reason – though he has been apologetic – for his saying that in all these 20 months the Education Ministry has not been able to make up its mind definitely with regard to the introduction of a more comprehensive measure. He says he could nto do so because of the fact that the States Reorganisation Bill was pending. I for one cannot understand how this question of States reorganisation can stand in the way of important monuments being declared monuments of national importance by means of a meausre which may be introduced in this House. What does it matter whether one State after the States Reorganisation Bill is passed, is called A, B, C, D or E? After all, those monuments will remain where they are irrespective of the name of the State. And so far as Rajasthan is concerned, which, according to Dr. Das, contains many monuments, that should have been incorporated in the measure; it is going to remain undisturbed both in respect of its area, excepting for the inclusion of Mount Abu, and in respect of its name. Why could not, even in this measure, an amendment be suggested by the Education Ministry for the inclusion of those monuments that exist in the State of Rajasthan? Dr. Das should have adopted a little more helpful attitude in this matter and should have given us a list of those important monuments to be included as of national importance. Perhaps he could do it even now.

Sir, my hon. friend, the Minister incharge of this meausre suggested that it may be postponed but he has not told us as to what useful purpose will be served by its postponement. He only says that at a later stage the Education Ministry would come before us with a more comprehensive measure. That will be well and good. But if these few monuments that are intended to be declared as monuments of national importance are going to be included in that comprehensive measure, why cannot they accept this Bill with good grace straightway and whatever monuments are left out may be included in that comprehensive measure.

Sir, it is not very easy for a non-official member to get his Bill passed by this House and I am happy that for the first time in the history of this House this non-official Bill is, I hope, going to be accepted. It may also be that it shall remain hereafter a historical monument itself for surely private Members' Bills are not going to be accepted thereafter except on some rare occasion. So, I should congratulate Dr. Raghubir Sinh once again and I hope that this measure will be adopted not only with unanimity but with very good grace in the thrid reading of this measure when Dr. Das will have once again an opportunity to speak on this Bill.

Shri H.P. Saksena (Uttar Pradesh): Sir, I wholeheartedly support the motion moved by my hon. friend, Dr. Raghubir Sinh. Whether the Education Ministry at the Centre does it or not, the historical monuments and archaeological sites and remains have got to be preserved as a national necessity. If anybody ignores that necessity or neglects the discharge of that paramount duty, there are Indians in sufficient numbers to see that none of their ancient historical monuments are allowed to fall in to decay. Of course, the Education Ministry is only an instrument through which this work ought to be done. If this Ministry does not discharge its duties properly, the subject will have to be removed from the Central List and put in the List of those subjects which are to be looked after by the States themselves, by the various units of the Indian Union. All these monuments and sites are situated in one part of the country or the other. So I would be very happy if this is removed from the Central List and the discharge of these functions is entrusted to the care of the States because none but the mother herself takes greater care of the child. Therefore if this subject had been in the Concurrent List, I am sure that this neglect, this criminal neglect of duty, would not have been noticed today. As I said, the important point is the preservation of the monuments and that must be done. This motion of my friend, Dr. Raghubir Sinh, reminds this House and particularly the Education Ministry to wake up and do the very imperative and important function which should have been discharged by now and which should be properly and carefully discharged at least in future. Who would like the Taj to be forgotten? Who would like the Ellora and the Ajanta caves to be put into oblivion? There are so many monuments – Kurukshetra is one of which each and every Indian is proud; not only Indian but some of our monuments are even the wonder of the world. Therefore it is not wise and proper to be neglectful of this rich heritage, and I wholeheartedly support the Bill and hope that the Ministry concerned will do what it has neglected to do up till now.

Mr. Deputy Chairman: Mr. Saksena, you just remarked the action of the Ministry as criminal neglect of duty. I want you to withdraw that word 'criminal'.

Shri H.P. Saksena: I withdraw it. If it is unparliamentary, I gladly withdraw it and apologise to you for the use of that word.

Shri Bhupesh Gupta (West Bengal): Sir, I rise only to indicate our support to this Bill and we are indeed very grateful to the hon. the mover of this Bill who has taken upon himself the task which rightly belongs to the Government, and taken the initiative in this matter. We are all the more grateful to him because at times we feel that instead of discussing some of the other things, perhaps it would be more profitable for ourselves, for the country and for the Parliament, if we discussed subjects such as these. For one thing they provide a common ground for our coming together in order to preserve the treasure house of various things that we have got in our country. Whether you like the word 'criminal' or not, whether it is parliamentary or unparliamentary, it is beside the point; but the fact remains that despite our best intentions there is neglect in this matter. I do not say anybody in this House would not like to preserve our historical and archaeological monuments. But whatever the intention, some of these things are in neglect today. We are not giving proper attention to those things and taking proper care of them. Everybody is responsible for it in a way; but I say the responsibility is on the part of the Government because it has got the machinery and the resources to look after them. Such things are not to be left to the private care. Not that private individuals are not interested in such matters. It is the Government which must preserve these cultural heritages that are there with all their resources and all the care that they are capable of bestowing on them.

Now, Sir, a number of items have been mentioned in this list. Probably the list could have been made a little longer. In this matter we should take into account various factors, not only the religious temples and other things, but also other historical sites, buildings and all that. To me the residence in which Rabindranath Tagore lived and worked is a place of historical importance. That should be preserved in the same way as the place where Shakespeare lived and worked is preserved. Now, if you go to Calcutta, you will find that this is in neglect. Not that there are not individuals who are not interested, but the fact remains that proper care is not shown to such things. Sarat Chandra – an eminent name in Bengal that many hon. Members in this House are familiar with – his birth place and the institutions he started, where he began his work, are also not being looked after and are neglect. These are facts. And, therefore, I say that a policy has to be adopted by the Government which should have a broader horizon than this Bill suggests. I support this Bill. I support the spirit behind this Bill. I support everything that is intended to be done by it. Yet I would like to broaden the field of activity as far as this matter is concerned. Now there are well-known historical monuments and archaeological sites and remains which bear testimony to the great civilization that we possess. It is through these monuments that one gets a glimpse of the great past or heritage that we have got bequeathed to us. Therefore, it is important that the States' resources are mobilised for looking after them. Therefore, I say the Government should have some kind of departmental, or proper arrangement to look after these. I do not say another bureaucratic institution should be started, but the State Governments should be properly inspired to look after these and given specific responsibility.

Pandit S.S.N. Tankha (Uttar Pradesh): May I interrupt the hon. speaker? Are we not rising for lunch today? Today is a non official day.

Mr. Deputy Chairman: There is no break for lunch today. Yesterday it was made clear that we should sit through the lunch hour and also till six o'clock. We have got other Government business.

Pandit S.S.N. Tankha: I am sorry, Sir. The hon. Member may now resume his speech.

Shri Bhupesh Gupta: I wish the hon. Member a wholesome lunch. Now, I shall forego it, I have decided. Now, the Central Government, I must say, is taking a little more interest in the matter and I have read some of their writings and publications. And I also get information through the press that some such activities are being conducted by them. But if you go to the States, you will find that whatever is there is not being well looked after and the Central Government's responsibilities are not, in actual practice, discharged there. That is my complaint. Therefore, I do not know whether the Government has any advisory body in regard to this matter. If not, the Government should have a proper advisory body consisting of people who would be competent to give advice on such things, so that the Government can work on such advice and look after these things.

Then, Sir, it is also necessary to impress upon the State Ministries that they must give due attention to the historical monuments, archaeological sites and all that. You pass a Bill. You have regulations and measures. Then you do not know exactly what is being done. In some sites of historical importance you do not know what is happening. Some officials are there, some people are interested in the task of looking after them, but then you do not know exactly how things are being done. Visitors have often complained that they feel that proper attention is not being given. There is lack of care, lack of sympathy, lack of human imagination in regard to such matters. I think our Government should not be open to this charge at all. Therefore, it is very important that some such thing, an advisory committee and a proper machinery should be set up.

Now, Sir, by 'historical importance' I do not mean the past history. There are certain places which are of importance from the point of view of contemporary history. Places which are associated with the struggle for our national liberation are very impotant. Surely I can speak for my part of India, that is to say, Bengal. You get a number of places which are associated with certain great developments in the political struggle in our country. Now, I am glad that certain cells in certain jails are being preserved as a monument. The prison where Gandhiji stayed should be preserved as a monument or as a place of historical importance. The cell where Pandit Jawaharlal Nehru lived in prison should undoubtedly be kept as a site or place of historical importance and every care should be given to that. Similarly, in this matter I think a partisan attitude should not be followed, a narrow attitude should not be followed. There are places where some of our martyrs – not necessarily belonging to the Congress creed, whatever it is, non-violence has gone by now – took part in the national struggle. Anyway they made the sacrifice. They inspired the country. We have got the example of Bhagat Singh....

Shri H.P. Saksena: We honour them today as martyrs.

Shri Bhupesh Gupta: But the place in which they lived is a historical place according to me. Therefore, these should be preserved. I say that the scope of this Bill or the scope of such a measure should be broadened in order to cover all these. I would like the places where Gandhiji lived and worked, including the prison cells where he lived, to be covered by such a provision.

Similarly, there are other people also, other important people who fought for our freedom, for our independence, and dedicated and gave their lives. Such places should also be preserved.

Then, Sir, there are certain places where struggles took place, bitter struggles took place, between the British and the Indian people. They may not always be constructed as monuments, but there may be a particular site where such struggles took place, where the Indian people fought the British oppressors and fought alone. These are sacred. They have dim and inspiring memories. These should be marked and looked after so that you can know that these are the places. It would give one an impression as to how widespread our struggle was and how the country is decorated and adorned with such sacred places. Therefore, I say there you want a broader view of the matter. You must cover everything that is historical -- not from the point of view of the great and glorious past that we have got, but from the point of view of living history that we are making. That is what I say in regard to this matter.

Similarly, I would not include except for archaeolgoical reasons or for architectural reasons some of the places within the historical places. More for architectural reasons I do not know whether you can include the Victoria Memorial Hall. It has not much of good architecture. Anyway it is there. A lot of money has been spent on that. Look after it. We were told some time back that it was going down. I do not know whether it is because of the weight of the empire or some such thing, but it was going down. We do not want it to go down. Let it remain, but except for architectural reasons, I would not call it a historical place or a monument.

Then, Sir, you have got even now in the Calcutta Maidan certain big Colonel Blimps riding a horse, sitting on a horse, brandishing their sword, and they used to be called historical monuments. Remove them as quickly as possible. Put the monuments of Rabindranath Tagore and other leaders of our national life there, no matter to which party they belong. They are historical monuments. But we do not like to have the sight of these. Colonel Blimps and Generals there. We want to get rid of the whole bunch of them. In the course of these seven or eight years they have not been removed. I would like to know from the Government what the policy is in regard to this matter. We are not at all justified in spending any money on such monuments. They should be removed. Remove these things. Bengal, whatever she may or may not have got, has got an unending list of martyrs. Place the monuments of these people there, the martyrs who laid their lives shooting the oppressors, the Englishmen. There are also other national leaders, political fighters, literary men, artists and so on. Put them in such places. The whole place will look serene and would look good to the eye and to the foreigners who come there. I would say to the Government -- I do not know if anybody representing the Government is here -- yes, there are some including the hon. Parliamentary Secretary -- that these things should be removed, and anything that reminds us of our past should not be included within the scope of the Bill or within the operation of the law which provides for looking after the historical monuments. I make it very clear that everything of this character should be removed. But you will say "These are some good structures. Sometimes the horse looks very nice. In that case keep them somewhere else. Sometimes I find in the Maidan some structure of a horse almost life-like, as if it is about to jump on you. I do see such things. Remove them. It is not necessary to keep them, because it is not a question of a horse or how it is done from the point of view of architecture or from the point of view of the monument. It reminds us of a very very lamentable past. Therefore, these things should be removed.

Now, I am glad to say that the Government is giving some attention to this matter and I find that some of the Colonels and Generals are disappearing from the Maidan. There are still some of them left but some have disappeared. I would like to see none present there. Similarly, Sir, there are certain other places which the British thought had something to do with their history, but they have nothing to do with our history. They belong to their history. I do not know how many such places are being looked after at the expense of the public exchequer. Unless a place or a monument or whatever it is connected with our tradition, tells a fine story of our country, is in conformity with our present outlook and understanding and with our great heritage, it should not be brought within the purview of measures such as this. This is what I want to say. I wish the Government would take all possible measures and I hope, Sir, the Members of Parliament will realise their responsibility in this case. We are too busy with politics, we are dealing with politics too much. Sometimes I do not find enough time. I think it is the duty of the political workers and the political party men to take an active interest in such matters, because politics is something which is not divorced from your cultural heritage, from your great past, and whatever bears testimony to our great past has to be taken care of by the combined efforts of the country as a whole and most certainly by the people who consider themselves the leaders of our nation. That is why responsibility in a measure also belongs to every political party, no matter which that party is, no matter what its ideological or political affiliations are. As far as India and its cultural heritage is concerned we are at one. We want to preserve the great heritage, the great culture, the great archaeological and architectural monuments that we possess today. I say these are our invaluable assets which we must preserve at all costs, and there should not be any dearth of finance, there should not be any lack of care, there should not be any negligence or indifference whatsoever. We must preserve these things at all cost and by all means.

Sir, this is all that I want to say and I hope the Government will accept this Bill and that it will become the law of the land.

Dr. Raghubir Sinh (Madhya Bharat): Mr. Deputy Chairman, I am happy to have got this opportunity of giving a reply to the long debate that has in a way continued for more than twenty months, for, as the House knows, this Bill was first introduced and discussed in the month of December 1954, and then further consideration was postponed till some future date. Now, Sir, I do not want to speak at length about other matters, because quite a few have already been answered. I would only limit myself to the remarks made by my hon. friend, Dr. Das, in respect of the various points he has raised in his speech. Firstly, he said that the States reorganisation picture had not become clear and so a comprehensive Bill could not be brought in. Now some other speakers have already dealt at length with this matter. My only wonder is as to how the fact that the States Reorganisation Bill has not been finally passed would have stood in the way of this Bill being brought in. I still wonder whether, as a result of the passing of the States Reorganisation Bill, it will be necessary for the Government to completely amend and remodel the earlier Bill, because the descriptions are there and the places are there, and even if such a Bill had been brought in, this thing would have been equally clear.

Another observation I want to make is this. What little I know about the intention of the Ministry is this. Last year at this time, in October 1955, I addressed a letter to the Ministry asking as to what was happening to the Bill. Then I was told that the Bill was going to be introduced in the last winter session, and they added that if for some reason they could not introduce it in the winter session, it was definitely going to be introduced in the last Budget session. If these considerations had been there, I am afraid that sort of letter could not have been written then. Probably it was an after thought. We all have got to explain away such delays and similar things.

Mr. Deputy Chairman: You have to define the district and the State. That is now in the hotch-potch as it were in the States Reorganisation Bill.

Dr. Raghubir Sinh: What I say is if they had brought in this comprehensive Bill it would have followed the present pattern and the States Reorganisation Bill would have come in later.

Mr. Deputy Chairman: That means that another amending Bill should have been brought.

Dr. Raghubir Sinh: It was not necessary. I would like to know if the hon. Minister is going to bring in an amending Bill in respect of the original Bill where all the details of the States and districts are given.

Mr. Deputy Chairman: That is according to the old set up.

Dr. Raghubir Sinh: It can be understood according to the new set up also. We all have got the States Reorganisation Bill; we all have got maps. We would not have had any difficulty in locating them. Now, Sir, my friend has said that my Bill brings in only a couple of monuments to be added. I admit it, Sir, as that is actually so, but as my friend must have seen, my original Bill included the Part C States' monuments in the list. Sir, I think the Central Government had somehow got an idea that there was no need at all for declaring those Part C States' monuments to be of national importance. Now, Sir, while moving for consideration of this Bill, I seem to have had a very prophetic vision. I must congratulate myself for that. At that time, Sir, I stated in my speech as follows:

> "I know for this for certain that many of the Part C States, as they are now, are not going to continue. So if these monuments are not to be declared to be of national importance today, I say – and I say it with full confidence – that if not today, within another year these monuments shall be declared by this very Parliament to be of national importance."

Now, Sir, I have had the satisfaction of seeing that in clause 126 of the States Reorganisation Bill, 1956, all these monuments have been declared to be of national importance. My prophecy seems to have come true. Now it is true that actually only a couple of monuments are going to be added in the list of monuments. My friend asks me to withdraw the Bill or to postpone it. But my contention is that we have already waited for 20 months, and by no stretch of imagination I can think of a comprehensive Bill being brought forward before the present Parliament. It is going to take a very long time, probably another 16 months, because such a comprehensive Bill will have to be introduced in Parliament, and Parliament will have to pass it. At the most there can be only one more session of the other House, and it will not be possible for that House to take up and pass such a comprehensive Bill during that session. Therefore, in any case, such legislation cannot be enacted till after the autumn session, next year and that means another sixteen months. Now, Sir, my friend may say that the Government are bringing forward an amendment to the Constitution by which it will not be necessary to get all these lists passed by Parliament. Merely making an amendment to the Constitution will not empower the Government to declare the monuments to be of national importance. For that purpose, an enabling legislation will have to be enacted. And I feel that such a legislation cannot possibly be enacted during the life-time of the present Parliament. Therefore, Sir, my submission is that no action can possibly be taken in respect of these monuments for another 16 months. Therefore my appeal to the Government is not to follow the policy of "Either all, or none." Even if these few monuments are declared to be of national importance, the number in future will be reduced to that extent.

Dr. Mono Mohan Das: Only by two.

Dr. Raghubir Sinh: If the Government takes this additional burden of two, I will be more than satisfied. And I will give you the reasons for it.

Now, Sir, I was pursuing the point about Rock inscription within the Parsvanath Temple compound (12th century)'. Now that is an inscription of very vital importance to the history of the country.[1] And then that description has been edited more than once. One of the important historians, Dr. Bhandarkar, also was particularly keen on editing it. But because of certain reasons he could not do it. Now, Sir, that inscription is on a rock which is very undulating, and not smooth. Actually, Sir, certain portions of the rock have begun to peel off. As you know, Sir, these stones, once they start cracking, God alone knows what may happen to them, and one does not know whether they will last for ever. In the case of this particular edict, Sir, I might add that it gives at length the chronology to which belonged the last Hindu King who ruled over this city of Delhi, that is Prithviraj. His whole genealogy cannot possibly be traced correctly, but I might submit that the national importance of this Rock edict cannot possibly be denied, for that Rock edict plus the incomplete manuscript of the poetical work 'Prithviraj Vijay' Mahakavya are the only two sources for the chronology of that Chauhan Dynasty. Therefore, Sir, even if that one monument had been accepted, I would have been very much satisfied. As I said, Sir, 16 months are bound to elapse before any of these monuments can be declared to be of national importance by the Government, and I am

1. Inscription in Hindi (material not included).

anxious that this valuable time of another sixteen months should not be lost. That is why I would beg of my friend for the sake of future historians and the rich heritage which we have to preserve to accede to my request.

Mr. Deputy Chairman: He is not opposing it.

Dr. Raghubir Sinh: If he is not opposing it, then let it be accepted by the House.

Mr. Deputy Chairman: The question is:

> "That the Bill further to amend the Ancient and Historical Monuments and Archaeological Sites and Remains (Declaration of National Importance) Act, 1951, be taken into consideration."

The motion was adotped.

Mr. Deputy Chairman: Now we take up the clause by clause consideration of the Bill.

Clause 2 – *Amendment of Schedule, Act LXXI of 1951*

Dr. Raghubir Sinh: Sir, I move:

3. "That at pages 1 and 2 for lines 9 to 16 and 1 to 21, respectively, the following be substituted, namely :

(1) In Part I, in the Table appended to Item II, in the entries under the heading 'Rajasthan State'.–

(a) after the entries under the sub-heading 'District Bharatpur' and before the sub-heading 'District Bikaner' the following sub-heading and entries shall be inserted namely :

'District Bhilwada

23A.	Maha Kal and two other temples . .	Bijholi
23B.	Rock inscription (12th century) . .	Bijholi
23C.	Rock inscription within the Parsvanath Temple Compound (12th century) . .	Bijholi

(b) after the entry under the sub-heading 'District Bundi' and before the sub-heading 'District Dholpur' the following sub-heading and entries shall be inserted. namely :

'District Chittorgarh

28A.	Fort of Chittor as a whole .	Chitor
28B.	Ghateshwar Temple .	Badoli

28C.	Shringar Chawri .	Badoli
28D.	Temple of Ganesh .	Badoli
28E.	Temple of Trimurti .	Badoli
28F.	Temple of Ashtamata .	Badoli
28G.	Temple of Vamanavatar known as Narad Temple .	Badoli
28H.	Kund .	Badoli
28I.	Temple of Sheshashyan .	Badoli
28J.	Temple of Shiv and Kund .	Badoli
28K.	Menal (Mahanal) Temple and Math .	Menal;'

(c) for the sub-heading 'District Udaipur–*contd.*' the sub-heading 'District Udaipur' shall be substituted;

(d) entries 73, 75 and 76 shall be omitted;

(e) entries 74 and 77 shall be renumbered 73 and 74, respectively'."

4. "That at pages 2, 3 and 4, lines 22 to 45, 1 to 42 and 1 to 5, respectively, be deleted."

5. "That at page 4, for lines 6 to 26, the following be substituted, namely :

'(2) In Part II, in the Table appended to item II, under the heading 'Rajasthan State' sub-heading 'District Udaipur', entry 40 shall be omitted'."

Mr. Deputy Chairman: The clause and the amendments are now before the House.

(No remarks)

Mr. Deputy Chairman: The question is:

3. "That at pages 1 and 2, for lines 9 to 16 and 1 to 21, respectively, the following be substituted, namely :

'(1) In part I, in the Table appended to Item II, in the entries under the heading 'Rajasthan State',–

(a) after the entries under the sub-heading 'District Bharatpur' and before the sub-heading 'District Bikaner' the following sub-heading and entries shall be inserted, naemly :

'District Bhilwada

23A.	Maha Kal and two other temples	Bijholi

23B.	Rock inscription (12th century)	Bijholi
23C.	Rock inscription within the Parsvanath Temple Compound (12th century)	Bijholi;'

(b) after the entry under the sub-heading 'District Bundi' and before the sub-heading 'District Dholpur' the following sub-heading and entries shall be inserted, namely:

'District Chittorgarh

28A.	Fort of Chittor as a whole	.	Chitor
28B.	Ghateshwar Temple	.	Badoli
28C.	Shringar Chawri	.	Badoli
28D.	Temple of Ganesh	.	Badoli
28E.	Temple of Trimurti	.	Badoli
28F.	Temple of Ashtamata	.	Badoli
28G.	Temple of Vamanavatar known as Narad Temple	.	Badoli
28H.	Kund	.	Badoli
28I.	Temple of Sheshashayan	.	Badoli
28J.	Temple of Shiv and Kund	.	Badoli
28K.	Menal (Mahanal) Temple and Math.	.	Menal;'

(c) for the sub-heading 'district Udaipur – *contd.*' the sub-heading 'District Udaipur' shall be substituted;

(d) entries 73, 75, and 76 shall be omitted;

(e) entries 74 and 77 shall be renumbered 73 and 74, respectively'."

The motion was adopted.

Mr. Deputy Chairman: The question is:

4. "That at pages 2, 3 and 4, lines 22 to 45, 1 to 42 and 1 to 5, respectively, be deleted."

The motion was adopted.

Mr. Deputy Chairman: The question is:

5. "That at page 4, for lines 6 to 26, the following be substituted, namely :

'(2) In Part II, in the Table appended to Item II, under the heading 'Rajasthan State', sub-heading 'District Udaipur', entry 40 shall be omitted.' "

The motion was adopted.

Mr. Deputy Chairman: The question is:

"That clause 2, as amended, stand part of the Bill."

The motion was adopted.

Clause 2, as amended, was added to the Bill.

Clause 1 – *Short Title*

Dr. Raghubir Sinh: Sir, I move:

2. "That at page 1, line 5, for the words and figure `Second Amendment Act, 1954', the words and figure `Amendment Act, 1956' be substituted."

Mr. Deputy Chairman: The clause and the amendment are now before the House.

(No remarks)

Mr. Deputy Chairman: The question is:

2. "That at page 1, line 5, for the words and figure `Second Amendment Act, 1954', the words and figure `Amendment Act, 1956' be substituted."

The motion was adopted.

Mr. Deputy Chairman: The question is:

"That clause 1, as amended, stand part of the Bill."

The motion was adopted.

Clause 1, as amended, was added to the Bill.

The Enacting Formula

Dr. Raghubir Sinh: Sir, I move:

1. "That at page 1, line 1, for the word 'Fifth', the word 'Seventh' be substituted."

Mr. Deputy Chairman: The Enacting Formula and the amendment are now before the House.

(No remarks)

Mr. Deputy Chairman: The questions is :

1. "That at page 1, line 1, for the word 'Fifth', the word 'Seventh' be substituted."

Mr. Deputy Chairman: The questions is :

"That the Enacting Formula, as amended, stand part of the Bill."

The motion was adopted.

The Enacting Formula, as amended, was added to the Bill.

The Title was added to the Bill.

Dr. Raghubir Sinh: Sir, I move:

"That the Bill, as amended, be passed."

Sir, I might mention here with moving this motion that I am very grateful to the House and also to Dr. Das for not having opposed the Bill.

Mr. Deputy Chairman: Motion moved:

"That the Bill, as amended, be passed."

Dr. Mono Mohan Das: Sir, I take this opportunity to place before the House some of the facts which apparently the House has forgotten.

Sir, some uncharitable, unwanted and unwarranted remarks have been hurled against the Government during the discussion on this Bill. I cannot immitate hon. Members in using the vitriolic language that they have used. But I will try my best to place before them the facts regarding the criticism that they have made. Sir, the Government of India are taken to task because of the fact that during the last twenty months they have not done anything for introducing an amending Bill. May I draw the attention of the hon. House to the fact that the first Bill declaring certain monuments and archaeological sites and remains to be of national importance was passed in November 1951. Then, Sir, in January 1954, three years after, the first amending Bill was brought before the House and passed. During those three years we gained experience by visiting different parts of the country which were previously under the Indian States, and the results of that experience of our officers were embodied in the second amending Bill. It was passed in January 1954, and only twenty months or two years have passed, and we are now preparing for another Bill. Is such a gap too big for any amending Bill to be placed before the House? Moreover, as I stated, the reason for not bringing forward a Bill earlier was the S.R. Bill. I have been ridiculed for that. I am very sorry for it. I anticipated that hon. Members would know the importance of the S.R. Bill so far as this particular Bili regarding the declaration of certain monuments as of national importance is concerned. I submit to them the following facts regarding ancient historical monuments and archaeological sites and remains. Now, here there is mention of Part A, B and C States. Now, under the new reorganisation of States which is now before the House, we are going to do away with Part B States. Probably Jammu and Kashmir will be the only Part B State. Now, all Part B States will be effected from the map of India. Several of our States which are archaeolgoically very important such as Bhopal, Vindhya Pradesh, Madhya Bharat, Indore, Gwalior, Mysore and most of all Hyderabad, are all going to be effaced from the map of India. Hyderabad is going to be disintegrated and the most famous monuments archaeologically, historically and aesthetically, will be going to a different State. That particular portion will be merged most probably with Bombay. So, all these have to be considered and taken into consideration. Naturally, this Act will have to be amended in the light of the new reorganisation of the States. I may point out once again to hon. Members the great important bearing the S.R. Bill has got upon this subject.

Then, I find that the minds of hon. Members are working under a wrong impression. They think that archaeology is completely and wholly a Central subject. That is not a fact. In my speech I tried to make it clear, but I am sorry if I could not be properly heard or could not be properly understood. During the time of the Britishers, so far as British India was concerned, archaeology was a Central subject, and archaeological monuments, etc. were managed by the provisions under the Ancient Monuments Preservation Act. This Act was applicable to the whole of British India, and the provinces at that time had nothing to do with archaeology. Archaeology was a Central subject so far as British India was concerned, and they were governed by the provisions of this Act. Now, after independence when the Indian States were integrated and before the coming into force of the Constitution, this Act was made applicable to the Indian States. So during the interim period after independence in 1947 and the coming into force of the Constitution, archaeology became a completely Central subject, but when we passed our Constitution, the Constitution envisaged that archaeology should not be a Central subject. The makers of our Constitution in their wisdom thought that we should select certain monuments – historical ancient monuments – and archaeological sites which were of national importance and declare them to be of national importance, and entrust the maintenance of these to the Central Archaeological Directorate and that the monuments, archaeological sites and remains of lesser importance should be left to the States. So, the importance of declaring these monuments and sites to be of national importance comes in. It does not mean that only monuments and sites which are declared to be of national importance are looked after and the rest are not. That is not a fact.

Shri V.K. Dhage (Hyderabad): May I ask the hon. Minister whether there is any arrangement in the States with regard to the preservation of ancient monuments and, if so, what are the Budget provisions for this?

Dr. Mono Mohan Das: I am afraid that Information is not at my disposal, because it is a provincial subject.

Mr. Deputy Chairman: Each State has its own Department of Archaeology.

Dr. Mono Mohan Das: I will refer the hon. Member to two items in our Constitution: One is item 67 of the Union List which declares that the Central Government has got authority only over those monuments, archaeological sites, etc. which are declared by Parliament to be of national importance. Then I refer the hon. Member to item 12 of the State List which says that monuments, archaeological sites, etc. which are not declared to be of national importance by Parliament should belong to the States and should be looked after by them.

Shri V.K. Dhage: The hon. Minister stated that they are being looked after by the States. My point is that, if it is fact, then the State Governments must make some provision for that in their Budgets and also for having a Department to look after these monuments.

Dr. Mono Mohan Das: It is not possible for me . . . .

Shri H.C. Dasappa (Mysore): There are certain State Governments who are looking after them.

Shri V.K. Dhage: Is his State Government having any provision for this?

Dr. Raghubir Sinh: So far as Mysore is concerned, they have handed over all their monuments lock, stock and barrel to the Central Government.

Shri H.C. Dasappa: We have a Department called the Muzrai Department, which is looking after some of the monuments.

Shri V.K. Dhage: My information is that two or three States only have Archaeological Departments but that even they are not sufficiently provided to look after the monuments, etc.

Mr. Deputy Chairman: That is a matter which has got to be agitated in the State Legislatures.

Shri H.C. Dasappa: There is an Archaeological Department in Mysore, which spends several thousands of rupees on Belur and other various temples. Also the monolithic statue at Shravanbelgola of Gomateswara is being partly financed by the local Government.

Shri Bhupesh Gupta: The hon. Member said that they spend several thousands of rupees. Will it be of any use?

Mr. Deputy Chairman: We are not concerned with it here.

Shri B.K.P. Sinha (Bihar): I fail to understand the relevance of this explanatory speech at the third reading stage.

Dr. Mono Mohan Das: Some remarks were made and I wanted to explain the position so far as the Government is concerned. So it is not a fact that if a monument....

Mr. Deputy Chairman: It is not that Mr. Gupta does not know it; still he wants to have a fling.

Shri Bhupesh Gupta: I do know that the Department is there but in Bengal there is practically none. He comes from my State and he will bear me out. If the hon. Minister pleads ignorance, I cannot help. It is the duty of the Government of India to keep abreast of such things.

Mr. Deputy Chairman: Only for national monuments.

Shri Bhupesh Gupta: We have heard of that Bill but our point is, when certain monuments have been left with the States and they are of no less importance, and they are being neglected by the State, the Government of India should be concerned and if necessary the Bill should be suitably amended.

Mr. Deputy Chairman: You must agitate in the State Legislature.

Dr. Mono Mohan Das: I hold no brief for any State Government but I wish to remind that the voters or the people who have sent us here have sent their representatives to the Legislative Assembly of the State also and my hon. friend cannot claim more representative character than the Members of the Assembly there. We don't say that all the wisdom has been concentrated in the heads of Members of Parliament or Central Ministers.

(Interruptions)

Mr. Deputy Chairman: Anyway it is not relevant here.

Shri V.K. Dhage: The point is this: Dr. Das has been stressing that the monuments of archaeological importance are looked after and the point that I am stressing is that it is not the case.

Mr. Deputy Chairman: If that is not the case, you have to agitate in the State Legislature.

Shri V.K. Dhage: It is not necessary.

Mr. Deputy Chairman: Please hear me. The Centre is responsible only for such monuments as have been declared as monuments of national importance.

Shri V.K. Dhage: My point is ...

Mr. Deputy Chairman : There is no point. He has been saying that the States are responsible for certain monuments which have not been declared as of national importance and the Central Government is responsible only for mational monuments. That is the law and that is in the Concurrent List. You have to agitate in the State Legislature.

Shri V.K. Dhage: Then he should say that they are not responsible and not that they are being looked after.

Mr. Deputy Chairman: That is another question.

Dr. Mono Mohan Das: Our Constitution does not entrust the Central Government with the responsibility for all the archaeological monuments etc. They have divided them into two groups – the most important monuments that are declared by the Parliament as national monuments which are to be looked after by the Centre and the rest of lesser importance to be looked after by the States. That is the arrangement under the Constitution of India. Now, if the allegations of my hon. friends are correct, that the State Governments are not dong their duties properly, then it is the State Legislatures who should intervene and force the State Governments to do what their duties are, to look after the monuments properly. That is my point. My hon. friend Mr. Mahanty is not here.

Mr. Deputy Chairman: You need not answer all that. Dr. Sinh.

Shri Bhupesh Gupta: Sir, I want to speak on this....

Mr. Deputy Chairman: No.

Shri Bhupesh Gupta: Why not?

Mr. Deputy Chairman: I have not called you.

Shri Bhupesh Gupta: You may not call me but I would like to speak.

Mr. Deputy Chairman: I have called Dr. Raghubir Sinh.

Shri Bhupesh Gupta: You have called him, I know, but I don't see why you should not look at this side. In the Third Reading everybody can speak.

Mr. Deputy Chairman: All right.

Shri Bhupesh Gupta: Thank you very much.

Shri Abid Ali: On a point of order. The same thing happened during the First Reading also. When my good friend Mr. Das replied, you called upon.....

Mr. Deputy Chairman: Dr. Raghubir Sinh has to reply.

Shri Abid Ali: I mean Government's point of view, then he should have been given an opportunity to explain his point of view....

Shri Bhupesh Gupta: Why is he....

(Interruptions)

Shri Abid Ali: I am talking to the Chair. Now if you are allowing the hon. Member to speak, I cannot raise objection but certainly the Minister should be allowed to explain again the Government's point of view....

Shri Bhupesh Gupta: I think you are very right, Sir, in calling me but he need not have any apprehensions about it. I don't mind listening to the hon. Minister again.

Mr. Deputy Chairman: Go on. It should be relevant....

Shri Bhupesh Gupta: As relevant as one can make it after an irrelevant speech. You set the tune. After having set the tune, you need not very much complain if I am a little out of tune. If I say anything which requires any reply on the part of the Government, there is another Minister, a formidable Deputy Minister, sitting beside the Deputy Minister who has spoken and he can speak as a private Member.

Mr. Deputy Chairman: All this is irrelevant.

Shri Bhupesh Gupta: Anyway what we were trying to impress and to our great regret so unsuccessfully upon the hon. Minister is this that in spite of the Constitution, if you think that there are certain monuments which are not declared as monuments of national importance by the Parliament and therefore they are not within the jurisdiction of the Parliament but are yet being neglected because the States are not looking after them, there is undoubtedly room for taking this matter up in their hands. At the same time one should also think whether the existing law requires a little change in regard to this matter so that the Central Government could come into the picture a little more than it has come. It is perfectly relevant, when we are dealing with a Bill of this sort. It rests with the Government of India to declare any monument in India as one of national importance and thereby assume the responsibility of looking after it. Is it or is it not a fact? Is it or is it not a provision of the Constitution? Therefore it is very important and legitimate on our part to pose this question before the hon. Minister and require an answer from him. I very much regret that the hon. Minister completely misunderstood us and I can see his plight. He is getting used to this kind of thing, and it will take a little time but I thought the matter was so simple that he should have understood it. So instead of....

Dr. Mono Mohan Das: Don't be too much patronizing. I don't require your patronage.

(Interruptions)

Shri Bhupesh Gupta: He comes from my State, and I have all sympathy and affection for him. I am not provincial by nature or by temperament but I would like to see people from my part of India to shine in whatever position they may be. The point is this. He, instead of trying to appreciate the point of view that was placed by Mr. Dhage and by us and some other speakers, suddenly said that the State Legislature was there to discuss it and "we don't know about it." Then he said that wisdom is not our monopoly and that they represent some majority in the States....

(Interruptions)

Could there be anything more highly irrelevant to the subject? Whether majority or minority the question is one of neglect. It does not matter whether it is a majority, or a minority. We are now concerned with the fact of whether a neglect is there or not. Then you should think whether the Government of India should assume wider responsiblity in this matter. If your majority is not looking after, then your majority can also assume the powers. We have never claimed monopoly of wisdom in this matter of....

Mr. Deputy Chairman: You can bring an amending Bill.

Shri Bhupesh Gupta: I resist this kind of attitude. We are glad that we are passing the Bill but I very much regret the mentality displayed today by the hon. Minister, because the mentality displayed is depressing. Even when they have not opposed the Bill, later on the hon. Minister said that vitriolic language was used. But he had not quoted a single item from anybody's speech which could be described as vitriolic language.

Mr. Deputy Chairman: All that is not relevant.

Shri Bhupesh Gupta: I don't know whether he has consulted the dictionary but no vitriolic language was used nor anything which was not right. Therefore I object to this kind of reply being given to a subject about which all are agreed. Maybe there are differences in accents and differences in opinion and outlook and approach in regard to this matter. But this is by no means a controversial matter. Then we are told that the States Reorganization Bill was before us....

Mr. Deputy Chairman: Don't go back to these things....

Shri Bhupesh Gupta: Everybody knows....

Mr. Deputy Chairman: You cannot repeat your arguments.

(*Interruptions*)

Shri Bhupesh Gupta: If the States Reorganization Bill is to stop all measures, we need have only the Home Ministry and....

(*Interruptions*)

Mr. Deputy Chairman: Don't repeat.

Shri Bhupesh Gupta: Therefore I say if the hon. Minister makes such replies, then of course an answer will also be forthcoming.

Mr. Deputy Chairman: You have not understood his point.

Dr. Mono Mohan Das: I want the right of reply.

Shri V.K. Dhage: Just one minute, Sir.

Mr. Deputy Chairman: No, no.

Shri V.K. Dhage: Sir, I will not speak for more than a minute or two. My only point is that there are monuments in the States which are not considered as of national importance. My point is not whether these are monuments of national importance or not.

Mr. Deputy Chairman: That point has been made sufficiently clear, Mr. Dhage.

Shri V.K. Dhage: But they should be looked after and the difficulty arises, as I have been able to understand from some of the States, with regard to finance. I would, therefore, say if they are not taking them over as national monuments to be looked after by the Centre, I would like the Government to consider whether sufficient finances could be provided by the Central Government to the State Governments so that they may be able to look after these monuments properly. That is the only point I wanted to make.

Dr. Mono Mohan Das: Sir....

Mr. Deputy Chairman: No, no further speech.

Dr. Mono Mohan Das: No, Sir. Only a few points. The point that my hon. friend, Shri Dhage, raised just now is a very important one. As a matter of fact, we are actually taking over more and more monuments and that is why our Schedule is increasing and that is the main reason why amendments are required and we have to bring forward an amending Bill. We have already done it once and we want to do it again. That is because we find that important monuments are not being properly looked after, maybe for various reasons, in some of the States at least. That is why we are gradually taking them over.

So far as Mr. Gupta is concerned, I would like to remind him that we are a democratic country and we are administering the country under a Constitution which is not totalitarian. It is not a totalitarian State.

Shri Bhupesh Gupta: Sir, he is delivering a speech and there I object.

Shri Mono Mohan Das: Why object? (*Interruptions*) I am not giving way.

Shri Bhupesh Gupta: Sir, on a point of order.

Dr. Mono Mohan Das: I am not giving way.

Mr. Deputy Chairman: Order order. He is not yielding.

Shri Bhupesh Gupta: But he is delivering a speech, Sir.

Mr. Deputy Chairman: Leave Mr. Gupta alone, it is not necessary to reply to him. At this rate we cannot go on.

Dr. Mono Mohan Das: But, Sir, the first point is that there is our Constitution and although we do not regard every letter of it as unchangeable, we except through proper Parliamentary methods, do not want to change our Constitution. Neither can we do it. So our activities, the activities of the Government of India, are all guided by the provisions of our Constitution. So what I have said is according to the provisions of the Constitution.

Mr. Deputy Chairman: All right.

Dr. Mono Mohan Das: Just one point more, Sir. Mr. Gupta wants to know....

Shri Bhupesh Gupta: No, No. I don't want to know anything from him. I have not asked him for anything. Sir, he is making another speech.

Mr. Deputy Chairman: I am not allowing him.

Dr. Mono Mohan Das: I will not give way, Mr. Gupta. About vitriolic language as you yourself suggested, Mr. Saksena....

Mr. Deputy Chairman: He withdrew it.

Shri Bhupesh Gupta: I definitely rise on a point of order.

Mr. Deputy Chairman: That will do. Dr. Raghubir Sinh.

Dr. Raghubir Sinh: Sir, I am very happy that my Bill has raised so much interest and has received so much support. It had made hon. Members so much interested in it that the Bill actually took more time than I expected. I am very thankful to the House for the interest that has been shown and for the support that the hon. Members have given to my Bill. I thank you, Sir.

Mr. Deputy Chairman: The question is:

"That the Bill, as amended, be passed."

The motion was adopted.

WHO'S WHO

Bose, Subhas Chandra	: Great patriot, was elected president of Indian National Congress in 1938 at Haripura and again in 1939 in Tripuri, was founder of the Forward Block (1939), Indian National Army and the Indian National Government, was imprisoned several times during the Liberation movement for India.
Das, C.R.	: A renowed Swarajiaist leader who was elected President of the Indian National Congress at Gaya in 1922.
Jinnah, M.A.	: First Governor General of Pakistan, was the Vice-Chancellor of Osmania University, was elected to the Indian Legislature Assembly in 1930 and 1934.
Mukhtar Ahmed Ansari	: A prominent Congress leader from Delhi, was elected president of the Indian National Congress in 1925.
Nehru, Motilal	: A well known barrister of Allahabad and a prominent Congress Leader, was elected president of the Indian National Congress in 1928. Was elected to the Indian Legislature Assembly in 1924.
Patel, Vallabhbhai	: Maker of the Modern India as well as the Iron man, was the president of the Indian National Congres in 1931. Was appointed Deputy Prime Minister of free India in 1947.
Zulaikha Begum	: Wife of Maulana Abul Kalam Azad and a courageous household women.

Glossary

Ahimsa	:	Non-violence
Bapu	:	Literally father, a generic term to denote respect to elder, a term widely used by Indian people for Mahatma Gandhi.
Civil Disobedience Movement	:	Non-violent or Satyagraha Movement of Gandhi to resist British Rule in India.
Harijan	:	The term used by Gandhiji for the people belonging to Scheduled Castes in India.
Lahore Resolution	:	Resolution passed by the All India Muslim League in March, 1940 at Lahore, under the presidentship of Mr. Jinnah to launch an agitation to get India divided into two nations.
Mahatma	:	A title bestowed on Gandhiji by Dr. Rabindranath Tagore.
Swaraj	:	Self Rule
Young India	:	A weekly started by Mahatma Gandhi since 1919.

Chronology of Events
1956-57

1956, August, 20	:	Laid a statement on table of the Rajya Sabha regarding the meeting of the National Committee of Archivists of India.
November, 22	:	Made a Statement in the Rajya Sabha giving informations of study of Hindi in the various Universities in India.
December, 18	:	Clarified the position, in the Rajya Sabha about the erosive threat to the house of Sant Tulsidas.
1957, July, 25	:	Made Demands for Grants of Education Ministry in the Lok Sabha, for 1957-58 year.

Index